WITHDRAWN

Playhouse Law
in Shakespeare's World

Playhouse Law in Shakespeare's World

Brian Jay Corrigan

Madison • Teaneck
Fairleigh Dickinson University Press

© 2004 by Rosemont Publishing & Printing Corp.

All rights reserved. Authorization to photocopy items for internal or personal use, or the internal or personal use of specific clients, is granted by the copyright owner, provided that a base fee of $10.00, plus eight cents per page, per copy is paid directly to the Copyright Clearance Center, 222 Rosewood Drive, Danvers, Massachusetts 01923. [0-8386-4022-2/04 $10.00 + 8¢ pp, pc.]

Associated University Presses
2010 Eastpark Boulevard
Cranbury, NJ 08512

The paper used in this publication meets the requirements of the American National Standard for Permanence of Paper for Printed Library Materials Z39.48-1984.

Library of Congress Cataloging-in-Publication Data

Corrigan, Brian Jay, 1957–
    Playhouse law in Shakespeare's world / Brian Jay Corrigan.
      p.   cm.
    Includes bibliographical references and index.
    ISBN 0-8386-4022-2 (alk. paper)
    1. English drama—Early modern and Elizabethan, 1500–1700—History and criticism. 2. Law in literature. 3. Theater—Law and legislation—Great Britain—History—16th century. 4. Theater—Law and legislation—Great Britain—History—17th century. 5. English drama—17th century—History and criticism. 6. Shakespeare, William, 1564–1616—Knowledge—Law. 7. Law and literature—History—16th century. 8. Law and literature—History—17th century. I. Title.

PR658.L38C67 2004
822′.3093554—dc22

2003023958

PRINTED IN THE UNITED STATES OF AMERICA

> The law hath not been dead,
> though it hath slept.
>
> —*Measure for Measure*

Contents

Preface	9
Acknowledgments	13
Introduction	17
1. 'A Must, Then, to the Inns o' Court Shortly	25
2. Tricks and Quillets that Thunder at a Playhouse	51
3. Thy Love's Use Their Treasure	102
4. I Knew a Wench Married in an Afternoon: Secret Marriages *per verba de præsenti* and *per verba de futuro*	134
Conclusions	191
Notes	195
Bibliography	236
Index	257

Preface

THE PURE STATEMENT OF THE LAW IS OFTEN RATHER DIFFERENT from the attitudes that control it or the opinions that shape its practice. Therefore, the application of a law can often seem mysterious and even contradictory. It is not the black letter of the law, then, but rather the application, mystery, and contradiction that shape the popular perception of law. The written law, it might fairly be claimed, is no more than a snapshot of society in flux, attempting to regulate itself. The regulation, the black letter on the Statute, is often if not usually out of step with society—sometimes overly harsh or arcane (witness *Measure for Measure*), other times simply beyond the weft of actual human interaction (witness *The Staple of News*).

There has been a substantial pot of ink spilt over the question of law in Shakespeare. The unhappy fact in this field of study is that there is (at least among many—though not all—literary commentators) a general confusion over what law is. At a very recent seminar on Shakespeare's Law, papers were presented on societal ethics, civil custom, gender sensibility, political office, royal prerogative, and public execution (including the expected "stage scaffold equals state scaffold" observation). Valuable and interesting though these studies are, they are only in the very broadest sense handling law (and in most cases dealing merely with the formation, penumbra or consequence of law or with the indistinct notion of legal institutions). Many of these scholars—legal commentators though not trained legal historians—blur the line between law (the set of rules established by legislation and applied by a judicial body) and fact (an occurrence, as determined by a jury, out of which a point of law arises). Papers founded upon this confusion can (and often do) yield interesting arguments on societal patterns, but they seldom illuminate and often obscure the law itself. They fail to recognize that, although law presupposes control, not all instances of control or containment are illustrations of law.

On one side of the discussion stands a determined group of literary scholars hanging tenaciously to legal ideas and terminology that Bacon and even Shakespeare might have found curious. *Exempli gratia:* modern commentators on early marriage law often fix doggedly upon notions that certain rituals (such as ring exchange or "handfasting") were required to create matrimony. The law made no such demands upon sponsalia although such rituals might fairly be called customary. What has emerged, then, is a body of interdependent modern literary criticism that has succeeded only in creating legal fictions that have little useful relation to historical legal theory or practice. As such, these fictions (which have rather unfortunately entered the modern literary critical lexicon under the rubric Early Modern Law) shed precious little light upon the law as it appears in early modern drama.

Legal historians, conversely, sometimes tend to view legal history backward: the legal institution makes the law and society obeys. However, in a civilization that recognizes some concept of common law, society determines its customs and comportment and legislators attempt to craft language to codify, protect, and enforce those behaviors. The language becomes the law. When that language fails, as it regularly does, society reacts. Literature is often part of that reaction. A study of the literary reaction to law is not always the same as the study of legal history (although too often it is narrowly deemed to be so). The titular term "Playhouse Law" was therefore chosen with purpose.

My friends in the legal profession, legal historians and practitioners alike, who have read drafts of this book, have correctly pointed out that "the story of the law's evolution" (as one put it) is not fully treated. To this criticism I plead guilty and recommend to the reader the many fine works by the likes of the Sokols, J. H. Baker, and S. F. C. Milsom (who have been influential to my study and may be found in the bibliography of this work). Throughout this study, however, I have indeed attempted to remain on the side of solid legal scholarship even though my discussion by necessity exists within the world of literary criticism.

It is quite true, for example, that in my discussion of the Statute of Uses I neglect to fall into a discussion of how within a decade of its enactment Henry VIII carved out exceptions to it in his Statute of Wills. It is equally true that the discussion navigates around the many honest motivations there were for creating a use; by focusing upon the unscrupulous transactions involving the use, the discussion almost certainly does create a wholly wrong social impression. Wholly wrong, that is, from the perspective of the legal historian. It is, however, quite in accord with the impression given from the early modern stage, the popular perception if you will.

The purpose of this examination is to reveal the law not as it is presently perceived to have been but only as it found voice in the world of the playhouse. Unlike several modern investigations, this work does not begin with the assumption that the early modern dramatist necessarily understood the *minutiae* of the law. Rather, this study attempts to elucidate the law (as briefly and accurately as possible) before exploring how that law was presented from the stage. As the chapter on the use law should make clear, the playwrights of the period understood that chicanery could be involved in creating a use. This chicanery became a feature of their drama—not because it was "the history of the law" but rather because it formed the exploitable dramatic side of that history. Their understanding of the law, how that understanding might have been formed and how expressed dramatically, is the basis of this study. Therefore, if the discussion concerning the history of the use law leans very heavily upon misdealing, it does so with purpose. Misdealing under the Statute of Uses explores and explains the use law as it appeared in the early modern playhouse.

Likewise, in the chapter on secret marriage, the discussion might perhaps be guilty of creating the impression of a separation between church and state. This impression would be anachronistic and possibly even presentist if it were not for the fact that the drama of the time does rather seem to make that distinction. It is not a separation of church and state that is revealed, of course, but rather a bright distinction between man's law (whether practiced in the ecclesiastical or common law courts) and God's law (which is beyond the ken of legal institutions of any stripe). This chapter undeniably creates the perception of a civil marriage distinguishable from the sacred act. That perception does seem to reflect the ahistorical ideology of presentism (an ideology I reject). The fact remains that the playwrights themselves—through their characters—create a dichotomy similar to a modern understanding of church–state separation. Although the Ecclesiastical Commission asserted its plenary authority over marriage, the civil union is attested back to ancient times, and the period's drama clearly perceives an enforceable marriage—Natural or humanistic, but certainly outside the benediction of the church. In law, the church reserved the right to pass judgment on marriage formation until long after the time of Shakespeare. In drama, this right was seriously questioned and often rejected. Therefore, when this discussion states categorically that there were two forms of marriage (the humanistic and the sacred), it reveals not necessarily the understanding of the jurist but rather the perception of the layman (and, *a fortiori*, the playwright and the fictive world of his drama).

The primary purpose of dramatic legal images might have been to foment revolution—or at least evolution—in legal institutions. These images might have served a commercial purpose to lure in the Inns of Court student and entice him to spend his money. Or perhaps they were intended merely to draw upon interesting dramatic situations for the entertainment of laymen. They might have served some combination of all three motivations. I tend to believe that this synthesis of motivations regularly controlled dramatic legal imagery. Therefore, it should come as no surprise to discover that a single legal image might provide, on the lay side, a character motivation while simultaneously developing an esoteric commentary aimed at the legal practitioner. It is possible, nevertheless, to compare the presentation of these images over a series of plays, to examine attitudes toward the laws, and to uncover how those laws and attitudes might have been derived. What is thereby revealed is not necessarily legal history as the legal historian would have it—with all of its color and conflict pigeonholed into accessible dicta—but rather the literary (and popular) expression of and reaction to received jurisprudence. This popular (and perhaps more revealing) literary understanding is what I have chosen to call "playhouse law."

Acknowledgments

A PROJECT SUCH AS THIS SEEMS TO THRIVE UPON AN ONGOING ACcumulation of debts of gratitude. Numberless helpful librarians and work-study students at reference desks, circulation desks, and reshelving areas—the names of whom I never knew—have earned my heartfelt gratitude. I here express my sincerest appreciation to those countless, vital individuals on the permanent and temporary staffs of the libraries and collections at Tulane University, the Huntington Library, Harvard University, the University of Texas, Lincoln's Inn, the British Library, and Borthwick Institute of Historical Research, York. Thanks also to Bill Richards and the staff of the Stewart Library Interlibrary Loan department for their assistance.

I would also like to thank Robert F. Willson, Jr., Ted Tucker, A. R. Braunmuller, Herbert Berry, William Ingram, Susan Cerasano, Nicholas W. Knight, Marvin Morillo, Richard A. Posner, J. L. Simmons, Gerald Snare, and the participants in the Shakespeare Association of America's *Legal Institutions* seminars in Austin, Texas, and in Kansas City, Missouri, and also the *Theatre History* seminar in Minneapolis, Minnesota, for reading and providing invaluable commentary on draft portions of this work. I am grateful for the early guidance of Lloyd Bonfield of Cambridge and Tulane Law School and for his encouragement of this project. Sheldon Bernstein, LL.M., provided invaluable insights into modern legal philosophy and interpretation and generously gave his time to lengthy discussions of many of the most challenging questions arising from this study. Thanks also to Thomas Austenfeld and Phil Buckheister for helping to secure development funding for this work. Over the years, throngs of Renaissance drama and Shakespeare students in my classes and seminars patiently sat through readings of large portions of this work and provided valuable questions and commentary; for this I have incurred a debt I can never sufficiently repay. Damaris Moore Corrigan, my wife, herself a superior legal scholar and linguist, offered much advice and encouragement on the final drafts and throughout this project volunteered her expertise in Latin to translate, *inter alia,* Manorial court rolls; to her am I most indebted and dedicate this work.

All errors in this text, of course, are entirely my responsibility.

Playhouse Law
in Shakespeare's World

Introduction

THE THEATRICAL WORLD IN THE TIME OF SHAKESPEARE WAS NOT, I suspect, elementally different from the current entertainment industry. Screenwriters today must meet certain regulations and once had to kowtow before the Hayes Commission (and must still dance attendance to the MPAA). Performers must belong to their own form of guild—Equity, SAG, AGVA, and the like. And, ultimately, the whole jumbled morass accompanying any show business venture, the contracts, personal interactions, petty artistic rebellions, the need to hire a hall, and all of the none-too-entertaining commercial aspects of the modern entertainment industry, also occupied (in its own idiom) a large portion of the Renaissance theatrical enterprise. This was and is the stuff of show business. Recent criticism, however, has endeavored to "understand" Renaissance drama under such titanic rubrics as "New Historicism" and such notional signposts as "Containment vs. Subversion"—attempting to view flesh-and-blood drama from within the vacuum of theory. These approaches have been in equal measure politicized and overly generalized to be of any real assistance in recapturing the essence of the time. It is the minutiae, the individuality if you will, of social and political machinations that provide meat for artists. The human face, the soul in torment, these are the ingredients of drama.

There is a human face to Shakespeare's theatrical world. It has been captured and preserved in the amber of litigious activity. Contracts for playhouses represent human aspiration: an avaricious hope for profit or an altruistic desire to provide for a family. Lawsuits have preserved the declarations of rights and the righteous indignations as well as the fictions and half-truths under which the Renaissance theatre flourished. Leases and agreements preserve the intentions, honest or dishonest, of the men who wrote, performed, and bankrolled the drama of Shakespeare and his contemporaries. The period 1590–1623, the limits of the original Shakespearean enterprise, resembles nothing so much as a third of a century of the sort of squabbling, shoving, and place-seeking familiar to every modern theatrical professional. And this human comedy of Renaissance theatre business is in some measure recoverable. It can be found in the contracts and theatrical records that have been left behind, the chronologies that can be reconstructed, and within the plays themselves. The reconstruction that follows is primarily legal. Legal because regulation haunts every business, laws construct society, contracts bear witness to understandings, and litigation leaves in its record books a snapshot of lives. Much can be adduced regarding the unique symbiotic relationship of the legal and the theatrical world during the Renaissance.

In the General Introduction to *The Law of Property in Shakespeare and the Elizabethan Drama,* Paul Clarkson and Clyde Warren state that, within the intended scheme for their work, "the reader must constantly bear in mind the fact that the legal background which [is presented] for any group of allusions is not under any circumstances to be read into the dramatic passages."[1] The intention of their work, as with many such works seeking to explore Shakespearean and Elizabethan legal acquirements, is to develop an encyclopædic examination of some field or fields of law that are suggested in Renaissance drama.[2] The value of such work is, of course, that it produces an invaluable reference guide, which does, indeed, lay bare the field. The difficulty with this approach has been the scholarly reticence in taking the next step, the step that Clarkson and Warren specifically resist in the quoted passage. The weakness in such works is their failure to apply the legal concepts directly to the plays in which the concepts are found. A significant study might be made into how certain legal backgrounds inform specific Renaissance dramatic works. Such a work has not been forthcoming. Clarkson and Warren suggest that the "ideal author for the subject would be a combination of legal historian and specialist in the field of Elizabethan drama."[3]

Moreover, the discoveries made by such an inquiry can and do reveal a great deal about who was writing for the theatre. Additionally, these discoveries reveal to us the political, social, and personal concerns that interested playwrights and presumably interested their audiences. They tell us what sold admissions and playbooks. They reveal a lot about audience tastes and knowledge. Allusion to law leads us to the perceptions of the laws themselves. The perceptions lead us to a society of individuals (the Renaissance ideal) rather than to the modern, muddy reception of society as an agglomeration of ideas, exemplars, and political agendas.

Since 1790, the date of Edmond Malone's published commentary on Shakespeare's legal acumen,[4] the field of research concerning Shakespeare's legal knowledge has been mostly limited to a relatively unprofitable attempt to identify the author of the Shakespearean canon. For the two hundred years following Malone's conjectures, scholars choosing to address the question of Shakespeare's legal imagery have been content to argue whether the law in Shakespeare's plays was "good law" or "bad law."[5] This line of inquiry grew out of the desire to reconstruct Shakespeare's educational achievements.

Several commentators, Lord Penzance most notably, began to advance the theory that, because of the wealth of accurate legal knowledge demonstrated in Shakespeare's plays, the author must have been well-versed in the law; and a number of authorities began to suggest that Sir Francis Bacon himself wrote the Shakespearean canon.[6] The main success enjoyed by this type of examination, wherein legal imagery is used as evidence of a legal mind at work behind Shakespeare's plays, has been to shift the focus away from Shakespeare's law as it pertains to the text.[7] To argue, rather, the relative merits and demerits of the law as it is expressed in the Shakespearean canon merely begs the question. To posit, for example, the legality of Shylock's bond as it reflects the reality of English (or Italian!) law during the seventeenth century, or to suggest that Bacon alone could have written the bond with such precision is an academic form of woolgathering. We are better employed in searching into the significance of the legal imagery as it appears in Shakespeare's work and asking what it tells us about the play and the world in which the playwright wrote.

In 1947, the Annual Shakespeare Lecturer of the British Academy struck a well-tempered chord regarding the question of Shakespeare's relation to the law, and, by extension, the relation of Renaissance drama to the law when he said:

> [A]ll we can safely affirm of Shakespeare, and that I believe we can affirm, is that he mixed in a society where the terms of the law were current coin and wrote for an audience which accepted them as such.[8]

Shakespeare, along with Marston, Jonson, Middleton, Webster, Massinger, and a number of other playwrights, used law primarily as an image to buttress a character, underscore a plot, or present a theme and perhaps only secondarily to sate any personal interest in the law or comment upon current affairs.

The hermeneutic imperative is strong in a work attempting, as does this, to develop a picture of a theatrical world by reference to its literature. The better we understand how an image works within the context of its fictive structure, the better we are able to understand how it would have been appreciated by both playwright and audience. Hence, the more we recover the detail of the drama, even where that detail plays a very minor part in the drama—indeed especially where it is minor—the better we can appreciate how well legal concepts were understood within the world of the playhouse. Therefore, an off-handed reference to a contract term in *The Merchant of Venice,* a term that seems complex to the modern reader, reveals that the term was not at all beyond the reach of the playwright nor of a significant part of the audience.

In order successfully to demonstrate the Renaissance use of law as an image, one is obliged to select a single area of the law and follow it through several plays. By such comparison three goals are reached. First, the perception of the technical legal aspects of a line is adduced. Next, the popular currency of the legal expression is proved through demonstration of its usage by more than one playwright of the time or in more than one play. Finally, by application of the technical aspects of the law to the expression of a specific character in a specific situation, we come to appreciate the depth of the expression on a legal-dramatic level. A simple example of this last process may be drawn from King Henry's lines in *1 Henry IV.* In reference to Richard II, Henry says:

> The skipping King, he ambled up and down
> With shallow jesters and rash bavin wits,
> Soon kindled and soon burnt; carded his state;
> Mingled his royalty with cap'ring fools;
> Had his great name profaned with their scorns

> And gave his countenance, against his name,
> To laugh at gibing boys and stand the push
> Of every beardless vain comparative;
> Grew a companion to the common streets,
> *Enfeoff'd* himself to popularity;
> That, being daily swallowed by men's eyes,
> They surfeited . . .
>
> (3.2.60–71) [emphasis supplied]

The legal term, *enfeoffed,* involves one of the oldest methods of conveying property.[9] The verb, *to enfeoff,* means to make a gift to.[10] The phrase, "Enfeoff'd himself to popularity," therefore makes little logical sense. Lord Campbell called it "forced and harsh."[11] It is rather awkward to say that one may make a "gift to oneself *to* popularity." Shakespeare probably employed the word as a legal synonym for the verb "gave," and thereby failed to demonstrate much legal sophistication. The significance of the choice, however, goes beyond the usual willingness to quote the passage as proof of Shakespeare's unfamiliarity with the underlying meanings and usages of legal terms.[12]

Set in its context, awkwardness notwithstanding, the word choice is in line with the images of rashness and commonality the King is attempting to convey. The feoffment to which Henry alludes is the least complex, most mundane manner of conveyance. It is technically called a *feoffment with livery of seisin*[13] and is no more ceremonial than giving the physical object into the possession of the intended recipient. Handing out a party political button or a theme park bumper sticker are good modern examples. No writing is required for ownership to be transferred. Hence, when juxtaposed with figures used in the remainder of the quoted passage—mingling with rash bavin wits,[14] giving his countenance against his name, carding his estate—the image of Richard II engaging in a feoffment, a quick, unceremonious gift that succeeds in mixing his royalty with the masses, is most appropriate. Shakespeare here demonstrates that he understood the sense of the verb even if he did not employ its proper grammatical formulation. The choice is even more appropriate when the circumstance of the pronouncement is considered. King Henry is, by analogy, admonishing Prince Hal against *"enfeoffing* himself to popularity," so to speak, through his connections with Falstaff and his companions. Furthermore, we must accept as an empirically demonstrated fact that not only did Shakespeare know what he was about when he employed the term but also that he expected his audience to understand it.

The trick of the structure throughout the present work demonstrates a trifurcation of intention. First, the entire argument may be read *in toto* to support the overriding hypothesis that legal language is used in the period drama in such a cavalier and dynamic fashion as to demonstrate a presupposition of an audience *au courant* in the terms of the law (at least in the popular perception). Furthermore, the currency of the legal language suggests the symbiotic nature of law and the Renaissance theatrical world in which Shakespeare wrote. Second, individual chapters may be read in isolation to demonstrate the workings of certain legal motifs throughout a body of Renaissance work in order first to understand how the law was understood and second to see the interrelationships between several plays which use that motif. Third, and finally, the structure of this discussion invites individual examination of each play. This final point is intended to be of benefit to the neophyte Renaissance scholar studying the work for the first time, the lecturer wishing to annotate his lecture text, and the dramaturge mounting a production of the play under consideration.

The purpose of this book is not to create a Procrustean bed of legal interpretation against which every play is to be "understood," but rather to draw into the light some often overlooked and more often misunderstood legal references found in Renaissance drama. By abjuring but not discounting the encyclopædic method of listing cant legalese found in the drama and instead focusing on several specific legal points and tracing those points through the plays in which they appear, I hope to achieve several goals. First, for my colleagues engaged in the study of Renaissance drama, this discussion covers both New Critical and New Historicist approaches.[15] It is intended to reward interests in close reading as well as in the discovery of cultural textuality in fictive texts. I intend this inquiry to develop a greater understanding of how certain images resonate within the structure of each play as well as how those images reflect and shape cultural attitudes. Second, for my colleagues in the legal profession, the attorney-scholar interested in Law and Literature and legal history, this examination may help to illuminate attitudes to and perceptions of specific (and often troubling) laws that attracted attention in the sixteenth and seventeenth centuries. It is also intended to offer evidence on the character of and interest in legal studies during the period. Third, for my colleagues devoted to practical dramaturgy, I intend this investigation to offer possible character motivation in performance situations. Finally, and romantically, I intend this work to help in the revaluation of several worthy, but too often dismissed, plays from the period. This I do for the dramatists themselves.

The overriding intention is to reassemble a number of works including dramas, contracts, wills, court records, and recorded business dealings. This work will demonstrate how the theatrical world surrounding Shakespeare and his contemporaries may have functioned not only to form companies, create literature, develop play writing collaborations, and build playhouses, but also to dissolve corporate entities, cheat partners, and generally lead theatre people into court. The first level of inquiry must by necessity be an enquiry into the relationship between the Renaissance legal and theatrical worlds. The latter half of this book will focus on specific legal concepts found in particular plays.

Had I but world enough and time, this discussion would be many chapters longer than it is. There are dozens if not hundreds of legal concepts, each with its own compelling history, broached within the early modern drama. I have selected two. In the scheme of the following discussion I hope first to demonstrate something not too well understood, and that is the place of the lawyer in early modern drama—the lawyer as playgoer, playwright, critic, and character. I then intend to demonstrate a commonplace (no less true for being common) that the early modern playhouse world was a litigious place, a place well acquainted with the terms and strategies of the law. Having established the role of law in the early modern playhouse, this discussion turns to the drama itself and two very different but intriguing laws: use and clandestine marriage. These two legal concepts I select for several reasons. Because they represent diversity in legal approach, laws of land on the one hand and of persons on the other, they accurately represent the sort of discussion law in drama can encompass. Next, because these concepts have a well-documented history—ancient and early modern—they lend themselves to an evolutionary examination. Next, these laws have a history of misconception in the criticism of early modern drama, which cries out for correction and clarification. Finally, because these legal concepts find expression in a large number and variety of period plays, they may be examined in depth and with breadth. Still, the discussion covers only two laws. It is merely a taste, and not enough to satisfy even the author of this work, but one hopes it may provide an appetizer and starting place, if not a model, for other such examinations.

1
'A Must, Then, to the Inns o' Court Shortly

THE FIRST QUESTION TO ARISE MUST BE WHETHER THE RENAISsance audience would be capable of formulating the nice distinctions suggested by the legal imagery under consideration. An examination of the composition of the Elizabethan, Jacobean, and Caroline audience suggests that an influential portion would. The audience, at least in significant part, comprised young men whose interest in the law and legal matters was at least as much a reflection of social position as it was of scholarly attention.[1] References to the patrons of the drama throughout the period ranging from 1562 through 1642 regularly refer to the students from the Inns of Court.

Around 1603 John Stow described the Inns of Court in detail.[2] According to him, "There is in and about this Citie, a whole Uniuersitie, as it were, of students, practisers or pleaders and Iudges of the lawes of this realme, not liuing of common stipends, as in other Uniuersities it is for ye most part done, but of their owne priuate maintenance, as being altogither fed either by their places, or practise, or otherwise by their proper reuenue, or exhibition of parents & friends: for that the yonger sort are either gentlemen, or the sons of gentlemen, or of other most welthie persons. Of these houses there be at this day 14. in all, whereof 9. do stand within the liberties of this Citie, and 5. in the suburbs thereof, to wit:

Within the liberties	Sergeants Inne in Fleetstreete Sergeants Inne in Chancery lane The Inner Temple The Middle Temple	for Iudges & Sergeants only in Fleetstreete, houses of Court.
	Cliffords Inne in Fleetstreete Thauies Inne in Oldborne Furniuals Inne in Oldborne Barnards Inne in Oldborne Staple Inne in Oldborne	houses of Chancerie.
Without the liberties	Grayes Inne in Oldborne Lincolns Inne in Chancerie lane by the old Temple.	houses of Court.
	Clements Inne New Inne Lions Inne.	houses of Chancerie, without Temple barre, in the libertie of Westminster.

"The houses of Court bee replenished partly with young studentes, and partly with graduates and practisers of the law: but the Innes of Chancerie being as it were, prouinces, seuerally subiected to the Innes of Court, be chiefly furnished with Officers, Atturneyes, Soliciters and Clarkes, that follow the Courtes of the Kings Bench, or Common pleas: and yet there want not some other, being young students that come thither sometimes from one of the Uniuersities, and sometimes immediately from Grammar schooles, and these hauing spent sometime in studying vpon the first elements and grounds of the lawe, and hauing performed the exercises of their own houses (called *Boltas*,[3] *Mootes*,[4] and putting of cases)[5] they proceed to be admitted, and become students in some of these foure houses or Innes of Court, where continuing by the space of seuen yeares, or thereaboutes, they frequent readinges, meetings, boltinges, and other learned exercises, whereby growing ripe in the knowledge of the lawes, and approued withall to be of honest conuersation, they are either by the generall consent of the Benchers, or Readers, being of the most aunciente, graue, and iudiciall men of euerie Inne of the Court, or by the speciall priuiledge of the present reader there, selected and called to the degree of *Vtter Barresters*, and so enabled to be common counsellors, and to practise the law, both in their chambers, and at the Barres.

"Of these after that they be called to a further steppe of preferment, called the Bench, there are twaine euerie yeare chosen among the Benchers of euery Inne of Court, to bee readers there, who do make their readings at two times in the yeare also: that is, one in Lent, and the other at the beginning of August.

". . . Nowe from these of the sayd degree of Counsellors, or *Vtter Barresters,* hauing continued therein the space of fourteene or fifteene yeares at the leaste, the chiefest and best learned are by the Benchers elected to increase the number, as I sayd, of the Bench amongst them, and so in their time doe become first single, and then double readers, to the students of those houses of Court: after which last reading they bee named Apprentices at the lawe, and in default of a sufficient number of Sergeants at law, these are, at the pleasure of the Prince, to be aduaunced to the places of Sergeants: out of which number of Sergeants also the void places of Judges are likewise ordinarily filled . . . But from thenceforth they hold not any roome in those Innes of Court, being translated to one of the sayde two Innes, called Sergeantes Innes, where none but the Sergeants and Iudges do conuerse."

The number of members from the Inns of Court was never great. Even if one included the benchers and utter barristers along with the students,[6] all of their numbers would fill a coterie theatre perhaps twice, and it is reasonable to assume that, even of this relatively small number, not every student, bencher, and utter barrister was interested in attending dramatic performances. Even so, the lawyers and law students who were interested in the drama appear to have been dedicated patrons.[7] The members who attended plays, and attended regularly, would have likely exercised a disproportionate influence upon the emerging dramatic industry.[8]

The likelihood of the influence of the Inns of Court upon Renaissance drama may be premised upon three considerations. First, along with noblemen and visiting foreign dignitaries, the students of the Inns of Court were a cynosure in the theatre, or at least they believed themselves to be important patrons and acted accordingly. Second, as the sons of gentry and wealthy merchantmen, they were educated, viewed themselves as erudite and sophisticated, and spent more money as a group at the playhouses and bookstalls than did citizens and apprentices.[9] Third, the students of London's third university helped supply the market for playwrights. This contribution by the Inns of Court to the emergent drama of the Renaissance has been too often overlooked during the past three hundred years.

One of the unspoken doctrinal truisms of Renaissance dramatic studies holds that The Drama, by which we mean the dramatic movement that produced Shakespeare, began around 1587 or 1588 with the production of Kyd's *The Spanish Tragedy*. The Great Age of English Drama, some will argue, may be traced directly back to 1576 and the construction of the Theatre in Shoreditch. Most competent discussions of the subject acknowledge that some admixture of Greek and Roman sources, Native Drama, Chronicle History, and Academic *Histrionica* has a claim on Renaissance dramaturgy. But the prevailing view of the age was most apt to be a vision of a late-1580s *Überbühnenautor* springing full-grown, Athena-like, from the fertile Shoreditch fields and flourishing on the rich Southwark flood plain. Though the dynamic improvement in dramatic literature between 1587 and 1590 is remarkable, we have perhaps lingered too scrupulously upon this period and come to regard it too rigorously as a period of spontaneous genesis. Recent scholarship has begun to focus upon the patterns and traditions leading to the vernal moment in Renaissance drama.[10] The recently furrowed field of New Historicism asks questions concerning the rationale underlying some of the dramatic elements we have come to regard as typical of the English Renaissance. One such element, the thread of jurisprudential interest running through Renaissance drama, is almost certainly linked directly to the social, personal, and commercial influence practiced on poets and theatrical entrepreneurs by members of the Inns of Court.

From early in the history of the modern theatre, the Inns of Court have made contributions to the emerging art form. Before there was a permanent theatre structure in England, members from the Inner Temple and Gray's Inn were presenting courtly performances of intramural, didactic plays.[11] These plays represent the earliest known English attempts at verse structures, genres, and source influence, which are each characteristic of the popular period.[12]

1 : 'A MUST, THEN, TO THE INNS O' COURT SHORTLY   29

- *Gorboduc,* written by members of the Inner Temple, is the first blank verse play written in English.
- *Jocasta,* written by members of Gray's Inn, continued the tradition; *Jocasta* also represents the first known English adaptation of a Greek play.[13]
- *The Supposes,* also written by a member of Gray's Inn in the same year as *Jocasta,* not only represents the first prose comedy written in the English language, it also introduced the use of the prose prologue and supplied the subplot for Shakespeare's *The Taming of the Shrew.*
- *Gismonde of Salerne,* a tragedy written by members of the Inner Temple, is the oldest example of an English play based upon an Italian novella. It was later rewritten, "newly revived and polished ... according to the decorum of these daies," and published as *Tancred and Gismund* during the height of the dramatic Golden Age.
- *The Misfortunes of Arthur,* written by members of Gray's Inn, was contemporaneous with *The Spanish Tragedy*[14] and represents the first English play to treat the Arthurian legend.

Throughout the quarter of a century from *Gorboduc* to *The Misfortunes of Arthur,* therefore, the Inns of Court plays demonstrate a sensitivity for both linguistic and dramatic invention and artifice.[15]

The interrelationship between the drama and the Inns of Court neither begins nor ends with the five significant academic dramas produced between 1562 and 1588, however. Evidence has been uncovered to suggest Inns of Court connections with the drama as far back as the fifteenth century.[16] In 1505, the Inner Temple listed a *magister jocorum* in its records. This Master of Revels suggests that some revelry, perhaps including drama, was occurring in the Inner Temple in the earliest part of the sixteenth century. Four years later the Middle Temple paid 6s.8d. to a group of players *(ludatores).* The Inner Temple records an occasional allowance for actors *(pro istruonibus)* during this period.[17] And in 1526 Cardinal Wolsey was offended by a play written by John Roo of Gray's Inn. Hall[18] describes this incident thus:

> The xviij. Yere of Kyng Henry the viij. This Christmas was a good disguising plaied at Greis inne, whiche was compiled for the moste part, by master Ijon Roo seriant at the law. xx. yere past, and long before the Cardinall had any aucthoritie, the effecte of the plaie was, that lord gouernance was ruled by dissipacion and negligence: which

caused Rumor Populi, Inward grudge and disdain of wanton souereignetie, to rise with a greate multitude, to expell negligence and dissipacion, and to restore Publik welth again to her estate, which was so done. This plaie was so set furth with riche and costly apparel, with straunge diuises of Maskes & Morrishes that it was highly praised of all menne, sauyng of the Cardinall, whiche imagined that the plaie had been diuised of hym, & in a greate furie sent for the said master Roo. and toke from hym his Coyfe, and sent him to the Flete, & after he sent for the yong gentlemen, that plaied in the plaie, and them highly rebuked and thretened, & sent one of them called Thomas Moyle of Kent to the Flete, but by the meanes of frendes Master Roo and he wer diliuered at last. This plaie sore displeased the Cardinall, and yet it was neuer meante to hym as you haue harde, wherfore many wisemen grudged to see him take it so hartely, and euere the Cardinall saied that the kyng was highly displeased with it, and spake nothing of hymself.

The description of the action suggests a production similar to early allegorical drama such as *Magnificence* and *Respublica*. The art of disguising, by which we should probably read drama, was so valued by Henry VIII that, in the year following the incident recorded by Hall, 1527, the king divided the Great Hall at Greenwich Palace into a Banqueting Hall and a Disguising Theatre. It was in this Disguising Theatre sixty-one years later that the gentlemen of Gray's Inn would present their play, *The Misfortunes of Arthur,* before Henry's daughter, Queen Elizabeth.

Several elements of this account are worthy of notice. First, that the play was presented before the King in Gray's Inn and was written by a Sergeant of the law indicates the importance of drama to the Inns of Court by 1526. Second, the performance in question, referred to as both a disguising and a play, is something more than a Masque or a dance, because it is said to include "Maskes and Morrishes."[19] Third, it is significant to note the lavish display associated with the performance. Such costly array is often hinted at in the disguisings and interludes of the Inns of Court,[20] and such hints suggest the gravity with which these performances were viewed. Fourth, Hall indicates quite clearly that Roo compiled the play twenty years before the incident recorded. If the play was, indeed, written in 1506, at approximately the same time the Inner Temple was installing a *magister jocorum,* one must ask whether it was performed at that time, where, and for whom. Furthermore, one may conjecture from this evidence that, during the first quarter of the sixteenth century, the Inns of Court were presenting drama. Therefore, although many of the plays devised for performance at the Inns of Court have been lost, it seems likely that such plays were being produced regularly.

There is, for example, no record of a play being presented by or for the Inns of Court between the 1526 incident described by Hall and the production of *Gorboduc* in 1562. Alfred Harbage and Samuel Schoenbaum (*Annals of the English Drama 975–1700* [London: Methuen & Co. Ltd., 1964]) allude to a Moral Comedy in 1556 by William Baldwin, now lost, called *The Way to Life (A Discourse of the World)*, which may have had an Inns of Court auspice. The only other evidence that the Inns of Court were active in drama during the middle third of the sixteenth century comes in the form of negative evidence.

In 1551 Gray's Inn passed an injunction stating that there should "be no Comedies, called Interludes, in this House, out of Term times, but when the Feast of the Nativity of our Lord is solemnly observed." The conclusion to be reached is that such comedies, called Interludes, were an occurrence common enough during vacations to require a rule against them, except during Christmas. There is no suggestion of the character of these Interludes, whether written in-house or brought in by wandering players. The evidence suggests only that drama in some form was a regular feature of Inns of Court life during the middle of the sixteenth century.[21]

The period from 1560 to 1569 appears to be a decade of great theatrical activity within the Inns of Court. Lincoln's Inn hosted performances of the Chapel boys in 1565[22] and 1566. The Lincoln's Inn accounts of 1565/66 show a payment of £2 to the boys of the Queen's Chapel. The Inner Temple presented *Gorboduc* on 28 January 1562. The Revels Account from 1564/5 lists at "Shroftid . . . new and diuers showes made by the gentillmen of Greys Ine." In the margin is written "Gentillmenne of ye Innes of Court. Diana, Pallas" (fol. 117). In 1566 Gray's Inn not only produced a Shrovetide masque[23] but *Jocasta* and *The Supposes* as well. And in 1568 the Inner Temple produced *Gismund of Salerne*. Although the evidence would appear to suggest that the 1560s represent a Golden Age of Inns of Court drama, it actually proves only that our records for this period are more complete. There is little information about performances during the 1570s. Lincoln's Inn had a play by Lord Rich's Men in 1570. The "lusoribus" of "Lord Roche" received £1 for their efforts. Few other plays are recorded, which might suggest that the young law students began frequenting the Theatre, the first Blackfriars, and the Curtain to the exclusion of intramural performance. But the possibility also exists that, like the period spanning 1526 to 1562, theatrical productions were simply not recorded by any source currently known.[24]

On 9 February 1579/80 the Black Books of Lincoln's Inn record a payment of £3 6^s 8^d "to Mr Ferrand one of the Queen's chaplains *pro commedia.*" We have evidence that *Damon and Pithias* by Richard Edwards, Master of the Revels for Queen Mary, was performed at Lincoln's Inn in 1582, sixteen years after the playwright's death. Gray's Inn had a "play at Shrovetyde" in 1581 of which nothing is known. During 1587 Gray's Inn presented a "comedy or shew set forth by the gentlemen of this house last Christmas."[25] On 16 January 1587/88 Gray's Inn gave *Catiline* at home before Lord Burghley. We also know that the gentlemen of Gray's Inn presented *The Misfortunes of Arthur* before Queen Elizabeth at Greenwich on 28 February 1587/88.

In a letter from Bacon to Lord Burghley, which Spedding believes is pre-1592,[26] reference is made to two Masques of which we have no other record.[27] Bacon writes,

> There are a dozen gentlemen of Gray's Inn that, out of the honour which they bear your Lordship and my Lord Chamberlain, to whom at their last masque they were so much bounden, are ready to furnish a masque: wishing it were in their power to perform it to their minds.

Bacon's letter indicates that, at least at Gray's Inn, performances continued to be produced even though there remains no official record of those productions.

When stage plays became popular in the early years of the last decade of the sixteenth century, we have a clearer idea of the import of drama to the Inns of Court. In 1592 Gray's Inn performed a masque. In 1594 the celebrated entertainments for the Prince of Purpoole took place at Gray's Inn. On December 28 Shakespeare's *Comedy of Errors* was presented in the Hall. Although it is not impossible that this was the premiere performance of the play, as many commentators have suggested, it seems unlikely that the play was written specifically for this production. The sport was suggested and begun on December 12. Unless one is prepared to suggest that the play was written, rehearsed, and made ready for production in sixteen days, it is difficult to believe that the play was prepared for this particular occasion. That the play was "fire new" at this time and the coincidence of the law sports and the new play provided a happy accident is, of course, entirely possible. At least one commentator, Dunbar Plunket Barton in *Shakespeare and the Law* (pp. 63–66) sees a reference to the case of *Underwood v. Manwood* in the gold chain business of the play. If this *cause célèbre* from 1592 was alluded to for the benefit of the law students, we need not conclude that the play was written especially for an Inns of Court performance. The thesis of the present work is that such references were common in the literature of the popular theatre in order to attract and compliment the legally inclined audience members.

The infamous incidents of that "Night of Errors" required a *Masque of Amity* on January 3 to reunite the Grayans with the affronted Templarians. During that evening the king-at-arms read the articles of the Order. The context of the articles implies that the Knights of the Order would be required to do what they would do in any event. One article clearly states, in the high good humor suited to the occasion, that each Knight of the Order should "frequent the Theatre, and such like places of Experience."[28] The students of Gray's Inn, if not the students of the other Inns of Court, were already frequenters of the popular houses in 1594, as evidenced by the king-at-arms' easy familiarity with the haunts of public performances. Gray's Inn also produced the *Russian Masque* on Twelfth Night and the *Masque of Proteus* on Shrovetide of 1595 in connection with their revels.[29]

Much the same event occurred at the Middle Temple in 1599. During their *Prince d'Amour* revels of that year the champion of the prince, in the same vein as Purpoole's king-at-arms five years before, voiced his regret that the modern Knights Templar had forsaken public shows. In a humorous investing of the newly created *Knights of the Quiver* the herald read the articles of the Order. Item 24 of the articles states that the knight should "learn no speeches out of Playes to entertain the time," indicating that attendance at and memorization of popular drama was a recognized practice in the Hall. The Middle Temple also presented their *Masque of the 9 Passions* in conjunction with their 1599 revels.

The initial decades of the seventeenth century demonstrate no abatement in the zeal for drama within the Inns of Court. In 1601 the Middle Temple was host to Shakespeare's *Twelfth Night*. Plays were performed at the Inner Temple on Candlemas (February 2) from 1605 through 1612, and another on All Hallows day (November 1) from 1608 through 1612. The Candlemas performances of 1605 and 1607 each cost the Inner Temple £5, and the 1612 performance cost £6 13s 4d. The price of the performances suggests that they had engaged professional players. On Candlemas of 1612 a second company had been appointed to play. They were paid a mere 30s, presumably because the Inner Temple canceled their performance. In 1608 the Candlemas play at the Inner Temple was *The Oxford Tragedy*, the title of which has been suggested to be a corruption in transmission of *The Yorkshire Tragedy*. Also in 1608 the Inner Temple held three revels during the Michaelmas term which may have included dramatic performances. In 1610 the Middle Temple presented *The Fleire* by Edward Sharpham. In 1613, on February 15, the Middle Temple and Lincoln's Inn presented a masque written by George Chapman to honor the marriage of the Princess Elizabeth and Count Palatine of the Rhine. Five days later, on February 20, the Inner Temple and Gray's Inn cooperated to present Francis Beaumont's masque of *The Marriage of the Thames and the Rhine*. In the next six years the Inns of Court presented at least five grand-scale masques:

- Gray's Inn's *Masque of Flowers* on Twelfth Night, 1614;
- The Inner Temple's *Ulysses and Circe* by William Browne on 13 January 1615;
- The Middle Temple's masque for the Earl of Buckingham on 17 January 1617;
- Gray's Inn's Candlemas *Masque of Mountebanks,* 1618 (which Collier, without proof, ascribes to Marston); and
- The Inner Temple's Christmas *Masque of Heroes,* 1619, written by Middleton and played by members of Alleyn's troupe from the Fortune Theatre.[30]

An unpublished manuscript at the Folger Shakespeare Library, written by Archpriest William Harrison and dated 9 March 1617/18, prohibits priests from attending theatrical productions. A rejoinder by Father John Colleton, dated 28 April 1618, specifically excepts from Harrison's prohibition plays presented at the Inns of Court.[31]

Although documentary evidence dwindles shortly after the second decade of the century, the dramatic engagement in the

Inns of Court from 1620 to the Interregnum would appear to continue unabated. Except for one masque by the Middle Temple on 13 February 1621, and two Templarian masques in 1628, only Shirley's *Triumph of Peace* in 1633 and Davenant's *Triumphs of the Prince d'Amour* in 1634 appear to have been produced. But, as was true in the sixteenth century, there is a possibility that the record is silent on this point because performances were too common to record.[32] We know by the record left by Dugdale that, during the Restoration, stage plays were commonly associated with Reader's Feasts in the Inns of Court. Whether this association is atavistic, however plausible, is a matter of the purest conjecture.

A number of scholars have presented evidence that, besides the *Comedy of Errors* and *Twelfth Night*, at least two other plays by Shakespeare were performed in the Inns of Court. Leslie Hotson makes a strong case for *Troilus and Cressida* being a Middle Temple play written in 1598.[33] In another work, Hotson seeks to demonstrate that *Love's Labour's Lost* was performed at Gray's Inn during the Christmas of 1588,[34] and in doing so recants an earlier position he took that it had been a Middle Temple play.[35] Phillips quotes Hotson's evidence with apparent approval.[36] Although the evidence in question is ultimately unrecoverable, it is nevertheless credible and demonstrates the likelihood of the existence of other Inns of Court performances that have never been recorded.

At this point one should reflect upon how the knowledge of the connections with the *Comedy of Errors* and *Twelfth Night* has come down to us. In the first case the appropriateness of the play to the situation caused comment that succeeded in finding print nearly one hundred years after the fact. In the second, a law student—John Manningham—mentioned in passing his attendance at the performance in his diary, which survived unheeded until 1828, some 226 years after it had been written. Neither performance is recorded in the official record of either Gray's Inn or the Middle Temple. The temptation is great to conclude that other—perhaps many other—professional and intramural performances have gone unrecorded. Scholarship has attempted to demonstrate, for example, that *Timon of Athens* and *Measure for Measure* also had significant Inns of Court auspices.[37]

Besides the plays produced at and by the Inns of Court, the members of the law schools of London were known frequenters of the popular stage and followers of its bruits. In 1580 (April 13) the Privy Council minutes note the imprisonment of two members of the Earl of Oxford's players "for committing of disorders and affrays appon the gentlemen of the Innes of the Courte."[38] The fight occurred just after Oxford's Men had merged with the playing troupes of Dutton and the Earl of Warwick's Men. This transfer of service had been seen as an act of disloyalty and cause for a satire in which the men "wrot themselves his COMOEDIANS, which certayne Gentlemen altered and made CAMOELIONS."[39] It is not difficult to imagine the disgruntled satirists as Inns of Court men and the merger of companies the instigation of both the satiric barb and the fight that succeeded in chasing Oxford's Men into the provinces to play.

In 1581 there was another encounter between members of the Inns of Court and a professional acting troupe. The "dysordered companye of gentlemen of the Innes of Courte" were apparently mixing to some degree with professional actors on the day they encountered and fought with members of Lord Berkeley's players.[40] By interesting coincidence, this fight also ended in the players escaping into the country to continue playing. They played *What Mischief Worketh in the Mind of Man* at Stratford-upon-Avon in that year. They played in Stratford-upon-Avon again the next year, and it is alluring to think that Shakespeare, at the ages of seventeen and eighteen, may have had his first serious encounter with the London theatre by virtue of this company's brawl with Inns of Court men.

By 1592 Nash commented that "men that are their owne masters (as Gentlemen of ... the Innes of the Courte ...) do wholy bestow themselves upon pleasure, and that pleasure they devide (howe vertuously it skils not) either into gameing, following of harlots, drinking, or seeing a Playe."[41] In 1593 Sir John Davies,[42] himself an Inns of Court man and frequenter of the popular drama, wrote:

> *Rufus,* The Courtier, at the Theater,
> Leaving the best and most conspicuous place,
> Doth either to the stage himselfe transferre,
> Or through a grate, doth shew his double face,
> For that the clamourous fry[43] of Innes of court
> Fills up the private roomes of greater price:
> And such a place where all may have resort,
> He in his singularity doth despise.[44]

1 : 'A MUST, THEN, TO THE INNS O' COURT SHORTLY

Four years later another Inns of Court man with connections to the theatre, John Marston, characterized his contemporaries as ardent play fanciers:

> *Luscus* what's playd to day? faith now I know
> I set thy lips abroach, from whence doth flow
> Naught but pure *Juliat* and *Romio.*
> Say, who acts best? *Druscus,* or *Roscio?*[45]
> Now I have him, that nere of ought did speake
> But when of playes or Plaiers he did treate.
> H'ath made a common-place booke out of plaies,
> And speakes in print, at least what ere he sayes
> Is warranted by Curtain *plaudeties,*
> If ere you heard him courting *Lesbias* eyes,
> Say (Curteous Sir) speakes he not movingly
> From out some new pathetique Tragedie?
> . . . O what a tricksie lerned nickering straine
> Is this applauded, sencles, modern vain
> When late I heard it from sage *Mutius* lips,
> How il me thought such wanton Jiggering skips
> Beseem's his graver speech.[46]

In 1598 Francis Meres was cultivating Inns of Court connections. While himself not an Inns of Court man, his close connection with the Middle Temple is well documented. On 11 May 1598 Meres dedicated from his London address his *Granados Devotion* to Will Sammes of the Middle Temple. In that same year Meres produced the much celebrated *Palladis Tamia, Wits Treasury,* and it is not beyond reason to see in it an attempt to reflect the opinion of the crowd in which he moved. Dekker makes reference in 1609 to the twelve-penny rooms at a new play where one is allowed "a stoole as well to the Farmers sonne as to your Templar."[47] Thomas Overbury epitomized the 1614 "Fantasticke Innes of Court man" as having "heard one mooting, and seen two plaies."[48] A detailed description of a private theatre has been left us in *Certaine Observations at Blackfryers* (1617), written by Henry Fitzgeoffrey, who is identified on the title page as being "Of Lincolnes-Inn Gent."

In 1628 John Earle said of the gallant, which many Inns of Court men fancied themselves to be, that "his business is the street: the Stage, the Court, and those places where a proper man is best showne," and goes on to say of the stage player that "[y]our Innes of Court men were undone but for him, hee is their chiefe guest and imployment, and the business that makes them Afternoones men."⁴⁹ Of the few Inns of Court students' library catalogues that survive, four include Jonson's folio *Works*. In 1629 Francis Lenton described the idle young law student as addicted to Jonson's plays and that

> The Cockpit heretofore would serve his wit,
> But now upon the Fryers stage hee'll sit . . .
> His silken garments, and his sattin robe,
> That hath so often visited the Globe,
> And all his spangled rare perfum'd attires
> Which once so glistered in the Torchy Fryers,
> Must to the Brokers . . . ⁵⁰

From 1628 to 1631 Edward Heath of the Middle Temple saw nearly fifty plays and purchased ten playbooks.⁵¹ The Prologue to Thomas Nabbes's *The Bride* laments the dearth of financial success for plays when the lawyers are between terms:

> Vacation still: so little custom comes
> To buy or Merchandize, and fill our roomes,
> It would perswade us but for after hope
> Of better takings quite to shut up shop.⁵²

John Greene, the Lincoln's Inn diarist, mentions four visits to the Cockpit and Blackfriars in February of 1635 and additional visits to those houses in March, April, and June of the same year.⁵³ He also writes that, in October of 1635, "9 or 10 of Lincoln's Inn . . . were at a play, some at cockpit, some at Blackfriars."⁵⁴

One effect of the law students' interest in drama, not surprisingly, was that playwrights began writing to them. This is not to suggest that lawyers and law students were the exclusive aim of Renaissance playwrights, but rather that one level of their imagery added an extra dimension of meaning for their legal auditors.⁵⁵ Gurr, for instance, sees in the satire of Jonson's early work for the Lord Chamberlain's Men a conscious attempt "to put Inns of Court satire on stage and to broach the practice of 'railing,' as it came to be called."⁵⁶ In fact, the argument has been made that the railing characters of the Renaissance stage were a direct reaction to the 1599 ecclesiastical burning of the satirical literature favored by students of the Inns of Court.⁵⁷ The Inns of Court stu-

1 : 'A MUST, THEN, TO THE INNS O' COURT SHORTLY   39

dents' love of satire is directly responsible for the popularity of *Every Man Out of His Humour,* which went through two printed editions in a single year. Jonson's popularity might have been due in part to his intimate understanding of Inns of Court tastes. In *Satiromastix,* Dekker accused Jonson of "bumbasting out a new Play, with the olde lynings of Jests, stolne from the Temples Revels." But this is not to suggest that Jonson was the only playwright indebted to the drama of the Inns of Court.[58] The fictitious roaring boys of the public playhouses, therefore, provided a literary outlet for the Inns of Court gallants and a guaranteed audience for the theatres that catered to the gallant's taste. Gibbons notes that at about this time a stratification of tastes—noble versus common—began to stratify theatrical literature:

> Towards the end of Elizabeth's reign, plays at Blackfriars, Paul's, and, increasingly, the Globe, register a note of discontent with public affairs . . . [and] this divergence in attitudes to government and monarchy reflects a progressive split in the political attitudes of the two audiences: the first includes lawyers, members of the Commons, merchants and Inns of Court students, nobility and gentry, the second more predominantly tradesmen, citizens, labourers, carriers, apprentices, servingmen.[59]

The Induction to *Bartholomew Fair* seems to bear out Gibbons' suggestion. In it, Jonson writes to the "wity young masters o' the *Innes o' Court."* The many commentators, therefore, who suggest that Shakespeare and his contemporaries moved in a company where a knowledge of the law was presumed, where the terms of law were current coin, and where such knowledge and language was as much a mark of social rank as of pedagogical interest, would appear to have struck the mark precisely.

We should not find it surprising, then, that playwrights mixing in such company should acquire a certain amount of legal understanding. Certainly the reverse was true, and the members of the Inns of Court were well equipped to appreciate the drama. In 1594 a Grayan commentator was able to apprehend the source of the new play he witnessed, "[A]fter such Sports, a *Comedy of Errors* (like to *Plautus* his *Menechmus*) was played by the Players." John Manningham's oft-quoted diary entry demonstrates the law student's familiarity with four separate dramatic works and his ability to see correlation between them:

At our feast wee had a play called 'twelve Night, or what you will'; much like the commedy of errores, or Menechmi in Plautus, but most like and neere to that in Italian called *Inganni*.[60]

Authors of the period relied upon a portion of their audiences to appreciate the subtleties of their works, and commentary such as Manningham's suggests that the Inns of Court men were an audience best suited to appreciate linguistic and dramatic subtlety. Therefore, as seems likely, these attuned, affluent young men influenced the early-modern drama.

But perhaps the most telling, and most overlooked, connection between the Inns of Court and the drama is to be discovered in the number of Inns of Court men who were themselves dramatists, whether in the academic, popular, or coterie tradition. Thomas Sackville, whose contribution to English letters through both *The Mirror for Magistrates* and *Gorboduc* is overshadowed only by his political contributions, was a member of the Inner Temple, as was his literary collaborator, Thomas Norton. Sackville and Norton were pledges—that is, sponsors—for Arthur Broke's admission to the Inner Temple. Broke was admitted without fee "in consideration of certain plays and shows at Christmas last set forth by him." Broke also wrote the verse narrative, *Romeus and Juliet,* which provided the major source for Shakespeare's play.[61] George Gascoigne, influential pamphleteer who gave us *Certayne Notes of Instruction* and wrote *Jocasta* in collaboration with Grayan Francis Kinwelmarsh, and both translated and adapted *The Supposes,* was a member of Gray's Inn. Gascoigne and Kinwelmarsh are also responsible for the *Princely Pleasures of the Court of Kenilworth,* which may have inspired Oberon's "fair vestal" speech in *A Midsummer Night's Dream*. Robert Wilmot, Henry Noel, Christopher Hatton, and a Rod. Staf[ford] of the Inner Temple wrote *Gismonde of Salerne*. Wilmot went on to rewrite the work as *Tancred and Gismund* for the genteel closet market in the nineties in an attempt to capitalize upon the growing popular market for drama.[62] Christopher Hatton became one of Elizabeth's favorites and came to be known as "the dancing Chancellor."

Christopher Yelverton, who became a Sergeant of Law and one of the most famous statesmen to have come out of Gray's Inn, wrote the epilogue to Gascoigne's *Jocasta* and was one of the eight who wrote *The Misfortunes of Arthur.* Another collaborator on *The Misfortunes of Arthur* was Francis Bacon, also of Gray's Inn, whose legacy in both the pursuit of letters and the law need not be belabored here. The other Grayans involved in *The Misfortunes of Arthur* were Thomas Hughes, Francis Flower, Nicholas Trotte, John Lancaster, John Penruddocke, and William Fulbecke. Fulbecke distinguished himself as a legal pedagogue in his most famous work, *A Direction or Preparation to the Study of the Law* (1600). He also wrote *A Book of Christian Ethicks, or a Moral Philosophie* (1587), *An Historical Collection of the Continuall Factions, Tumults, and Massacres of the Romans* (1601), *A Parallele, or Conference, of the Civil Law, the Canon Law, and the Common Law of England etc.* (1602), and *The Pandectes of the Law of the Nations etc.* (1602). The aforementioned John Roo, whose play of *Lord Gouernance* enraged Cardinal Wolsey, was a Sergeant of Law out of Gray's Inn.

Thomas Lodge entered Lincoln's Inn on 26 April 1578 and demonstrated his interest in the drama almost at once. In 1579 he defended drama against the attacks of Gosson's *The Schoole of Abuse*. In his *Defense of Poetry, Musick, and Stage Plays*, Lodge stated,

> For tragedies and comedies, Donate the gramarian sayth, they wer inuented by lerned fathers of the old time to no other purpose but to yeelde prayse vnto God for a happy haruest or plentiful yeere ... As for Commedies, because they bear a more pleasanter vain, I will leaue the other to speake of them. Tulley defines them thus: *Comedia* (saith he) is *imitatio vitæ, speculum consuetudinis, et imago veritatis;* and it is sayde to be termed of *Comai* (emongste the Greekes), which signifieth *Pagos,* and *Ode, Cantus.*[63]

Lodge, besides being a defender and specious historian of the drama, was also a dramatist. In collaboration with Robert Greene, he wrote *A Looking Glass for London and England* in 1594, the same year his play, *The Wounds of Civil War,* was printed. His "Rosalynde," from 1590, provided a source for Shakespeare's *As You Like It*. He was cited by Meres as one of the best poets for comedy and satire in 1598. In 1614 he published *The Works of Lucius Annaeus Seneca*.

Although William Warner's connection with a particular law school is unknown, he was most assuredly an attorney. He was born in 1558. His translation of the *Menæchmi* is a possible source for Shakespeare's *Comedy of Errors*. His sudden death in

1609 was registered at Amwell, Hertfordshire. The parish register of that year calls attention to his bifurcated talents in the law and letters:

> 1608–9. Master William Warner, a man of good yeares and of honest reputation; by profession an attornye of the common pleas, author of "Albion's England."

George Chapman may have been accepted into the Middle Temple. He was certainly appreciated by that institution. On 15 February 1613 he wrote the masque for the Middle Temple and Lincoln's Inn to celebrate the marriage of James I's daughter, Elizabeth. His drama was written for the coterie audiences, and his collaboration with two other darlings of the Inns of Court, Jonson and Marston, is suggestive of Inns of Court connections if not of his personal membership.

Thomas Middleton, whose plays often contain legal motifs,[64] was one of two Thomas Middletons admitted to Gray's Inn in the mid-1590s. The *Dictionary of National Biography* identifies him as the Thomas Middleton who entered in 1593 (age 13), but the possibility remains that he was the Thomas Middleton admitted in 1596 (age 16). He later matriculated at Queen's College, Oxford. He was appreciated by the Inns of Court and wrote the Inner Temple's *Masque of Heroes* in 1619.

Ben Jonson, though not himself an Inns of Court student, was greatly influenced by his connections at the Inns of Court. His works reflect an intimate understanding of the inner workings of what has been termed "London's Third University" and an appreciation of its members. Several of his plays, as will be discussed, not only use Inns of Court settings but also characters drawn from Inns of Court men. He dedicated his *Every Man Out of His Humour* to them thus:

> TO THE NOBLEST
> NOVRCERIES OF HVMA-
> NITY, AND LIBERTY,
> IN THE KINGDOME:
> THE INNES OF COURT.
> I Vnderstand you, Gentlemen, not your houses:
> and a worthy succession of you, to all time, as
> being borne the Iudges of these studies. When
> I wrote this *Poeme,* I had friendship with

diuers in your societies; who, as they were
great Names in learning, so they were no lesse
Examples of liuing. Of them, and then (that I
say no more) it was not despis'd. Now that the
Printer, by a doubled charge, thinks it worthy
a longer life, then commonly the ayre of such
thing doth promise; I am carefull to put it a
seruant to their pleasures, who are the
inheriters of the first fauour borne it. Yet,
I command, it lye not in the way of your more
noble, and vse-full studies to the publike.
For so I shall suffer for it: But, when the
gowne and cap is off, and the Lord of liberty
raignes; then, to take it in your hands,
perhaps may make some Bencher, tincted with
humanity, reade: and not repent him.
                                By your Honorer,
                                Ben. Ionson.[65]

Jonson includes Inns of Court men in his plays, as in *Bartholomew Fair, The Staple of News,* and *The Devil is an Ass.* He was a frequenter of the Apollo Club, which also figures prominently in *The Staple of News* and was located in the Middle Temple at the Devil's Tavern, No. 2 Fleet Street, under the sign of St. Dunstan tweaking the devil's nose. *The Devil is an Ass* has at least one scene that depicts a student's room at Lincoln's Inn. Jonson has one other interesting connection with Lincoln's Inn. Legend holds that Jonson and his stepfather erected one of the brick walls located at Lincoln's Inn.[66]

John Marston's father was a member of the Middle Temple. The dramatist lived in his father's lodgings at the Middle Temple during his career, from 1595 to 1606. Marston's father's will indicates that the playwright studied for the law but did not continue in those studies. In willing his law books to his son, the elder Marston lamented in 1599, "man proposeth and God disposeth." At least one study has been made of Marston's connection with the Middle Temple and the symbiotic relationship of the law and literature as it applies to him.[67]

Edward Sharpham, who wrote *The Fleire* and *Cupid's Whirligig,* wrote for the children's companies popular among gallants. His plays appear to have been popular reading fare; both received four printings. The first was printed in 1607, 1610, 1615, and 1621, and the second in 1607, 1611, 1616, and 1630. Sharpham was a member of the Middle Temple, having entered on 9 October 1594.

John Webster, the dramatist, could well be the "Master John Webster, gentleman, son and heir apparent of John Webster of London, gentleman," who entered the Middle Temple on 1 August 1598.[68] If so, we have a better idea of how the dramatist acquired his interest in the law and legal trials evinced in such works as *Sir Thomas Wyatt, The White Devil, The Devil's Law-Case,* and *Appius and Virginia*. The Webster of the Middle Temple does not seem to have completed his studies, which seems to indicate that he began to follow another profession, perhaps play writing. All that we may say with certainty is that, four years after a "John Webster, gentleman" entered the Middle Temple, John Webster, dramatist, is noted in Henslowe's diary, in May 1602, as working on a play entitled "sesers ffalle."

Francis Beaumont is arguably the most famous dramatist to have been a member of one of the Inns of Court. He entered the Inner Temple on 3 November 1600. Beaumont did not begin publishing until after his arrival at the Inner Temple despite his having been at Broadgates Hall, Oxford from 1596 to 1598. He was obviously interested in appealing to the Inns of Court. In his first play, *The Woman-Hater,* he makes direct reference to "The whole frie in a Colledge, or in an Inn of Court." In 1613 Beaumont was chosen to write the *Inner Temple Masque,* performed on February 20 in honor of the marriage of the Lady Elizabeth.

Thomas Campion, who, like Thomas Lodge, later became a physician, was a masque writer while in residence at Gray's Inn. He was involved in the revels of 1594, when he wrote a hymn to Neptune. He is probably best remembered for his conflict over "ranting rime" which he waged with Samuel Daniel between 1602 and 1603.[69]

John Ford was born in 1586 and entered the Inner Temple on 16 November 1602. Though he was never called to the bar, Morris has suggested that he practiced law.[70] His plays are representative of the type of play favored by the coterie audiences during the Stuart reign. His plays were generally performed in small, upper class playhouses, most usually the Cockpit or Phoenix, but also Blackfriars. Ford's intertextuality, what Butler calls the "distinctive feature" of Ford's work,[71] is remarkable for its allusions to other dramatic works—*'Tis Pity She's a Whore* alludes to *Romeo and Juliet; The Lady's Trial* to *Othello; The*

Lover's Melancholy to *King Lear;* and *The Broken Heart* to *The Malcontent.* Such allusiveness can point only to his audience's familiarity with popular drama, and, given Ford's reputation as an Inns of Court writer, one is irresistibly drawn to the conclusion that the Inns of Court were well acquainted with the popular writers of the day and especially, it would seem, with Shakespeare. The dramatist William Heminge left us an epigrammatic sketch of the playwright in *An Elegy on Randolph's Finger:*

> Deep in a dump Jack Ford alone was got
> With folded arms and melancholy hat.

William Browne lived from 1591 through 1643. He is best remembered for his masque of *Ulysses and Circe* presented at the Inner Temple on 13 January 1615. This masque was presented "to please ourselues in private." Browne was a member of the Inner Temple from November of 1611.

James Shirley came to live at Gray's Inn in 1625 where, according to the *Dictionary of National Biography,* he "set up for a play-maker." After his sojourn in Ireland, he returned to apartments close to the Inner Temple gateway and was living there in 1666 when the Great Fire destroyed his lodgings and left both Shirley and his wife to die on the streets. In addition to his numerous stage plays, Shirley is responsible for writing *The Triumph of Peace,* which was performed in 1633 by all four Inns of Court.[72] The interest in this masque is well reflected in a record of the time from the Inner Temple:

> Whereas there having been no representation of any mask or other show before the King's Majesty by the four Inns of Court or any of them sithens his Highness' access unto the Crown, a consultation hath been lately had by the several benchers in their several Houses touching the same, whereupon it is unanimously agreed by them that a mask shall be jointly presented in this next Christmas before his Majesty, at the equall charges of the said four Houses ... every fellow of this House shall be taxed to pay as followeth, viz.: Every bencher, 5li.; every utter barristers of seven years' standing 50s.; every utter barrister under seven years' standing, 40s.; every gentleman under the bar ... 20s.

It has been suggested that this masque was a reaction to William Prynne's *Histriomastix,* a lawyer's Puritanical attack against plays ("the very Pompes of the Divell").[73] Prynne, relying on John Earle's *Microcosmographie,* attested that

> Inns of Court men were undone but for Players; that they are their chiefest guests and imployment, and the sole business that makes them afternoons men: that this is one of the first things they learne as soone as they are admitted, to see stage-playes.

The masque was dedicated "to the Four Equal and honourable Societies, the Inns of Court," and members from each of the four academies were represented within the production. The Inner Temple was represented at this masque by Sir Edward Herbert and John Selden; the Middle Temple by Edward Hyde,[74] who would become Lord Chancellor Clarendon, and Bulstrode Whitelock, who left an account of the masque in his *Memorials;*[75] Sir John Finch, who would also become lord keeper, represented Gray's Inn; Attorney General Noy represented Lincoln's Inn.

The well-known Essex trial provides an excellent example of how pervasive the dramatic background was to the practitioners of the law. On 19 February 1600/1601, the author of *Gorboduc,* Thomas Sackville, Lord Buckhurst, High Steward of England, sat in judgment. With Sackville sat dramatist John Ford's maternal uncle, Lord Chief Justice Popham. The author of the epilogue to *Jocasta* and the dumb shows of *The Misfortunes of Arthur,* Sir Christopher Yelverton, Sergeant of Law, appeared for the Crown. On trial were Shakespeare's erstwhile patron, Henry Wriothesley, Earl of Southampton, and the Earl of Essex. Attorney-General Coke, during examination of Sir Gilly, referred to

> the story of Henry 4th, being set forth in a play, and in that play there being set forth the killing of a king upon a stage: the Friday before, sir Gilly and some others of the earl's train having an humour to see a play, they must needs have the play of Henry 4th. The players told them that was stale, they should get nothing of playing of that, but no play else would serve; and sir Gilly gives 40 shillings to [Augustine] Philips the player to play this, besides whatsoever he could get.[76]

Henry IV (identified in most traditions as Shakespeare's *Richard II*) was chosen to give the conspirators the cue and motive for their treason presumably because Essex was identified with Henry IV in the popular imagination. After his rebellion, Elizabeth suggested to Francis Bacon that the author of *The Life and Raigne of Henry IIII* be placed on the rack to discover whether he had ulterior motives in writing it.[77] Apparently, however, the author was spared.

The authors of early modern drama who were also members of the Inns of Court account for a large portion of the extant drama from the period. An examination of only the works attributable to the major figures—Beaumont, Marston, Middleton, Shirley, and Ford—reveals nearly one hundred fifty plays and masques coming out of the Inns of Court connection. The number is substantially higher should one wish to include the works of Chapman, Webster, and Jonson, who each wrote specifically to please their patrons and friends at the Inns of Court, the former two having strong claims to membership. And again, if one were to add the contributions from the minor drama laureates of the Inns of Court—Davies, Browne, Campion, Bacon, Sharpham, Lodge, Warner, Wilmot, May—a strong case may be made for the dominance of the Inns of Court in Renaissance dramatic studies.

One need only examine a map of theatrical London between 1567 and 1639 to see the movement of theatres toward the Inns of Court.[78] Before theatrical speculators made the connection between their enterprise and the potential patronage from the Inns of Court, they built the Red Lion, Theatre and Curtain on the other side of the city, beyond Aldgate in the first instance and Moorgate and Finsbury Fields in the latter two. Within ten years, the clearly pronounced effect of law student patronage encouraged the construction of the Rose across the Thames and conveniently down river from the Temple Stairs. Within another ten years the Swan opened even closer to the Temple. When James Burbage lost his lease in Shoreditch, he purchased Blackfriars with the intention of presenting his plays within walking distance of the Temple. Burbage was almost certainly thinking of the first Blackfriars and the success that the children's company enjoyed during the early years of his own Theatre, both opening in 1576.

Although the move would have placed an adult company's theatre within walking distance of the Temple, the neighbors in the Blackfriars precinct were dubious. Their reticence indicates the novelty of an adult coterie theatre. A record remains of the protest lodged in the Blackfriars district in 1596 in reaction to Burbage's plan to bring in his adult company:

the said Burbage is now altering and meaneth very shortly to convert and turne the same into a common playhouse, which will grow to be a very great annoyance and trouble, not only to all the noblemen and gentlemen thereabout inhabiting but allso a generall inconvenience to all the inhabitants of the same precinct, both by reason of the great resort and gathering togeather of all manner of vagrant and lewde persons that, under cullor of resorting to the playes, will come thither and worke all manner of mischeefe, and allso to the great pestering and filling up of the same precinct, yf it should please God to send any visitation of sicknesse as heretofore hath been, for that the same precinct is allready growne very populous, and besides, that the same playhouse is so neere the Church that the noyse of the drummes and trumpets will greatly disturbe and hinder both the ministers and parishioners in tyme of devine service and sermons.

Evans's children's company rented the space from the Burbages for the same reasons Burbage had originally acquired the property and proceeded to enjoy success for nearly a decade serving Templarians, Grayans, and gentlemen from Lincoln's Inn. When the Globe was built, it was certainly situated to take advantage of the same trade that had been enjoyed by the Rose and Swan. At approximately the same time that the Globe was opening, another children's company began operating in St. Paul's, not far from Blackfriars and the noblemen and gallants in and around the precincts containing the Inns of Court.

The Fortune and Red Bull speculators set up in the same period in order to take advantage of the market not being served by the increasingly upperclass theatres along the river. They consequently built in the North. While these theatres ultimately appear to have attracted a lower-brow clientele, it is nevertheless suggestive that they were built on the same side of the city as the Inns of Court. The speculators' original intention in 1600 and 1605 may have been to draw the lawyers north and away from the Southwark and city playhouses. Theatres were moving indoors, however, and becoming more specialized. As they did, they became more exclusive. These new-style playhouses—Whitefriars, the Phoenix/Cockpit, and Salisbury Court—were later constructed in the front and back yards of the law fraternities in order to serve an exclusive market.

What is known for certain is that Beeston took a thirty-one-year lease on a property not far from the Blackfriars playhouse and equally close to the Inns of Court whose eight hundred students made up a conspicuous proportion of the hall playhouse's clientele.[79]

The Hope playhouse opened during this same period; however, with the higher-paying coterie audiences being well served by more convenient theatres, the Hope rapidly turned to baitings in order to remain open. In 1615, a year after the Hope opened, an ill-fated plan was launched to open a coterie playhouse at Porter's Hall, a playhouse variously known to modern theatre historians as Puddle Wharf and Rosseter's Blackfriars.[80] And, in the years just before 1642, Davenant tried unsuccessfully to build an indoor playhouse in Fleet Street at the very doors of the Middle Temple.[81] The influence of the Inns of Court upon the Renaissance drama, therefore, may well be seen to be in direct proportion to its influence upon the construction and location of early modern playhouses.

A number of dramatic works from the period are dedicated to the Inns of Court or their members.[82] Several plays feature Inns of Court men as characters.[83] The Inns of Court provide the locations of or are referred to in several plays.[84] In each case it is apparent that playwrights are attempting to curry favor with an identifiable sector of their audience. References such as that in Middleton's *A Mad World, My Masters* are obviously calculated to tease favored patrons. Mawworm tells Follywit that "there's none here but can fight for a whore as well as some Inns o' Court Man" (3.3.135–36).

It should, therefore, be readily apparent that an influential portion of the audiences attending the Globe, Blackfriars, Cockpit/Phoenix, Whitefriars, Paul's, Salisbury Court, Swan, Rose, and, to some lesser extent, the Fortune, Red Bull, and Hope theatres would appreciate the nuances appreciated by the members of the legal profession. Most commentators choosing to focus upon the tastes of this erudite group have emphasized their love of raillery and satire, which is not inappropriate. Butler, in his "*Love's Sacrifice*," p. 201, identified this facet of the Inns of Court literary tastes when he enumerated their "concern with politics, sex and skepticism, the sophisticated literary self consciousness, the verbal fireworks and clashing of violently opposed tones and styles, satire against pathos, tragedy against force [*sic*]." This editor would suggest "farce" over "force" as the more appropriate counterpoint to "tragedy" in the quoted passage, but Butler's point is still well taken.

Literary critics have focused upon these tastes because they reflect literate interests readily apparent to students of literature. But the membership at the Inns of Court, though certainly students of literature, were also students of law. Louis A. Knafla, in "The Law Studies of an Elizabethan Student" (*Huntington Library Quarterly* 32 [1969]: 221–40), demonstrates the rigor required of law students during this period. Our literary critics have been reluctant to trace the interesting connections between law and literature that grew out of the unique milieu of the Inns of Court. Here we have, perhaps for the only time in any period study, a large group of young literati who were also conversant in the law, both its technicalities and its pasquinades. To understand why the abstractions of the law were introduced into the drama of the Renaissance as motifs and images is to understand how the mind of the Inns of Court student was molded. Understanding the reasons behind the appearance of legal imagery in the works under consideration gives us a clearer understanding of the works themselves and, by extension, of the Renaissance theatrical milieu.

2
Tricks and Quillets that Thunder at a Playhouse

BEFORE THE THEATERS COULD THROW OPEN THEIR DOORS, THE theatre speculators had to navigate in legal waters. Questions of contract and property law plagued and in some cases influenced the construction of many of the playhouses. Shakespeare and his fellow playwrights were immersed in a litigious society simply by being in London. A London businessman of any stripe who did not know the law was at best a fool and at worst a gull. One either knew the law and used it or risked falling beneath its wheels. This is especially true in the case of the playwrights who had to deal with the likes of Philip Henslowe, Henry Evans, and the Burbages. They needed to know the law for their own self-preservation, for never has there been a more cagey fellowship of sharp dealers and legal rascals than are to be found in the confraternity of Renaissance playhouse entrepreneurs. There can attach no wonder then to the discovery of legal terms and juristic concepts in the drama of Shakespeare and his rivals. Their social and professional world was suffused with legal dealings. Complex contracts, litigation, and legal chicanery surrounded and shaped the building of many of the most famous London theatres and the founding of the most influential English playing companies.

THE THEATRE

If James Burbage was the father of the London playhouse, litigation was its mother. Adams has accurately stated that the "history of the first London playhouse [was] chiefly the history of quarrels and litigation."[1] The Theatre had been the brainchild of Burbage, who was unable to shoulder the cost of its construction. He brought in his brother-in-law, John Brayne, who had in 1567 attempted another such venture, the Red Lion, in Stepney.[2] Brayne paid the lion's share of the construction and demanded to be repaid out of the proceeds. Burbage objected to Brayne's plan for the division of the profits, and Brayne in turn accused Burbage of "indirect dealing" and hinted that Burbage had access to "a secret key" to the "common box" where the playhouse proceeds were kept. The two men then fell to brawling in a scrivener's office. Thus began the Golden Age of London playhouses.

Brayne and Burbage submitted themselves to arbitration. On 12 July 1578, the arbiters found that the debts on the property should first be paid from the playhouse profits and then Brayne was to be reimbursed for his expenditures above the amount Burbage had contributed. Only after all such debts were settled could the proceeds be divided equally between the partners. Burbage, however, failed to honor the arbiters' decision. In so doing, James Burbage established a pattern of ignoring legal orders and set in motion years of antagonism that would ultimately typify Renaissance playhouse history to the time of Cromwell.

The contentious partners soon had need for funds. They mortgaged their playhouse to John Hide for £125 8s. 11d. The debt was defaulted by year's end, and Hide gained title to the structure. While Hide continued to harass Burbage and Brayne (and, after 1586, Brayne's widow) for his money, the two parties attempted to strike a private deal with Hide. Each wished to exploit the opportunity to repurchase the structure outright and so cut the other out of the original agreement. Ultimately, in 1589, Cuthbert Burbage, James's eldest son, succeeded in redeeming the Theatre. Brayne's widow—Cuthbert and Richard Burbage's aunt—and her supporters did not accept the arrangement, however, and began agitating her nephews to be paid a share under the original contract.

While the fight over the playhouse structure boiled, another struggle over the land erupted. In 1582, Edmund Peckham claimed a right in the land that Giles Allen had leased to Burbage and Brayne. Peckham entered the playhouse forcibly, and Burbage "was fain to find men at his own charge to keep the possession thereof from the said Peckham and his servants." Because Allen had failed to deliver quiet leasehold to Burbage, Burbage withheld £30 rent. This act set Allen and Burbage at odds in court.

When in 1585 Burbage approached Allen to extend the lease, Allen refused. Under the original demise, Burbage was allowed to exercise an option within the first ten years of his twenty-one-year lease to extend the lease by an additional twenty-one years. This in essence gave Burbage an option of thirty-one years at the original rate, £14 *per annum*. Burbage had met the stipulations of the agreement, but Allen refused to allow the extension. The refusal greatly troubled the Burbages because, according to their original lease,

> Gyles Alleyn and Sara his wife did covenant and grant to the said James Burbage that it should and might be lawful to the said James Burbage . . . at any time or times before the end of the said term of one and twenty years, to have, take down, and carry away to his own proper use for ever all such buildings and other things as should be builded, erected, or set up in or upon the gardens and void grounds by the said James, either for a theatre or playing place, or for any other lawful use, without any stop, claim, let, trouble, or interruption of the said Gyles Alleyn and Sara his wife.

The longer Allen delayed renewing the lease, the closer Burbage came to losing the buildings he had erected, for once the twenty-one years had expired all buildings would revert to the original leaseholder, Allen. By 1596, Burbage saw the futility of dealing with Allen and bought the Blackfriars property with the aim of moving his enterprise there. That venture, after considerable expenditure, also proved futile when the neighborhood protested the playhouse, and the Privy Council took steps to halt the venture.

Allen continued to lease the Theatre property to Cuthbert Burbage after James died in 1597 only two months before the termination of the twenty-one-year lease. Cuthbert, however, was now a tenant-at-will paying £14 *per annum* on a year-to-year basis. Apparently fearing that Allen could close the Theatre on a whim, the company moved to the Curtain. By 1598, the Theatre was famous for being empty. In *Skialetheia* the old playhouse is referred to thus: "But see, yonder, one, like the unfrequented Theatre, walks in dark silence and vast solitude."[3]

The Burbage syndicate made plans to move to Bankside, and when Cuthbert heard of Allen's plans to convert the timber of the Theatre to his own use, he took matters into hand. What happened next is among the most famous moments in Shakespearean playhouse history. Allen, in his suit over the incident, described the event:

> The said Cuthbert Burbage, having intelligence of your subject's purpose herein, and unlawfully combining and confederating himself with the said Richard Burbage and one Peter Street [chief carpenter on this and the later Fortune playhouse], William Smith, and diverse other persons to the number of twelve, to your subject unknown, did about the eight and twentieth day of December, in the one and fortieth year of your highness reign [1598], and sithence your highness last and general pardon, by the confederacy aforesaid, riotously assembled themselves together, and then and there armed themselves with diverse and many unlawful and offensive weapons, as namely swords, daggers, bills, axes, and such like, and so armed did then repair unto the said Theatre, and then and there armed as aforesaid, in very riotous, outrageous, and forceable manner, and contrary to the laws of your highness realm, attempted to pull down the said Theatre. Whereupon, diverse of your subjects, servants and farmers, then going about in peaceable manner to procure them to desist from that unlawful enterprise, they, the said riotous persons aforesaid, notwithstanding procured then therein with great violence, not only then and there forcibly and riotously resisting your subjects, servants, and farmers, but also then and there pulling, breaking, and throwing down the said Theatre in very outrageous, violent, and riotous sort ... [and they] did then also in most forcible and riotous manner take and carry away from thence all the wood and timber thereof unto the Bankside, in the Parish of St. Mary Overies, and there erected a new playhouse with the said timber and wood.[4]

This truncated history of the first public playhouse opens several interesting insights into the Burbage syndicate and their treatment of questions in law. James Burbage had entered into a bond to abide by the arbitration concerning his dealings with Brayne. When he failed to do so, he surely forfeited the bond. His response was to ignore the forfeiture. There is no record of his ever having paid it. It seems clear from the suit filed during Michaelmas term 1588 that Brayne's widow had sued Burbage in common law on the bonds and for specific performance of the original agreement for one half of the Theatre. Burbage took her to Chancery for relief, a common tactic to slow proceedings. The suit continued through a number of Burbage's stalling tactics until 13 November 1590 when Chancery ordered that the parties abide by their 1578 arbitrament. This order Burbage also ignored. The case remained active through 1597 at least, but though the Burbages were clearly in default of several judgments there is no evidence those judgments were ever enforced.[5]

On the subject of the moving of the timbers to Bankside the case is cloudier. In strict law the lease had lapsed. The Burbages had no further claim on the materials sitting on Allen's land. Allen, however, had forced the lapse through a series of acts that could have been found fraudulent. Although they should have removed the materials before the end of the lease in 1597—to remain on the windy side of the law—the Burbages might in equity be found rightful owners of the timber and wood. This was the issue raised when Allen sued Cuthbert Burbage in the Court of King's Bench on 20 January 1599. The summary on the King's Bench roll is dated Trinity Term 1600. In late January of 1600, Burbage sought to stop Allen's common law suit by filing for relief in the Court of Requests. By 31 May 1600 the Court of Requests ordered Allen not to proceed with his suit in the King's Bench. Requests ordered Allen's arrest one month later when he continued to press his lawsuit in the common law court. On 18 October 1600 the Court of Requests found that Allen should have renewed his lease with Burbage. The Burbages therefore exercised their rights in removing the structure. Allen sued in Star Chamber, claiming that the Burbages used fraud to obtain their judgment in Requests. No record remains of the Star Chamber verdict, but it seems likely that the Court of Requests ruling remained in force.[6] The Burbages succeeded only then in acquiring quiet title to a building they had substantially stolen from Brayne, his widow, and (to a far lesser extent) Allen, and the Globe was born.

Francis Langley at the Swan and Boar's Head

Francis Langley, like so many other playhouse speculators of the period, was a businessman rather than a man of the theatre. Ingram's groundbreaking work on Langley leaves an indelible impression of a violent man, a devious entrepreneur, and a capitalist interested not in the art of performance but rather in its profits.[7] Langley's first recorded dealings with the emergent playhouse industry started in early 1594 when he mortgaged his profitable messuages in Cheapside. Langley was no doubt inflamed by the popularity of Henslowe's Rose, which he could not help noticing from the manor in Paris Garden where he had recently moved. He mortgaged his properties in the tenure of "John Terry, goldsmith, Robert Howe, goldsmith, Richard Langley, haberdasher, Hannibal Gammon, goldsmith, John Cornwall, goldsmith and Jane Clark, widow, citizens of London." These properties he used as collateral to secure a loan of £1,650 from Giles Simpson.[8] Ingram speculates that much of this money went to build the tenements and the Swan playhouse in Paris Garden.

Langley probably broke ground by late 1594. On 3 November of that year John Spencer, Lord Mayor of London, wrote to Burghley:

> I vnderstand that one Francis Langley, one of the Alneagers for sealing of cloth, intendeth to erect a niew stage or Theatre (as they call it) for thexercising of playes vpon the Banck side.[9]

Langley had placed his new theatre close to Paris Garden Stairs probably to waylay traffic heading to the Rose playhouse in much the same way the Curtain had been built closer to Bishopsgate originally to stem trade from the Theatre. The Swan was, in fact, built only twenty-six poles from the riverbank, a distance of only four hundred twenty-six feet.[10] By the most famous account, it was

> Theatrorum autem omnium prestantissimum est et amplissimum id cuius intersignium est cignus (vulgo Le Theater off te cijn) quippe quod tres mille homines in sedilibus admittat, constructum ex coacervato lapide pyrritide (quorum ingens in Brittannia copia est) ligneis suffultum columnis quae ob illitum marmoreum colorem, nasutissimos quoque fallere posse[n]t.[11]

On 21 February 1597 the Earl of Pembroke's company leased the Swan from Langley. The actors of the company each executed individual bonds of £100 to secure the property. They included Robert Shaa, Richard Jones, Gabriel Spencer, William Bird *alias* Borne, and Thomas Downton. Langley in turn "disbursed and laid out for making of the said house ready, and providing of apparel fit and necessary for their playing, the sum of £300 and upwards."[12] Langley was to receive a moiety of the proceeds from the galleries and was to be repaid his £300 from the other moiety. By 28 July of that same year Langley hand recouped £200, half of which was his profit from the galleries and the other half repayment of the loan. On that date the theatres were closed after the *Isle of Dogges* scandal. Because Shaa and Spencer were two of the players jailed over the incident, scholarship has reasonably concluded that the play had been presented at the Swan. By early August—mere days after the scandal—the relationship between the Pembroke's Men and Langley had failed. At that time Jones is found signing with Henslowe at the Rose. Soon afterwards, Shaa, Spencer, and Bird also removed to Henslowe's theatre, and Downton joined them in October. Henslowe had been able to obtain a new license for his playhouse following the general inhibition occasioned by the *Isle of Dogges,* but Langley—presumably because the Swan was responsible for the troubles—was unable to acquire one for his.

Chambers suggests that the new plays at the Rose after the *Isle of Dogges* incident, namely, *Black Joan, Hardicanute, Bourbon, Sturg-flattery, Branbolt, Friar Spendleton, Alice Pierce,* and *Dido and Aeneas* had all been played at the Swan and were brought over with the deserting Pembroke company.[13] Langley was obviously unhappy with the desertions, and it seems apparent that he tried to regroup and begin again. First, he managed to lure back two or possibly three of the original Pembroke "fellows." They along with other players continued to play at the Swan without license.[14] He thereby continued in modest sort to enjoy the profits of his enterprise. Next, he sued Shaa, Jones, Spencer, Bird, and Downton on their bonds, which had been breached by their defection to a rival house.

The five players moved the suit from the common law court to the Court of Requests,[15] maintaining that

1. they could not play because of the Swan's being unlicensed ("they durst not play ... w*i*thout lycence"; a plea of impossibility)
2. they were freed by Langley, who had acquiesced in their move to Henslowe (Langley had said they were "best to goe to him"; a parole modification of the original contract);
3. they could no longer appear as a company because Langley had split them when he returned the obligations of two or three of the players, perhaps as an inducement to encourage them to return (another plea of impossibility); and
4. they had not materially damaged Langley because he still had players at the Swan (an argument of mitigation).[16]

The players also countersued, claiming that Langley had failed to give them the costumes they had redeemed with the £100 from their moiety of the gallery takings. Further they claimed that Langley had converted "the same to his best profytt by lending the same to hyre."

It is impossible to say with certainty how the case was settled. No record has yet been discovered. In early 1598, however, Henslowe notes that Bird was still in some danger of being arrested and lent him £1 "to descarge the areaste betwext langley & him." It seems possible, judging from this scant evidence, that an out-of-court settlement or a judgment in favor of Langley had obtained and that Bird was in arrears by March. By September it seems an arrangement to buy out Langley's complaint was in the offing. Langley received £35 outright "A bowt the agrement betwext langley & them" and an additional £19, possibly more, to "feche home a Riche clocke which they had of mr langleys."[17] This sum, £54, is barely half of the £100 Langley had failed to recoup. Langley was presumably dogging the players for his losses. Chambers has seen a possible repayment in August concerning the "sewt agenste Thomas Poope" of the Chamberlain's, for which Henslowe advanced Bird 10s.[18]

Langley's dream of competing with the Rose came to an end on 19 February 1598, almost a year to the day of his contracting with Pembroke's Men. The Chamberlain's and Admiral's (now more appropriately Nottingham's) Men presumably conspired to call attention to the fact that the Swan was operating without a license. The Privy Council issued an order to the Master of the Revels and the Justices of both Middlesex and Surrey stating:

> Whereas license hath been granted unto two companies of stage players retayned unto us, the Lord Admiral and Lord Chamberlain . . . and whereas there is also a third company who of late (as we are informed) have by way of intrusion used likewise to play . . . we have therefore thought good to require you upon receipt hereof to take order that the aforesaid third company may be suppressed, and none suffered hereafter to play but those two formerly named, belonging to us, the Lord Admiral and Lord Chamberlain.[19]

Robert Wilson staged a contest in extemporaneous versification at the Swan later that year, and Peter Bromwell was licensed to perform his "feats of activity" there in May of 1600, but the Swan was effectively closed as a playhouse for the remainder of Langley's life. The playhouse and the manor of Paris Garden were transferred to Hugh Browker in January of 1602.

The Swan was only the beginning of Langley's foray into playhouse management, however, and he apparently learned much from his discomfiture there. In 1599 Oliver Woodliffe approached Langley to enter into a partnership with him and two other men, Richard Samwell and the actor Robert Browne. The three men, through a series of negotiations, owned the lease on the Boar's Head Inn, which they were converting into a playhouse.[20] The original leasee, Woodliffe, was obliged to make improvements amounting to £100 to the western side of the innyard. He was given seven years to complete the task from 1595 to 1602. Woodliffe brought in Samwell to help financially. They split the leasehold between them and came to an arrangement for dividing responsibilities and proceeds. The size of the project soon overwhelmed both men, and, while Samwell turned to Robert Browne to help him with his portion of the project, Woodliffe looked to Langley.

By late 1599 Samwell had defaulted on his obligations to Browne, who bought out his part of the lease for £360 and moved his company of players into the playhouse. The fact that Langley was interested in sharing in the venture so soon after the Swan failed is an indication of the potential he saw in the playhouse business. According to a later suit, Langley offered to "buy the whole interest of the said Woodliffe and his wife of the said Inn." He offered £400 for Woodliffe's interest, which amounted to the western gallery of the playhouse. Ingram points out the apparent inconsistency of Langley's offer of £400 for the western gallery compared to Browne's payment of £360 for the rest of the playhouse, observing,

> either Woodliffe and Langley agreed to collude in an effort to defraud Samwell and Browne of their rightful interest in the yard, or else Woodliffe consciously defrauded Langley by misrepresenting the matter to him. Either way, Langley's offer of £400 . . . suggests that Langley had in mind more than a mere half-share in the gallery.[21]

Langley borrowed £100 from his nephew Richard Langley and executed three bonds for £100 each to acquire Woodliffe's entire interest in the inn. In return Woodliffe executed a bond for over £666 as a "security for the same lease."[22] Langley began almost immediately a campaign to drive his partners from the playhouse. Woodliffe's original lease to Samwell, which Langley now controlled, allowed Samwell "ingress, egress, and regress" to the yard. Langley interpreted these terms literally and claimed that Samwell's structures, namely the playhouse galleries he had built and from which he earned his profits, were an act of trespass. Because Samwell had no interest to convey in the yard, according to Langley, his subsequent lease to Browne was a nullity.

Samwell took Langley to court at once. Langleys ignored the suits Samwell brought in the Court of Queen's Bench and Chancery. Samwell claimed that Langley was guilty of "unlawful maintenance" (the "officious intermeddling in a suit which in no way belongs to one," Black's Law Dictionary (BLD)), "champerty" ("a bargain by a stranger with a party to a suit, by which such third person undertakes to carry on the litigation at his own cost and risk, in consideration of receiving, if successful, a part of the proceeds," BLD), and "buying of pretensed rights and titles" (otherwise known as Bracery, outlawed under 32 Hen. VIII, c. 9). Langley retaliated by filing a complaint against Samwell in the Marshalsea Court. When Samwell failed to appear, Langley swore out a warrant for his arrest. Langley's true character then emerged.

On Friday, 13 December 1599, Langley accompanied what could only be described as a rout to Samwell's lodgings. Two bailiffs of the Marshalsea and their two servants, likely large men who in current parlance might be called *enforcers* or *bruisers,* and a carpenter named Owen Roberts besieged Samwell's rooms. According to Ingram, they made their entrance "most forcibly with bills, staves, swords and daggers."[23] Nothing more is known of this legal housebreaking. In three days' time, however, they returned just as violently with "swords, daggers, rapiers, pistols and other weapons." It is not difficult to conclude with Ingram that what happened next was nothing short of a skirmish. The bailiffs attempted to arrest Samwell and were succeeding when Samwell's son, Richard, arrived with friends and fought successfully to liberate his father.

Other such affrays occurred. Langley's apparent goal was to harass Samwell through both legal and physical means and make him give up his part of the Boar's Head lease. His harassment included leasing out his portion of the innyard to two of his creatures, Thomas Wollaston who subleased to Richard Bishop. Wollaston and Bishop at once began legal actions against Samwell for trespass. Langley's obvious goal in this was to, in Ingram's phrase, "multiply the occasions for litigation." Langley was no fool, however, and during the busy Christmas season the harassment ended abruptly so not to turn away trade at the playhouse. Likewise, Browne and his company went wholly unmolested during the entire period of Samwell's harassment. Presumably this was because Browne was the profit center of the enterprise despite the fact that his rights flowed from Samwell's lease.

One cannot help but wonder whether Langley had engaged in an analogous form of legal harassment the year before when he was trying to lure Pembroke's Men back to the Swan. Bird's legal difficulties remain tantalizingly suggestive in Henslowe's diary, but there is too little evidence to suggest Langley proceeded against Bird to the degree to which he badgered Samwell. Samwell took the matter to Star Chamber. Little is known of the outcome. Samwell's various complaints in various courts disappear after November of 1600. He tried to sue Browne, but withdrew the suit and died shortly thereafter.

But Samwell's death did not spell the end of the troubles. Browne's company proved popular, and profits appear to have been good. But in that same month, November 1600, Langley defaulted on the first £100 bond to Woodliffe. Woodliffe brought an action in common law on the bond. Langley responded by suing Woodliffe. Woodliffe had bound himself for over £666 to deliver a clear lease to the innyard. The troubles with Samwell (never mind they had been caused by Langley) demonstrated that the lease was anything but clear. Langley countered in equity and had Woodliffe's common law suit removed to the slow mill of Chancery. Woodliffe balked and offered an out-of-court settlement to return the three £100 bonds and repay the original £100 if Langley would agree to return his bond guaranteeing a quiet leasehold. Langley indicated that this would be an acceptable arrangement, but then Browne struck.

Browne, still claiming an interest in the playhouse through his lease with Samwell, brought suit in Chancery against both Woodliffe and Langley. Browne's suit complicated the suits already filed. If Browne could demonstrate that Samwell's—and consequently his own—lease were valid, the suits of the other two against one another would be jeopardized. In 1601, however, Browne had taken his company into the provinces and subleased the playhouse to Worcester's Men, Will Kempe's new company that would take up at the Rose in the following year to replace

Nottingham's Men, who had removed to the Fortune playhouse the year before.

Langley took a "rude company" into the playhouse during a morning rehearsal of the Worcester's company. Ingram quotes from the record what happened next:

> [O]ne of the said Langley's company with a halberd or such like weapon struck at this deponent's [carpenter John Mago's] servant [John Marsh], then working there, and almost wounded him, but as God would he hurt him not.

John Marsh elaborated upon his master's evidence, saying:

> [Langley] got the possession of the said stage and tiring houses [sic] ... and with a company of rude fellows kept the same, some of them swearing and vowing that they would kill or murder any that should resist them; and this he had cause to remember, for that one of the said company with a halberd or such like weapon had almost maimed this deponent in the thigh.[24]

Langley demanded that the players acknowledge him as their landlord. They were bound to pay him £3 per week for the privilege of playing at the Boar's Head. The payments apparently extended from Michaelmas to Shrovetide, a period of approximately twenty weeks.

Woodliffe was still at odds with Langley, who maintained that Woodliffe had passed the lease to him and therefore was guilty of trespass whenever he sought to enter the playhouse. Woodliffe, however, was still obliged to make the £100 worth of improvements to the western yard under his original lease, and he now had less than a year to complete the promised improvements. If he defaulted on the term, his lease would be nullified and with it all subordinate leases to Samwell, Browne, and Langley. Browne clearly saw the advantage in allowing the lease to lapse. He could negotiate his own lease with the owners and eliminate the problematic Woodliffe and Langley.

Langley, however, saw the wisdom in establishing a truce with Woodliffe. He leased to Woodliffe "certain rometh part of a messuage called the Boar's Head."[25] This lease would allow Woodliffe the right to enter and make the improvements necessary to keep the original lease in force. Langley, however, could not afford to have such a lease made public in case it would be construed as acknowledgment of Woodliffe's right. Instead of sealing the document, then, Langley gave it to Woodliffe who then transferred it to Hugh Browker, the man who was then negotiating to purchase Paris Garden and the Swan playhouse. According to Browker, the lease was "delivered by the said Woodliffe to [Browker's] custody to be kept to the use of the said Francis Langley."[26]

This document is the last dealing of interest in Langley's playhouse career and is worth a few words. When Woodliffe delivered the document to Browker he gave Browker a bond for £8. Browker executed a bond in return for £12, the probable price of the lease. The two gentlemen had created a use (to be discussed in detail in the next chapter) with Langley as the ultimate beneficiary. The bond for £8 probably acted as a guarantee to Langley (through Browker) for either the cost of the sublease or, more probably, the contemplated improvements to the western yard. The £12 bond assured both Woodliffe and Langley that Browker would not sell the leasehold to a third party, someone like Browne, while it was in his possession. By Langley's making himself the beneficiary of the use (a.k.a. the *cestui que use*), he ensured himself that he would have free and absolute access to the property even though he had demised it temporarily to Woodliffe. In this way Langley had estopped Woodliffe from claiming a new action of trespass against him. The Boar's Head, at least at the management level, was a roughhouse run by a group of rowdies masquerading as businessmen. Given Langley's tyranny toward his partners, it is no wonder he sought to protect himself in this way. The improvements were apparently completed, for the lease continued to run unmolested. The suits and troubles continued after Langley's death in 1602, but with his demise the intended scope of this discussion also comes to an end.

Langley's dealings at the Swan, where he was swindled not only of his profits but also of his playhouse, set the stage for his Boar's Head venture. Control became the central issue of Langley's later playhouse dealings. As merchant and landlord, Langley had not needed to worry about control. Where the commodity is tangible, wool or a tenement, control flows with the property. One may lock up one's wool or lock out one's tenant to maintain one's profits. The playhouse business, however, dealt in an uncontrollable commodity. Patrons bought nothing but a right to enter and watch. Players were at once tenants, commodity, and profit base. Words were the primary article of trade. There was nothing to lock up, no one to lock out if the enterprise careened out of control. Pembroke's Men taught Langley as much. Control of the playhouse business lay in the holding of the license and careful husbandry of the property. In a sense, then, the playhouse business would more properly be described as a crop rather than a mercantile enterprise. In Langley's dealings with Samwell, Woodliffe, and Browne one may readily see that the entrepreneur's first concern was holding and maintaining the property of the galleries and yard. These were where the fertile grounds of profit lay. He had earlier trusted Pembroke's Men to divide proceeds with him under their contracted terms, treating the playhouse as a shop rather than a cash farm, and he had the crows in to harvest his field. He did not make the same mistake with his new venture. What Langley learned through trial and error, however, seems to have come readily to other playhouse entrepreneurs, as we shall see.

Transfer of the Wooden O

When the Lord Chamberlain's Men decided to move south and build their own theater, they leased a tract of land from Nicholas Brend for £14 10s. per annum. The lease would run for thirty-one years. Six of the senior members of the company and an interested outsider signed onto the lease: Cuthbert and Richard Burbage each bought twenty-five percent of the paper while John Heminges, William Kempe, Thomas Pope, Augustine Phillips, and William Shakespeare each bought ten percent. Rather than having seven interests in the same document, however, the new syndicate divided the lease into two instruments. The Burbages owned an undivided interest in one half of the lease while the other five owned an undivided interest in the other half.

The complex agreement allowed all seven men to hold the entire property, but they did so in two separate instruments. Almost immediately the five players transferred their undivided half interest, or moiety, to two businessmen, Savage and Leveson, who in turn transferred their interest back to them for reasons which will soon become clear. Some two or three months later, when the playhouse was complete or nearing completion, William Kempe left the syndicate and assigned his portion to Heminges, Shakespeare, and Phillips thus raising their shares from ten percent each to thirteen and a third. Kempe excluded Pope from his transfer. Pope was a clown like Kempe,[27] and one wonders if Kempe slighted him from some sense of professional or personal animosity. Nevertheless, Heminges, Shakespeare, and Phillips transferred their new shares to one Thomas Cressey, who then transferred back four equal shares to the remaining four partners in the Globe moiety. After this transfer each partner held twelve and one half percent.

The first exchange is succinctly covered in a pamphlet prepared by the Public Records Office (PRO):

> Between the execution of the lease and the completion of the building these five men [Heminges, Shakespeare, Kempe, Pope, and Phillips] assigned their half share to William Levison and Thomas Savage who 'reassigned to ev[er]ye of them sev[er]ally a fift parte of the said Moitie'. The purpose in establishing the original tenancy in common may have been to prevent the scattering of the shares and to stop them passing into other hands through inheritance. If so the new arrangement defeated the purpose for shares did pass by inheritance, causing protracted litigation.[28]

The PRO's author is wrong in suggesting that the men created a tenancy in common. They created a joint-tenancy and in doing so wrote a strange chapter in the annals of playhouse dealings. No one has stopped to ask what the legal significance might be of this transfer to Leveson and Savage and the later transfer to Cressey. When Kempe left in 1599, not only did Shakespeare, Phillips, Heminges, and (eventually) Pope's shares increase from a fifth of the moiety (10% of the total) to a fourth of the moiety (12.5% of the total) but more importantly, the character of the leasehold estate changed. The householders owned something quite different after the transfers back from Leveson, Savage, and (later) Cressey than they held under the original lease arrangement. The alteration of the leasehold's character indicates that the sharers-cum-housekeepers were probably as nervous as Kempe had been. They, however, unlike their leading clown, decided to remain in the enterprise.

To understand the nature of what the men were doing, it is necessary to understand the rights and responsibilities they were creating with their transfers. There is a distinct difference between a tenancy in common and a joint tenancy, sometimes referred to as a jointure. To put it simply, a tenancy in common is an agreement wherein the multiple owners of a property do nothing more than share rights to the same piece of property. They must each respect one another's rights in the property and therefore may not waste or damage it, but beyond that they may treat the whole property as their own. They are allowed to will or sell their interest without harming the partnership. This is the sort of arrangement the Burbages had with the five players. Each side held half of the lease in a tenancy in common with the other side.

Conversely, a joint tenancy treats all the partners as though they are one person. There are four threshold considerations, called unities, in making a joint tenancy. They are the unities of interest, title, time, and possession. By interest is meant that all the partners must have the same claim to the property as the others have. No one partner in the Globe moiety could have more or less than the other four had. By unity of title is meant that all claims have been created under one and the same act or document. This unity was met under the original Brend lease (between the parties to the two halves of the lease) and later under the reassignments by Leveson and Savage and finally by Cressey (between the players sharing the moiety). The unity of time means that all partners must have the property vested in them for the same period of time. In this case, each partner held a leasehold of thirty-one years. Unity of possession means that all partners have rights in the whole property. The legal phrase for joint tenancy is that the property must be held *per my et per tout,* that is by the moiety as well as by the whole.[29] In short, a joint tenancy operates as if only one person holds the property. If one of the partners sells his share, that share is no longer held in joint tenancy because that new (sold) share was not created by the same document that created the rest of the tenancy. Understanding this helps to understand the original reassignment to Leveson and Savage and the seemingly peculiar actions of Heminges, Shakespeare, Phillips, and Pope after Kempe's resignation.

The first lease between Brend and the Globe syndicate was intended to be a tripartite lease between the landlord, Brend, and two distinct entities within the syndicate, the Burbages on one side and the five players on the other. There is a prejudice in contract law, however, that assumes that any devise to two or more persons creates a joint tenancy, and a contract must specifically state that it is to be a tenancy in common in order for it to be held as such. Brend's tripartite lease apparently failed to create a tenancy in common between the two main parties (the Burbages on one side and the five players on the other). Because the players found it advantageous to reassign their moiety, it seems likely that the Brend lease had somehow inadvertently created a joint tenancy between all seven men. The players destroyed the seven-way joint tenancy and successfully divided the moiety of the Burbages from their own through their subsequent transfer to Leveson and Savage. They thereby successfully created the tenancy in common with the Burbages the parties had originally sought.

When the paper was transferred back to the players, the unity of title was destroyed between the players and the Burbages, and the new instrument created a joint tenancy between the five men only. Heminges, in a later suit, depicted the transfer back from Leveson and Savage, saying, "[They] regranted & reassigned to euerye of [us] seuerally a fift parte of the said Moitie of the said garden and groundes."[30] Heminges's use of the word "severally" may cause the non-lawyer needless trouble. Though it seems that "severally" contradicts the notion of property to be held "jointly," such is not the case. Undoubtedly Heminges is using a shortened form of the usual contract phrase "jointly and severally" as it appeared in the original document. Blackstone elucidates: "But a *devise* to two [or more] persons, to hold *jointly and severally,* is a joint-tenancy; because that is implied in the word 'jointly,' even though the word 'severally' seems to imply the direct reverse."[31]

The proof of the joint tenancy between the five men can be seen most clearly when Kempe departs. The playhouse was nearly or recently erected when Kempe assigned his share to Heminges, Shakespeare, and Phillips, cutting out Pope. This transfer, in essence, destroyed the joint tenancy *in Kempe's share,* for, according to Blackstone, "if one of three joint-tenants releases his share to one of his companions, though the joint-tenancy is destroyed with regard to that part, yet the two remaining parts are still held in jointure."[32] This situation was anathema to the partners' original plan. According to Heminges, he, Shakespeare, and Phillips transferred the fifth part that had been Kempe's share:

> W^{ch} said Last mencioned fiveth parte did shortlie after come to Thomas Cressey by the gaunte & assignem^t of the said Wm Shakespeare the said John Heminges and Augustine Phillipps wch said

Cressey did shortlie after regraunte and reassigne the said fiveth parte to the said William Shakespeare John Heminges Augustine Phillipps & Thomas Pope.[33]

In essence, then, the five players now had two jointures: one full share each (10%) from their transaction with Leveson and Savage, and one quarter share each (2.5%) from Cressey. Because the two interests arose separately, the two jointures would be separate properties sharing identical characteristics. A nice legal distinction, to be sure, but also a necessary one.

There are certainly solid business reasons for what the partners did. Perhaps they were nervous. By making themselves jointly and severally liable for the debts of the property and not liable only for their own portion, they were protecting the new syndicate against any individual actions for debt. They had certainly extended their credit in the speculation. They were likely protecting the syndicate from the creditors from whom they had borrowed "more sums of money taken up at interest, which lay heavy on us many years" to quote the 1635 *Sharers Papers*. The transaction was probably not an attempt to raise monies, although it is true that Heminges did involve himself in a sale and leaseback to raise substantial monies on his home in Adlestreet and again used his neighbor Savage for the task.[34] It is possible, though not probable, that the transfers accomplished a dual goal of protecting the syndicate by making all parties liable while also raising additional monies. The latter does not seem likely, however, given the advanced stage of the playhouse's construction at the time of the transfers.

One of the player-sharers, Pope, died in 1603 and left his shares in both the Curtain and the Globe playhouses to Mary Clark (*alias* Wood) and Thomas Bromley. Bromley was a minor, and one Basil Nicoll, Bromley's guardian and Pope's executor, afterwards administered his interest. Augustine Phillips died in 1605. In his will Phillips specifically discouraged his widow from remarrying:

> yf the said Anne my wyfe doe at any tyme marrye after my decease, ... from thenceforth shee shall Cease to be any more or Longer [my] executrix, of this my laste will [and Testament] or any waies intermedle with the same, And the said Anne to haue no parte or porcion' of Goodes [and] {or} Chattells.[35]

When she did remarry in 1606, Anne Phillips's new husband, John Witter, sought to lay claim upon the share that Phillips had left his wife. What became of Shakespeare's share in the Globe has not been recovered. He did not specifically devise it in his will in 1616 unless it passed to Susanna and John Hall among his "leases." It is not unlikely that he assigned it before retiring to Stratford-upon-Avon—probably to Heminges, who seems to have acquired it by the 1620s.

Kempe is a puzzle. He entered into the Globe venture, became a householder, went to the trouble of transferring his undivided share to Savage and Leveson and taking back his divided share only to sell his interest to three of the four partners and quit the stage temporarily. He later joked, "I haue without good help daunct my selfe out of the world."[36] He reemerged after his "nine dayes wonder" as a leading member in Worcester's company. I can only guess from the slight evidence that Kempe had little faith in the new venture, or he had grown tired of service in the Chamberlain's company. His slighting of Pope in the share transfer may be telling. Professional jealousy may have played its part, but to make too much of that act would reside in the realm of pure conjecture.

Most likely Kempe's decision to leave was founded upon a combination of unease over the novel arrangement the Burbages had instigated and the offer Worcester's company doubtlessly made him. Burbage's company was in trouble in 1599. They had suffered a series of setbacks in their recent history. In 1596 the Blackfriars venture failed. They lost their lease on the Theatre within that same year and spent two years trudging between hired playhouses. The idea to build a new theatre all their own must surely have been born of desperation,[37] and they took no chances over their new location.

When the Chamberlain's players moved to a parcel only one hundred yards from the Rose, they must have known what they were about. Henslowe rapidly moved the Nottingham's company north where he built the Fortune, possibly to avoid the powerful Chamberlain's company eating into his profits. Henslowe wasted no time in reacquiring the services of son-in-law Alleyn for Nottingham's at the Fortune. Henslowe soon thereafter negotiated with Worcester's Men, whom he moved into the Rose in 1602 as a "second Company" to compete directly with Burbage's new venture. One wonders whether this new Henslowe venture was a competitive maneuver to undercut the Chamberlain's Men while maintaining his own "first company" safely to the north.

Henslowe probably liked the look of the reconstituted provincial company that played at the Boar's Head in 1601. There were a fair number of well-known actors recruited into Worcester's, including several old Chamberlain's Men such as John Duke and Christopher Beeston as well as Robert Pallant (the elder). The company also included Thomas Heywood of Nottingham's company. A young John Lowin also joined the company at the Rose and the next year moved as a hired man to the King's company at the Globe. Worcester's had also acquired the novice, Richard Perkins, just in time for the new Rose venture. Perkins would go on to win great praise throughout his career—not the least of which from John Webster for his work in *The White Devil*. Worcester's clearly had an astute eye for older men whose careers were becalmed or in decline and younger men on the threshold of success. Henslowe was a shrewd businessman and knew a good investment when he saw it. The company that looked to Henslowe good enough for the Rose would have clearly looked inviting to an aging actor being asked to risk his own money in the abnormal and speculative Globe venture. When Worcester's approached Kempe to join the rejuvenated company, Kempe apparently took his first opportunity to sell up and leave the Globe partnership.

From the actions the men took it is possible to reconstruct their relationship in the transfer. Kempe and Shakespeare would appear to have been syndicate men. Each seems to have sold his share back into the company rather than aliening it to a friend or relative. Pope and Phillips appear to be mainly interested in creating a devisable property, for so they used their shares. Heminges was the facilitator and probably the instigator of the transfer. Heminges ultimately seems to have fared best under the new arrangement.

The five men, working in concert as they must, and probably at the urging of Heminges and possibly of Pope and Phillips as well, took their moiety to William Leveson, a mercer and a churchwarden, and to Thomas Savage, a goldsmith. Both Leveson and Savage were neighbors and friends of Heminges.[38] The choice of Leveson and Savage was a sound one. Both men were financially stable and trustworthy. Savage died in 1611 and left a large estate including the generous sum of "£8 for a supper to be paid on day of burial" at the Worshipful Company of Goldsmiths and a further "£3 for a dinner to be paid immediately after death" for his "fellows, seacoalmeters of City of London."[39] Heminges, as a member of the "seacoalmeters," almost certainly ate at that dinner. The office of "seacoalmeter" was a profitable one. It carried the responsibility of measuring coal brought to London by sea. Leveson, too, left a sizeable estate when he died in 1621. Both honest, reputable, and moreover successful businessmen, not to mention friends of Heminges, Savage and Leveson were trustworthy and therefore excellent choices to hold and transfer the paper on the Globe moiety.

Once the moiety was transferred to Savage and Leveson, the two merchants transferred back the property to the five partners. This transfer legally changed the nature of the property held by Heminges, Pope, Phillips, Kempe, and Shakespeare and allowed them to alien it as they pleased. Having done so, however, the men—at least the three who seem most anxious to have the character of the property changed—created something of a legal monster. The subsequent transfers and wrangling over the Globe profits during the Jacobean period is beyond the limits of this discussion, but they have their roots in this original set of transfers. It should be noted, however, that all five men appear to have wished to safeguard the property within the family of sharers. The comradeship to which Adams alludes was probably in evidence,[40] but comradeship stood hand in glove with business. The transfer not only created of them a fellowship of actors, it also made them financially responsible for one another in playhouse affairs. The later wrangling over the shares by the devisees of the various wills was certainly far from the sharers' minds when they optimistically created their joint tenancy at the beginning of their hopeful—and highly successful—undertaking.

THE LEGAL HISTORY OF THE BLACKFRIARS SYNDICATE

Henry Evans, Scrivener, Playhouse Speculator

When in 1609 William Rastell and Edward Kirkham took Alexander Hawkins to court over a £200 bond, they were probably only tying up the loose ends of a failed business deal.[41] Much has been made of the animosity between the venture capitalists involved in the second Blackfriars, but the legal record does not necessarily reflect the personal feelings of the litigants. The popular reading of the 1609 suit maintains that the surviving partners wrangled over the playhouse's carcass. In modern parlance, however, the two complainants were probably doing nothing more than flying a legal kite. To be sure, no litigation is begun or conducted on strictly amicable terms. The process of filing alone, with its attendant complexities and costs, can create an atmosphere of ill will.

Pleadings, and the depositions that seek to support a litigant's position, are customarily biased. That Rastell and Kirkham appear acrimonious on the surviving record does not necessarily indicate they were so in fact. It is a legal truism that the weaker the case the hotter the rhetoric. On its face the suit appears to be a strongly worded legal speculation. The Bill of Complaint is striking in that Rastell and Kirkham "do not specify the manner in which the condition of the bond has been violated."[42] From the extant record it appears that Rastell and Kirkham found a technicality that might yield them a windfall of £100 each and hoped to capitalize upon the vague possibility that Hawkins and Evans had earlier breached an agreement with them.[43] They would have been dilatory not to exploit their possible advantage.

The Blackfriars speculators, all of them, were engaged from the beginning in a highly questionable legal arrangement. Shortly after the restoration of the children's company at St. Paul's, *circa* 1599, and its attendant success, Henry Evans, who had been centrally involved in the first Blackfriars playhouse, presumed to reestablish a children's company at the second Blackfriars. This theatre had lain dormant since James Burbage had purchased the property in 1596 with a view toward making it an adult playhouse. At that time the tenants around Blackfriars, including the Lord Chamberlain himself, moved to have the Privy Council deny to Burbage what amounted to a zoning variance. This community action successfully estopped Burbage from seeing the plan through, though it seems probable that he had already taken steps to turn the site into a playhouse.

Four years after James Burbage's disappointment, and now with his son and heir to the Blackfriars property, Richard, in possession, Evans approached with a novel solution to everyone's theatrical headaches. By installing a group of "choristers" in the empty building and designating a portion of the building to be a "schoolhouse," the property could pass under a legal fiction. Although it would be a playhouse in fact, in law it would be a school to train the Children of the Queen's Chapel. The children could present drama in their building—they might even charge admission. The enterprise operated under color of presenting a public rehearsal to "try out" their work and so perfect it for later presentation before the Queen. It was a clever bit of chicanery operating upon what Shakespeare would later term "the windy side of the law." Evans's dodge was not unlike the legalistic maneuvering in the first Blackfriars venture. During that first venture, landlord Sir William More complained that the subleasee, Richard Farrant, "pretended unto me to use the house only for the teaching of the Children of the Chapel, but made it a continual house for plays."[44]

Farrant died before Sir William could exact judgment upon him for his misuse of the first Blackfriars property. Farrant's death, however, did not end Sir William's problems. In fact it increased them, for Farrant's widow employed a loophole in the sublease that had passed to her after her husband's death. The agreement between Sir William and Farrant had allowed Farrant to transfer his lease to her through his will, but there was no stipulation that she would be restrained by the special covenants to which Farrant had agreed. In strict law, of course, she could not receive a property greater than her husband had to demise, but she was decidedly disinterested in strict law. She engaged in a transaction that was prohibited to her husband when she transferred the sublease to William Hunnis, Master of the Chapel Royal, to whom was joined John Newman, Hunnis's partner in the dramatic venture. Hunnis and Newman, possibly ignorant of the earlier covenants, transferred their sublease to Evans, who sold his interest to the Earl of Oxford, who in turn assigned all rights to John Lyly, his private secretary. The wild tangle of transactions succeeded in playing a legal game of keep-away from Sir William. While Evans was still in possession of the sublease, Sir William sought to wrest it from him in a court proceeding, but the Welsh scrivener knew how to delay the proceedings.

He demurred. That is, Evans admitted that the facts Sir William presented were true but asserted that they did not give rise to a cause of action in a court of law. Sir William recounted what happened next:

[This] was done in Trinity Term [*i.e.* late May/early June]. The demurrer being drawn, the said Evans kept the same [the lease to the property] in his hands all Michaelmas Term next following [*i.e.* through November], using many delays. After the demurrer had, I caused my learned counsel in Hilary Term [*i.e.* late January] to demand judgement . . . but the recorder argued against me [presumably because he had not yet alleged and proved a cause of action from which a judgment could flow]. The judges would not then give judgement, but required to have books of the whole proceeding delivered to them, whereof I delivered one to every one of them. At the end of Easter Term following [*i.e.* April/early May] I had judgement against Evans.[45]

The widow, through first pleading with Sir William and then engaging in subleases followed by Evans's legal maneuverings, managed to keep the first Blackfriars open and in business against the landowners' express desires. By way of a legal dance worthy of Terpsichore, the first Blackfriars' life was artificially extended from the death of Farrant in early 1581 to the time of Sir William's final judgment in Easter Term of 1584.

In 1600 Henry Evans was prepared to try again. He employed Farrant's old "schoolhouse" dodge and on 2 September secured the lease to the second Blackfriars from Burbage for £40 rental per annum.[46] He quickly brought in partners. Nathaniel Giles, Master of the Chapel Children at Windsor, had a royal patent to impress children into the service of the Queen's choir. Alexander Hawkins was Evans's son-in-law and would prove to be his cleverest choice for a partner. Between them, Evans and Hawkins executed a £400 bond to Burbage to secure the lease. It seems likely that Edward Kirkham's association also dates to the inception of the project. As Yeoman of the Revels, Kirkham was in charge of the Revels wardrobe, an invaluable asset to a fledgling company of players. He could have been made a sharer in the project without the formality of making him a partner in the syndicate.

But almost as soon as the project was under way, troubles began. Using Giles's royal warrant, the men began "taking up" children for their company. Their behavior in this undertaking was often questionable. In some cases they may have acquired children from their rival company, the Children of St. Paul's. At least one boy, Salathiel Pavey, was drafted in 1600 when he was ten years old and "apprentice to one Peerce."[47] This "Peerce" could be Edward Pearce, master of St. Paul's, who had taken charge of the new children's company some eight months earlier. However,

Evans and Giles also laid hands upon a thirteen-year-old named Henry Clifton in what could only be described as an abduction.

The boy's father, Thomas Clifton, was well connected in Court. After having secured the release of his son, Clifton took Evans to law. On 15 December 1601 Clifton filed a formal complaint before Queen Elizabeth,[48] and his case was referred to Star Chamber. Clifton's complaint is damning. In it, he alleges that the Queen's royal patent under the Great Seal "for the better furnishing of your Royal Chapel with well-singing children" was converted by Giles and Evans "to make unto themselves an unlawful gain . . . to erect, set up, furnish and maintain a playhouse or place in the Blackfriars." And while the chapel master had long been allowed to sustain his place and keep the children by raising funds through play acting, Evans had clearly overstepped the warrant in kidnapping Henry Clifton. The allegations, if proved, could place Evans in a very serious breach of the law. He stood to lose everything.

The Star Chamber censured Evans and forbade him from managing the playhouse or the children. Just after this judgment, the Blackfriars speculation was reconstituted. Articles of Agreement were drawn up on 20 April 1602 between four new partners—Edward Kirkham, who probably stepped up from a post in the company he already held, two investors (a haberdasher named Thomas Kendall and a merchant named William Rastall or Rastell), and Evans's son-in-law, Alexander Hawkins, who now claimed to hold the lease. A bond passed between these gentlemen. In it, Hawkins and Evans pledged £200 that Kirkham, Kendall, and Rastell would have free access to the playhouse and company. As a businessman and father-in-law to Hawkins, Evans would be allowed to indemnify his son-in-law's partners against loss without running afoul of Star Chamber's orders. Evans, at least in the eyes of the law, had obeyed the judgment of Star Chamber and removed himself from Blackfriars' business. He was now merely co-signing a note insuring a family member, Hawkins, as any loving father might.

Once again, however, Evans had stayed a step ahead of the law. Before appearing in front of Star Chamber, Evans transferred the lease to son-in-law Hawkins. The reason for the transfer, as noted in Smith and elsewhere, is not mysterious. Had Star Chamber ordered the seizure of Evans's property, he would have lost the lease. Loss of the lease would mean more than a loss of valuable property, and even more than the loss of future revenue. Evans had a twenty-one-year agreement with Burbage secured by a bond. Losing the lease would not break his contract with Burbage, and the rent would either continue to be paid or the £400 bond would be forfeit. These factors would surely provide reason enough for Evans to make the transfer to Hawkins and keep the playhouse venture active.

The £200 bond to Kirkham, Kendall, and Rastell was combined with the Articles of Agreement to invest Hawkins's partners with all the *de facto* rights of property holders without actually making them so. As partners, their names should have been on the lease. However, Burbage's agreement with Evans precluded assigning the lease. Evans had lost the first Blackfriars for the very reason he now stood to lose the second Blackfriars. He could not make over the lease to the new partnership without nullifying it. Instead, he oversaw the creation of two documents: the Articles of Agreement forming the partnership, and the £200 bond ensuring that the new partners would be allowed free access to the property just as if they themselves held the lease. Kirkham, Kendall, and Rastell were thereby enfranchised even though they did not—and could not—control the actual lease.

There is a mystery, however, that no commentator has troubled to identify or discuss. If Evans signed over the lease to Hawkins before the Star Chamber proceedings, which he must have done to avoid the fraud inherent in an after-judgment transfer, and, further, if Star Chamber forbade him from meddling in Blackfriars business again, what was his enforceable connection to the enterprise after the Clifton judgment? He certainly had one, as his history amply demonstrates. Furthermore, how did he assign the lease to Hawkins without violating his agreement with Burbage? The answer resides in that remarkable document, *Kirkham v. Pauton et al* (1612).[49] In his answer to the complaint against him, Evans attests that he "did upon mere trust and confidence, and of intent and purpose to save harmless the said Alexander Hawkins ... from one bond of £400 [to Burbage] ... grant and convey unto him ... all [my] goods, chattels and leases." Although he goes on to say that he specifically kept the Blackfriars lease to himself, that hardly seems likely. The fact that he assigned absolutely everything else to Hawkins in order to protect it from judgment, including his "household stuff, wares, commodities, and all his goods," would be enough to lead one to conclude that he also transferred his most valuable possession, the Blackfriars lease. Add to that the fact that Hawkins is specifically identified as the leaseholder in the Articles of Agreement, and it becomes clear that Evans lied in court when he said he did not transfer the lease to Hawkins.

The reason to lie about the Blackfriars transfer is obvious. He had contracted with Burbage not to alien the lease. To admit in court that he had done so would place him in breach of his bond. Although Burbage could not demand the bond in 1612, four years after the lease had been returned to him, an admission of past dishonesty would surely injure Evans in his current pleading. More importantly, he had represented himself as the leaseholder to Kirkham, Rastell, and Kendall, the partners in the 1602 Articles of Agreement. He could scarcely claim now that he was not.

Evans was between Skylla and Kharybdis in 1602. He could not alien the lease under his agreement with Burbage, but also he could not be involved in the Blackfriars venture by order of Star Chamber. Though he could privately declare to Kirkham, Rastell, and Kendall that he did indeed still retain control of the lease, he could not do so openly in a legally binding document. He had, after all, gone to great lengths to create the legal fiction that he was no longer part of Blackfriars. In the deposition of 1612, *Kirkham v. Pauton et al.,* Evans was in another tight spot legally. He had no wish to admit to his bad faith transfer to Hawkins and so craftily employed the proper dodge. The scrivener Evans had a legal turn of mind, and he seems never to have said anything in a legal document that he could not use to his advantage. Special interest must be taken, therefore, to a particular moment in his deposition.

Evans surely transferred the lease, but he had to do so in such a manner as to accomplish several goals:

1. He wished to keep control of the enterprise for his own profit;
2. He had to maintain a feasible arm's length (from a legal perspective) from the enterprise because of the Star Chamber order;
3. He could not breach his agreement with Burbage; and
4. He could not breach his agreement with his partners (and he was a silent partner) under the 1602 agreement.

His dual statements in the 1612 deposition—that he made the transfer to Hawkins "upon mere trust and confidence" and that his purpose was "to save harmless the said Alexander Hawkins [from the £400 bond to Burbage] . . . who married this defendant's daughter"—are legally interesting as well as dispositive of Evans's legal maneuver.

Evans employed a clever, though not uncommon, tactic. He transferred the paper to Hawkins but maintained the *use* of the property for himself. Under the laws of use, to be discussed in detail in the next chapter, a property holder could do just this. Briefly put, a use allowed the owner of property to transfer that property to a second person who would then be responsible for holding legal title to that property while it was enjoyed by yet a third person. In some cases the property owner would transfer the property to a second person and then name himself as the "third person" invested with the enjoyment and use of the property. This latter arrangement was Evans's scheme. Hawkins became the owner of the lease by right of possession of the paper. In this, the Star Chamber order was satisfied. Evans no longer held the paper. However, because the transfer was never set down under the Statute of Enrollments (a dodge common to and even anticipated in many use transfers), Evans was still the owner of the lease in the eyes of the business world. Thus he satisfied his obligation to Burbage. Furthermore, because of the peculiarities of the law of the use, both Evans and Hawkins had an enforceable property interest in the leased playhouse after the transfer. Depending upon the circumstances that arose, each had the right to claim the property was his own or conversely (in the case of a Star Chamber inquiry) not his at all. It was a workable, brilliant answer to Evans's legal and business dilemma.

In the 1612 deposition, Evans tells us as much. The creation of the use required both the actual transfer and a good (read "legal") reason to do so. Evans uses the phrase "trust and confidence." This is the correct formulation for the creation of a use, which in modern parlance amounts to a trust. Next, he asserts that his natural love and affection for Hawkins, as his daughter's husband, led him to protect his children. Natural love and affection was a recognized reason to make such a gift in English law since the middle of the sixteenth century. By phrasing himself carefully in his 1612 deposition, Evans successfully kept himself on the knife's edge of legality. He could legally claim, because he retained the legal use, that he did not alien the lease, but he was also giving himself the escape (should the situation warrant) that he had physically handed over the paper to Hawkins, who then became the Blackfriars' legal leaseholder. By creating a use in the Blackfriars property, Evans was able to alien the paper to Hawkins without announcing the assignment to Burbage. However, if the Star Chamber had ordered Evans's property seized and sold to satisfy Clifton, Evans could legally claim that the property belonged to Hawkins and thereby protect it from seizure. That was Evans's apparent pre-judgment plan in 1602.

When Star Chamber did not order the property seized but rather that Evans should merely desist from management of the playhouse, the use served another turn. Evans, who retained the use of the property, could continue as silent partner. The property was still legally and enforceably his. However, had Hawkins chosen to enforce his own right in the lease under the assignment, he could have caused Evans considerable trouble. The united force of Burbage's agreement and Star Chamber's order would keep Evans from claiming his right in open court. Had he been forced to do so, he would have found himself in breach of the £400 bond and haled up before Star Chamber for what would amount to contempt of court. Fortunately, Evans had chosen well when he entrusted the document to Hawkins. Not only was Evans's son-in-law willing to protect Evans's interest and allow him to continue on as silent partner in actual control of the venture, but Hawkins, as cosigner, stood to lose the £400 bond to Burbage if he did not. In all of the litigation that arose out of the second Blackfriars venture, Hawkins never proceeded against Evans. Apparently they shared a mutual loyalty. Understanding the character of Evans's control helps us to understand many of the other troubling conflicts surrounding the second Blackfriars project after 1602.

The Strange Affair of Edward Kirkham

When John Marston left St. Paul's in 1603 for Blackfriars, he apparently acquired a share in the new syndicate. We learn from court records that he acquired it from Evans.[50] Combined with the possibility that the boy actor Salathiel Pavey, and perhaps other boys, had been conscripted from St. Paul's, the evidence of luring Marston away indicates that the Evans syndicate was playing a hard game with Edward Pearce at St. Paul's. Thomas Woodford may have replaced Marston as manager of St. Paul's in 1603.[51] If he did, he lasted no more than one season. Whatever

Woodford's association with Paul's might have been, it all ended in tears with Pearce physically assaulting him and being made to pay damages of £13 6s. 8d.[52] Pearce perhaps tried managing on his own, but if he did he quickly discovered that he needed an experienced hand.

In 1604 or 1605 Pearce hired Edward Kirkham, partner and sharer of the rival company at Blackfriars. The choice seems conspicuously curious, especially when considered in light of what transpired. Within fifteen to twenty-four months, the popular Paul's boys were in shambles. The playhouse closed, the playbooks were registered with the stationers—sold off for publication[53]—and the Children of St. Paul's never performed regularly again. Paul's chief playwright, Thomas Middleton, was apparently caught short, surprised by the closure. His sudden activity and tremendous dramatic output in 1606 resembles nothing so much as the desperation of a man surprised to be out of a job.[54]

In the meantime, the Blackfriars syndicate was expanding. Though always controversial, the company gained in popularity and royal favor. When the new patent for the Blackfriars company had been issued on 4 February 1604, it named Kirkham, Kendall, Hawkins, and a Robert Payne as partners. The new patent gave the Children of the Chapel a new patron and name. They became the Children of the Queen's Revels. The royal favor did not last long, however. In 1606, the company was again in trouble. A play by John Day, *The Isle of Gulls,* enraged James. Of the players, "sundry were committed to Bridewell."[55] The Queen removed her patronage, the company became the Children of Blackfriars, and the syndicate remained out of favor until it folded in 1608. In the two years of the first Queen's Revels, 1604–6, the syndicate and playhouse remained in nearly continuous trouble.

Part of the reason for the trouble was that under the new patent of 1604 the poet Samuel Daniel was named to license plays for the children's company. The syndicate paid Daniel an annuity of £10 for this service, but modern scholarship has taken this payment to be no more than a sinecure.[56] The Blackfriars company was famous for skating close to the line of propriety, and that was no doubt part of its popular appeal. Because the children were technically not professional players, they did not fall under the purview of the Master of the Revels. Excluding their plays from Tilney and Buck's cautious eyes, however, proved too great an incentive for abuse. Far from keeping the Children of the Queen's Revels in check, their new censor Daniel was the first to offend. In the same year as the new patent issued, in fact within two weeks, on 20 February 1604, Daniel's *Philotas* cost the poet his position (though not his annuity). The play's resemblance to the Essex rebellion brought Daniel before the Privy Council to answer questions regarding the matter. He apparently acquitted himself, and the next year he is to be found writing a pastoral for Christ Church, Oxford. Edward Kirkham was the payee for the performance in Court that year, and shortly thereafter he is to be found managing the St. Paul's company.

The simplest interpretation of what happened is that both Daniel as poet and Kirkham as manager were censured and made to give up their positions with the Queen's Revels. This may be so. It certainly seems that Daniel retired temporarily—although he did return as payee a year later. However, Kirkham clearly did not leave the syndicate, and there is even confusion among the commentators on the point of his leaving the Blackfriars management. Gair insists that Kirkham's management of St. Paul's dates to 1604.[57] Adams and Nungezer both agree that Kirkham removed to Paul's sometime after the 1605 presentation of *Eastward Ho!,* which had landed Jonson and Chapman in jail and forced Marston into hiding.[58] Chambers, Fleay, and Smith, however, all maintain that Kirkham did not leave active management of the Blackfriars company until after the *Isle of Gulls* debacle of 1606, about the same time that Paul's was collapsing.[59] If Chambers, Fleay, and Smith are correct, whom Adams and Nungezer do not contradict, then Kirkham remained manager of both companies simultaneously for perhaps as long as two years, which would seem a highly unlikely situation.

In 1605, that is, after *Philotas* but before *Eastward Ho!,* Daniel and Evans were the payees for the Blackfriars children's appearance in Court on January 1 and 3, which indicates that Kirkham was not leading the company during that period—at least not leading them actively under James's eye.[60] There is no confusion, however, on the point of Kirkham's Blackfriars affiliation. Although he did indeed go to St. Paul's sometime between 1604 and 1605, he remained in the Blackfriars syndicate for as long as it lasted, that is to say until 1608 when Evans returned the lease to Burbage. Kirkham may well have made the most of a bad situation, using his discommendation over either the

Philotas affair in 1604 or the *Eastward Ho!* affair in mid-1605 as a springboard into the rival company. His reasons for doing so, however, would seem to be more suspect than commentators have suggested or supposed.

It is certain that Kirkham was with St. Paul's boys shortly after *Eastward Ho!,* for in the spring of 1606 we find him presenting himself, as Chambers puts it, "triumphantly before the Treasurer of the Chamber's paymaster the following spring [1606] as 'one of the Masters of the Children of Pawles.'"[61] The remarkable feature of this post-1605 season is that the Children of St. Paul's now performed plays drawn from the Blackfriars stock: Marston's *Parasitaster, or The Fawn* and Chapman's *Bussy D'Ambois.*[62] The commentators to note this odd concurrence follow Chambers in suggesting that Kirkham took these plays with him when he left Blackfriars.[63] While the suggestion is clearly possible, it overlooks several important factors. First, there is no strong evidence that Kirkham did leave Blackfriars when he went to Paul's. In fact, evidence exists contrary to that conclusion. He did, in fact, maintain a financial interest in Blackfriars. Second, as a man with a financial interest in the Blackfriars syndicate, it seems odd that Kirkham would steal from his own stock simply to enrich the St. Paul's company. Third, with a strong set of plays, mainly by Middleton, and a strong and popular set of players at Paul's, one wonders what would induce Kirkham to showcase the strengths of the Blackfriars stock rather than those of his new company. It seems extraordinary that Kirkham would complicate his new job by rehearsing his new charges in new plays when he could continue forward with their own already familiar and well received repertory. When one considers the potential added charges of building new stage devices and costumes, hangings, and special properties for the new plays, Kirkham's choice seems peculiar if not unwise.

His having done so cannot be seriously questioned in light of the printed record, however. Kirkham almost certainly did move plays from the Blackfriars company to Paul's during his residence there. Marston's *Parasitaster, or The Fawn* was printed in 1606 as acted "at the Blacke Friars by the Children of the Queenes Maiesties Reuels, and since at Powles." The tide, however, flowed in two directions. In 1608, two years after *Parasitaster* was published, Middleton's *A Trick to Catch the Old One* appeared in print as acted "both at Paules, and the Black-Fryers."

In each case the legend seems to indicate the direction of migration, first a Marston (Blackfriars) play moved to Paul's and next a Middleton (Paul's) play moved to Blackfriars. The likely conclusion is that Kirkham entered the Paul's company with a view to undermining it. It is not beyond the realm of possibility that he took several plays with him from Blackfriars as a Trojan horse. When Paul's crumbled, Kirkham returned to the syndicate with some of Pearce's play stock. What cannot be argued, however, is that the Paul's venture, once invincibly strong, faltered so badly under Kirkham's usually sure supervision that it was forced to close and liquidate within months of his entering its management.

We do not know how the Blackfriars syndicate faired financially during this period, but it is reasonable to conclude that it did well. There is no squabbling among partners during this time, and their plays were not rushed to press. Both factors suggest financial security. The company's history indicates that it was in fact a stable concern. The playing company begun by Evans in 1600 withstood a Star Chamber order, court censure in every year from 1603 to 1606, changes of leadership in 1604, 1606, and 1608, and reorganizations in 1604 and 1608. Nothing stopped them. The Boys grew up and ultimately merged with an adult company, Lady Elizabeth's Men, in 1613. The court's displeasure that Kirkham spawned in 1605, then, must have come when the syndicate was feeling reasonably secure, maybe even a little brazen. Perhaps the time seemed right to use Kirkham's apparent disfavor as an opportunity to sabotage Paul's and increase Blackfriars' profits.

Under Kirkham's management the Paul's company presented plays by Middleton, Beaumont and Fletcher, Dekker, and Webster. They performed in Court on several occasions, were invited to the Christmas Revels not once but twice, steered clear of all scandals, and in short seemed destined to remain strong. There may be many reasons why the St. Paul's playhouse and company closed abruptly in the middle of the 1606 season. Gair has suggested that a sweeping Puritanism was responsible—a putsch that managed unaccountably to strike only the one company. Still, it is difficult to overlook the curious accident that a sharer, partner, and manager of Pauls' deadliest rival was at Pauls' helm when it folded. It is also difficult to ignore the fact that two years later, in 1608 when the Blackfriars playhouse was returned to

Burbage and the King's Men, Kirkham was still closely associated with the Blackfriars syndicate and engaged in and indeed led the division of its spoils.

Blackfriars and Whitefriars:
Robert Keysar and George Androwes, Playhouse Gulls?

After the string of censured Blackfriars performances in 1603 (Marston's *Dutch Curtesan*), 1604 (Daniel's *Philotas*), and 1605 (Marston, Chapman, and Jonson's *Eastward Ho!*), the most dangerous blow came in 1606 with *The Isle of Gulls* by John Day. Kirkham was by that time forced to give up management, and the queen withdrew her patronage. Although the rival St. Paul's was now gone, and Blackfriars' business was promising, the syndicate was in its most serious difficulty with the authorities. At this time a relative newcomer to the theatre world, a goldsmith named Robert Keysar, took over management of the company.

Keysar was a strange choice. Past managers of the Blackfriars venture, Evans and Kirkham, had long experience in the theatre. Most likely, Keysar joined the theatrical world no earlier than 1604, probably as part of the reorganization of the Blackfriars company on 20 April of that year.[64] If this is so, he could have been little more than an investor, for there is no record of his active involvement in theatre until after *The Isle of Gulls*. Up to his entry into theatre speculation, Keysar could best be described as a sharp dealer. In 1593, while still a goldsmith's apprentice, he was accused of robbing his master and was bound over to his brother, John Keysar, another goldsmith, for the remainder of his apprenticeship. Three years later, in 1596, Robert conspired with his brother to witness a fraudulent bond. With it, John took two merchants named Wheatley and Taylor to court in order to extort money from them.[65] Robert Keysar's career as a goldsmith is riddled with fraudulent dealing, and the Wardens Accounts and Court Minutes to be found in the Goldsmiths' Library are filled with complaints against him and fines levied to correct his behavior.[66]

In 1606 Robert Keysar, now firmly associated with the Blackfriars venture, took Thomas Middleton to court over a debt. Middleton gave answer that the debt had been discharged. The playwright claimed to have delivered to Keysar a tragedy entitled *The Viper and Her Brood* in full payment.[67] Keysar evidently dropped the suit, presumably because Middleton had proven his case. This conclusion would be in keeping with what we know about Keysar and his extortive use of the courts. It is possible that Middleton had acquired the debt to Keysar in contemplation of moving to Blackfriars from Paul's as Marston had done three years before. In any case, Middleton did not ultimately shift his allegiance to Blackfriars, which would have seemed a most logical move under the circumstances. Keysar's attempt to defraud him or possibly indenture him through litigation probably induced Middleton to look elsewhere for employment. Nevertheless, Keysar, probably with the direct aid of Kirkham, managed to liberate Middleton's *A Trick to Catch the Old One* as well as *Your Five Gallants,* which was revived at Blackfriars in 1607. Add to these intellectual embezzlements the chicanery over *The Viper and Her Brood* and one has little trouble understanding Middleton's disinclination to join the Blackfriars enterprise.

Keysar had little to recommend him to a theatrical enterprise except money and apparent enthusiasm. Except for Woodford, he was, according to Ingram, "the youngest and among the most inexperienced" of the playhouse investors. He was also one of the most conspicuous.[68] It is not difficult to imagine that the Blackfriars speculators were preparing to extract themselves from their difficulties in 1606 when they placed Keysar at the helm. The sharp-dealing Keysar was himself being set up by the cleverer Evans.

Though it was true that Paul's was gone, and business should have looked promising for the Blackfriars syndicate, another rival company had sprung up to the west of Blackfriars. Michael Drayton had a patent to set up a children's company under the name "King's Revels" to perform in Whitefriars. They would compete directly with the Queen's Revels at Blackfriars. While this speculative venture was still germinating, however, the Queen's Revels lost its patron and was obliged to call itself the Children of Blackfriars. Additionally, Kirkham was required to give up management of the company. It is not hard to conceive the syndicate, along with Evans, always alive to the preemptive strike, looking for a way out of the company that now promised only decline and the wasting of their resources.

The syndicate appears to have wearied of the constant struggle and contented itself with allowing Keysar to do all of the work with little or no supervision. It was, at least for a time, an agreeable arrangement for the syndicate. Kirkham would later testify that, during this period, the syndicate's income increased by one hundred fifty percent "without any manner of charges whatever." This would appear to indicate that the syndicate extracted a heavy annual fee from Keysar and left him responsible for the entire playhouse overhead.[69] With the onus and responsibility shifted to Keysar, it is little wonder that the next two years resembled the past four not at all.

After Keysar took over management, the Blackfriars company changed character. Gone were the controversial plays that infuriated the Court and brought in the crowds. Keysar's management is remarkable for its lack of contention. For two years the Blackfriars Boys did nothing to incur the wrath of anyone. It is as though the syndicate had gone underground, perhaps looking for its chance to sell out. Keysar, as court testimony would later demonstrate, had no idea that he was to be left holding the bag when the syndicate made its final move.

That move, when it came, was as dramatic as it was obvious. Within the course of a single week in 1608, the Blackfriars company returned to its old habits with a vengeance. The sudden reintroduction of both Marston and Chapman into the repertoire, two of the syndicate's favorite dramatists (Marston even owned a share in the venture), indicates that the uncontroversial Keysar had been suborned by the partners. Abruptly the syndicate's old ways reappeared along with their old playwrights. First they produced a play on the king's silver mine venture in Scotland. In it James is portrayed as a bully and a foul-mouthed drunkard. His courtiers are mercilessly lampooned. Within two days of that performance, Chapman's *Byron* plays depicted the French court, and especially the queen, in a most unfavorable light. The reaction of later commentators is summed up by Hillebrand, who says with apparent bewilderment, "Hard as it is to believe that the same company could be so foolhardy as to defy the censorship twice in the same week, nevertheless it seems that the Revels children were thus guilty."[70]

The official reaction was swift and sure. The French ambassador, M. de la Boderie, lodged a formal protest and sent a letter describing the infamy of Chapman's work and the fallout: "Touttefois il ne s'en trouva que trois, qui aussi-tost furent en la prison où ilz sont encore." In it he also alludes to the silver mine play:

Un jour ou deux devant ilz avoient dépêché leur Roy, sa mine d'Escosse, et tous ses Favorits d'une estrange sorte; car apres luy avoir fait dépiter le ciel sur le vol d'un oyseau, et faict battre un gentilhomme pour avoir rompu ses chiens, ilz le dépeignoient ivre pour le moins une fois le jour.[71]

The two plays coming as they did in quick succession were enough to ensure the immediate closing of the Blackfriars playhouse. M. de la Boderie reported, "Mesme il a fait deffense que l'on n'eust plus à jouer de Comédies dedans Londres." While Wren and other scholars have interpreted the king's anger as aimed mainly at the *Byron* plays,[72] they rely upon de la Boderie's report.

We should not forget that de la Boderie was particularly affronted by Chapman's work. However, it was not Chapman who was arrested even though the ambassador states categorically that "[q]uand ledit Sieur Roy a esté icy, il a tesmoigné estre extrèmement irrité . . . et a commandé . . . qu'on eust à faire diligence de trouver le compositeur." It was Marston, who possibly went into hiding again as he did after *Eastward Ho!,* who was arrested eight months after the fact. He was committed to Newgate on 8 November leaving his new play, *The Insatiate Countess,* unfinished. His arrest has led many scholars to believe that he was the author of the silver mine play. Upon his release from prison, Marston left the theatre world forever. Before he did, however, he sold the share in the company he had acquired from Evans in 1603. The share did not go back to Evans or to one of the syndicate partners, who would be unlikely to buy him out of a disintegrating business. Instead Marston sold to Robert Keysar. Keysar claimed to have paid Marston £100 for what later proved a phantom share. Obviously, Keysar thought the Blackfriars venture would continue after the contretemps had dissipated. He was therefore clearly not privy to the syndicate's evident plan to dismantle the venture.

By 11 March 1608—within days of the debacle—the rumor of the playhouse closing was already being spread in official circles. Sir Thomas Lake, a clerk of the signet in attendance upon the King at Thetford, wrote on that day to Lord Salisbury:

His ma*je*stie was well pleased with that which your lo*rdship* advertiseth concerning the committing of the players y^t have offended in ye matters of France, and have commanded me to signifye to your lor*dship* that for ye others who have offended in ye matter of ye Mynes and other lewd words, which is ye children of ye blackfriars, That though he had signified his mynde to your lor*dship* by my lor*d* of Mountgommery yet I should repeate it again, That his G*race* had vowed they should never play more, but should first begg their bred and he wold have his vow performed, And therefore my lor*d* chamberlain by himself or your lor*dships* at the table should take order to dissolve them, and to punish the maker besides.[73]

Noting that Lake says that he is obliged to "repeate it again," there can be little doubt that the theatrical world knew something was in the wind by March 11. In an interesting coincidence, the Whitefriars company, that mysterious band known as the King's Revels, drew up its Articles of Agreement the day before Lake's letter was written, on 10 March 1608.

One cannot help remarking upon the extraordinary coincidences occurring in the children's theatrical community. In 1606 Paul's folds, Kirkham gives up management of Blackfriars, Keysar not only steps into Kirkham's shoes but also takes over all of the syndicate's responsibilities and expenses, and Drayton acquires a lease to Whitefriars from Lord Buckhurst. In 1608 the Blackfriars syndicate commits commercial suicide at precisely the same time that the Whitefriars company incorporates. It is difficult to ignore the possibility that the coincidence may be more than mere accident. Unfortunately there is too little evidence upon which to tie together the two business dealings. I cannot avoid the feeling that someone involved in the Blackfriars' destruction is also behind the amalgamation of the King's Revels at Whitefriars. Kirkham's involvement with the undoing of Paul's has a marked resemblance to the collapse of Blackfriars. Unhappily, the Whitefriars company is itself a riddle. If a plan was incubating to sabotage Blackfriars in furtherance of the Whitefriars' venture, it did not work. Nevertheless, the Whitefriars project was rife with its own brand of chicanery.

Thomas Woodford, who had an association with St. Paul's two years before, joined with Drayton to begin the Whitefriars/King's Revels project around 1606. This, it should be noted, was the same year that Kirkham was commanded to step down at Blackfriars. Within a year Woodford retired from the project and sold his share to Lording Barry. Drayton and Barry set up a syndicate and sold shares or part-shares to William Trevell, William Cooke,

Edward Sibthorpe, John Mason, and a silk weaver named George Androwes. Barry and Mason wrote plays for the new venture. Drayton was the leaseholder to the property and was to be made a partner under a new agreement, which never came to pass. The other sharers appear to be investors with no theatrical backgrounds whatever.[74]

The timing was bad for the King's Revels syndicate. Within three weeks of their incorporation, the king ordered all theatres closed. The difficulty at the Blackfriars over the silver mine and *Byron* plays led to an inhibition of playing in London that began 29 March 1608. Playhouses had been temporarily closed in the past, and this setback could have been weathered; however, before the inhibition was rescinded, plague struck and kept the theatres closed for the remainder of the year and well into the 1609 season. Logic dictates that the money put into the Whitefriars project dried up, the speculators counted their losses, and the company folded for no other reason than the perilous nature of business. And so it well may be.

When the Whitefriars venture ran into its difficulties, the syndicate apparently cut its losses with precipitous speed. Within a month of the inhibition, in April of 1608, King's Revels plays were registered and found their ways into print despite the prohibition against printing outlined in the company's Articles of Agreement. The syndicate immediately suspended paying their rental on the Whitefriars property, and the King's Revels manager, Martin Slater, was forced from his Whitefriars lodgings along with his wife and family of ten.[75] Slater reacted curiously. Rather than sue the syndicate, Slater sued only George Androwes. The likelihood of Androwes being the only sharer with money left after the project collapsed seems inescapable. It is from Androwes's countersuit in Chancery that we discover the background of the company and learn of its legal complexion.

Late in the franchise's development, after Barry had borrowed nearly £120 (mostly from or through Woodford) and Trevell, Sibthorpe, Mason, Sharpham, and Drayton had also tested their credit, the partners began what appears to be a desperate attempt to draw in more money by adding new partners. It appears from the sketchy records left by the venture that they separated ownership of the company from ownership of the leasehold and redivided each into shares and half shares. The tactic was plainly employed in order to have more to sell to new partners and resembles in some ways the modern concept of stock splitting. William Cooke, a haberdasher of St. Lawrence, Barry's parish, took back as surety on a loan "twoe twelue p*artes* of the Lease of the Whyte ffryars playe house, And of A p*arte* of the Shares as maye appeare by the wrighting*es* therof made by Barrey and Sybthorpe."[76] He later would testify that "he hadd [a] halfe a Share of the whyt ffryars playehouse . . . wch Coste him about ffyve and ffortye pound*es*."[77]

George Androwes, the silk weaver, was last to join the syndicate. The partners were by then apparently in financial straits, for we learn that even as Androwes was buying his share Trevell was borrowing £50 from an Elizabeth Brown.[78] Androwes had been importuned by Lording Barry to purchase one-third of the moiety Barry had acquired from Woodford—one-sixth of the total property equaling one full share in the enterprise. The share was to have cost Androwes £90, but Androwes haggled and got it for £70, which again seems to demonstrate the desperation of the enterprise. He had been shown costumes worth £400, and those were put up as surety against his investment. He expected that his share of the annual profits would reach £100. With these assurances, Androwes was prevailed upon to invest in excess of £300 for renovations to the playhouse space. By the time the inhibition and plague struck, however, Androwes still had not been assigned his portion of the lease, and he was left without recourse. The costumes that had indemnified him for £400 were found not to be worth £5. As Ingram has pointed out, at least some of the costumes and in particular several hats were already secured by preexisting bonds. Doubtlessly the haberdashers, hatters, cobblers, and creditors seized much of the costume stock as the playhouse foundered and bills went unpaid. In the end, Androwes paid some £370 in the venture, virtually building a playhouse from his own funds in the process, only to receive nothing in return. In a remarkable footnote to this remarkable venture, Lording Barry, who has long been misidentified as a "Lord Barry" by Nungezer and others, was not a member of the peerage at all but was rather a commoner and fled his Whitefriars creditors only to become a pirate.[79]

In the meantime, the Blackfriars syndicate was cutting its own losses. Evans was preparing what should have been the company's coup de grâce, a legal transfer that would successfully extricate the syndicate from future responsibility while keeping its profits intact. It seems likely that Evans, who had as early as 1603 tried to return the Blackfriars lease to Burbage,[80] had by 1608 negotiated the deal that would release him from the twenty-one-year lease and the £400 bond securing it. Burbage and the King's Men were by this time as interested in reacquiring the property as both Evans and Hawkins were in divesting themselves of it. Kirkham, too, was interested in quitting the syndicate and around 26 July 1608 asked Evans for a division of the company's stock.[81]

The transfer went smoothly. Evans's wife paid a call upon her son-in-law Hawkins, collected the lease that Evans had given him in trust back in 1602, and proceeded to deliver the document to Richard Burbage, John Heminges, or another person operating on behalf of Burbage and Heminges. In return, Burbage liberated Evans and Hawkins from the yearly rental of £40 and returned their £400 bond. The property was then back in the hands and exclusive control of Richard Burbage, and that should have been an end to the second Blackfriars enterprise. However, the end of the syndicate opened a series of suits through which we are able to see how the venture was organized and how the use transfer that Evans had made in 1602 played a central role in the playhouse's life.

There is calculation in the 1608 actions of the Blackfriars syndicate. Keysar testified that the partners had tried to buy him out of his portion and offered him £400.[82] The sum may be exaggerated. The offer may even be fallacious. Still, the possibility exists that the syndicate was ready to fold in that year. If so, Keysar would prove an obstacle if he refused to give up his portion. In 1608 Kirkham would have been in his fifties; Kendall was ill enough to redraw his will and would in fact die that year; Evans, the grand old man of the theatre, was already in his mid-to-late sixties. It is not difficult to imagine that these men were ready to end their association and divide up their assets. If so, Keysar's undoubted insistence that the venture should continue would have been a tremendous annoyance. He was a young man and would outlive the others by decades. Possibly he was theatre-struck. Nevertheless Keysar seems to have been committed to the enterprise and refused to sell back his share to the weary partners. He also apparently would not or could not buy them out of their shares. The syndicate had earlier, in 1606, decided to allow him to continue on while the named partners retreated into the background and collected what amounted to rent plus a healthy share of Keysar's profits. It was to this time in the Blackfriars history, 1606–1608, that Kirkham alluded when he affirmed that Keysar had an interest in the Children, who "were masters themselves [i.e., their own managers]."[83]

What actually happened to destroy the Blackfriars venture has been fully documented but never placed into its legal context.[84] In 1606 Day's *Isle of Gulls* incensed Robert Cecil, Earl of Salisbury, and the king's "little beagle," much more than it had annoyed James. Salisbury had turned a blind eye to the earlier satires of his power brokering in court and ignored the jibes from the Blackfriars stage concerning his hunched back. This changed in 1606. Day's play, with its caricature of James as Duke Basilius (noted often as "king" in the stage directions) and obvious burlesque of Salisbury as Dametus the "little hillock, made great with others ruines,"[85] had been enough to close the playhouse and have Kirkham removed from its management by royal order. Salisbury clearly sent the message that he would no longer tolerate Blackfriars defamation. When the Blackfriars syndicate decided finally to close their books in 1608, they needed to find a way of removing an unwilling Keysar from his position.

An earlier version of Chapman's *Conspiracie, and Tragedie of Charles Duke of Byron, Marshall of France,* had included a scene slighting Salisbury.[86] When the French ambassador, de la Boderie, had seen it during Lent of 1608 he had it forbidden before its first performance. Significantly, the syndicate arranged to have *Byron* performed in 1608 after the king and court had quit London but while both Salisbury and de la Boderie—the two men most insulted by the play—were still in the city. Indeed they were the very men who brought the outrage to the king's attention. Two days earlier, Blackfriars had staged the infamous play of the silver mines that lampooned James directly. The aging Blackfriars syndicate played a safe game, however. As in all of Evans's schemes, he secured for himself a plausible deniability. Keysar was manager; Chapman and (possibly) Marston were playwrights, and when the king's axe fell it splintered the business enterprise, which was Evans's goal, but did not reach the syndicate personally.

Keysar, however, remained unwilling to give up. If the silver mine and the *Byron* plays were, as I suspect, calculated to drive Keysar from management in the same way Kirkham had been driven out by royal decree after *The Isle of Gulls,* it did not work, and Keysar did not take the hint to quit. Rather, with the syndicate folded and counting its revenue, Keysar continued to support the children at his own cost. He made a powerful friend in court, Sir Thomas Monson, and took his children there during the Christmas of 1608. When the theatres reopened, Keysar moved his troupe into the abandoned Whitefriars—made ready by the generosity of an unsuspecting George Androwes the season before—and took the Children again to the court during the Christmas of 1609. When on 4 January 1610 Keysar succeeded in regaining royal patronage, he became a silent partner to the new syndicate. One month later, on 8 February 1610, Keysar haled Richard Burbage into court claiming a right in the profits that the King's Men were realizing at Blackfriars.

The lawsuit demonstrates why Keysar fought so diligently to keep the Company of Boys together after the 1608 catastrophes. He had believed all along that he was a sharer in the company. Scholars have been too willing to dismiss Keysar's assertion as an angry reaction to the loss of the Blackfriars lease. In fact, he could well have been telling the truth as he knew it. The actions of the syndicate would bear out his claim. According to an admittedly biased Keysar, "Henry Evans did for good and valuable consideration . . . grant all or some part of the said term . . . to one John Marston, gentleman." The portion amounted to "one full sixth part of . . . certain goods, apparel for players, properties, play-books and other things then and still used by the Children of the Queen's Majesty's Revels in and about their plays." Keysar maintained that he bought Marston's share for £100.[87] Keysar testified that he had heard rumors at the time that Evans and Burbage were conspiring to sell back the lease. Keysar went to Burbage and the King's Men and announced that he had what he thought to be a share in the lease and that it therefore could not be returned legally without his consent. Burbage and company assured him that they would not take back the lease unless all of the partners were satisfied with the transaction. Nevertheless, according to Keysar, the syndicate first attempted to buy him out for £400 and later, when Keysar had refused to sell, returned the lease to Burbage without Keysar's consent. There is enough detail in Keysar's account, I believe, to warrant an examination of his claim without summarily dismissing it as the unsubstantiated rantings of a man disappointed in business.

Because Keysar believed that he still owned a one-sixth interest in the Blackfriars lease, he claimed that he was owed his share of the profits regardless of who actually performed in the playhouse. Burbage and the other defendants agreed that the lease transfer from Evans to Burbage had taken place, but they denied Keysar had any interest in it. At this point Keysar lost his temper. He swore that everything was a plot against him. He claimed that Burbage conspired with the Blackfriars syndicate to encourage Keysar to buy out Marston. He went on to assert that they had hidden Evans from him in order to divide up the property behind Keysar's back. He continued by claiming that the defendants conspired with all the owners of all the private playhouses and paid them a dead rent to keep him and his company from playing anywhere in the city of London. The Burbages exploited Keysar's tantrum.

Burbage and the other defendants answered with a general denial, and the tone of their denial seems bemused if not condescending. They pointed out that Marston could never have purchased a share from Evans because "Henry Evans was restrained in and by his said lease . . . from granting, assigning or putting away the premises."[88] They argued that the supposed share Marston had was not attested: "neither is there any mention at all made thereof in any deed or writing made or passed from the said Marston." They admitted that a dead rent was indeed paid to Pearce to keep St. Paul's from reopening. However, the dead rent was instigated by Keysar's own partner, Philip Rosseter, and later entered into by the King's Men as a mutual benefit. Cuthbert Burbage offered to produce Marston, whom he suggested would contradict Keysar's claim of having bought a share from him. The case was apparently settled out of court, and scholars have suggested that the outcome cannot be recovered.

It is altogether likely that Evans, or Burbage, or some other party in interest bought Keysar out of his suit. Had Marston gained a share from Evans by virtue of the use transfer, which is not only possible but precisely why one might wish to create a use in the first place, then Keysar could have caused legitimate trouble. While it is true that Cuthbert Burbage's threat to produce material witnesses to contradict Keysar may have caused Keysar to withdraw his action, it is equally possible that Cuthbert Burbage was only sabre rattling—he could, in fact, even at that late date, have remained ignorant of Evans's use transfer. If so, he would have had reason to believe that Marston could have had no interest in the lease. Had Marston appeared in court or been deposed and able to verify Keysar's claim, however, Evans's use would have been made a matter of court record. Keysar could then have proceeded with his claim. Evans would have understood this even if Cuthbert Burbage had not. The danger of proceeding was probably too great, and an out of court settlement would have been the best answer for all concerned.

Keysar was not legally sophisticated. He used the law as a thug uses a blackjack. Perhaps he did not realize that his argument had potential merit. It could be that he aimed at an out of court settlement from the start. Litigious extortion had been Keysar's modus operandi years before in the nuisance suit he helped to file against Wheatley and Taylor[89] and was also probably his reason for suing Middleton in 1606. Perhaps the Burbages decided it was best to buy Keysar out and rid themselves of the troublesome suit.

Clearly Keysar's argument had not had its day in court, however, and Kirkham decided there was merit to it. Two years after the Keysar suit, Kirkham filed a suit of his own that used as its foundation Keysar's primary argument regarding his right to the King's Men's profit by virtue of Evans's lease. If Keysar had won a settlement, Kirkham may have been encouraged to imagine that he, too, could recover additional revenue from the defunct Blackfriars venture. His post-Blackfriars history suggests that Kirkham was indeed trying to engineer a suit to squeeze additional money out of the extinguished enterprise.

Tying Up the Loose Ends

Edward Kirkham did not waste time when the Blackfriars venture folded in 1608. By Easter 1609, he and Rastell had initiated suit against Hawkins over the original 1602 Articles of Agreement. By this time the third partner, Kendall, a close friend of Kirkham's, had died. In the 1609 suit, Kirkham and Rastell attempted to demonstrate that Evans and Hawkins had forfeited their £200 bond. On 20 April 1602 Evans and Hawkins executed the bond promising Kirkham, Rastell, and Kendall that they "shall or may from henceforth, during the continuance of the said lease, have the joint use, occupation and profit, together with the within-bound Henry Evans and Alexander Hawkins ... of and in the said great hall or room and other the premises, without the let or trouble of the said Henry and Alexander."[90] In 1609 Rastell and Kirkham claimed that "on the last day of February, 1604, 'the said Henry Evans shut up the said chamber above the chamber called the Schoolhouse, and then and there expelled the said William Rastall, Edward Kirkham and Thomas Kendall.'" Hawkins replied with a general denial of the claim, and the allegation ended in a nonsuit, meaning Kirkham's suit was dismissed for lack of proof.[91]

It seems clear that Kirkham was fishing. As the second Blackfriars venture disbanded, the series of suits that arose read not like personal animosity but rather like the stratagems of businessmen trying to exact money from a defunct venture. The usual reference to these suits as vindictive, vituperative, and malicious in nature does not appear at all clear on the face of the pleadings.[92] Rather, it is more likely that the parties all knew that Evans and Hawkins had made a number of sub rosa legal maneuvers and were now trying to find a way of working those questionable (and unrecorded) deals to their financial advantage. The 1609 case demonstrates their first trial balloon. Having failed with Hawkins, Kirkham tried to demonstrate that Evans had technically breached the £200 bond.

Evans, however, put a stop to Kirkham's exploratory suits. In 1612 Evans haled Kirkham into Chancery on a countersuit. It is this proceeding, *Evans v. Kirkham,* that scholars fix upon to demonstrate the vitriol of the partners after the Blackfriars demise. In it, Evans claims that Kirkham "carrying great spleen and malice against" Evans arrested him "by writ out of the King's Bench, upon several actions of £1,000 damages." Evans contends that Kirkham claimed £1,100 only to harass him. Kirkham, according to Evans, presumed that he would not be able to raise bail on the trumped-up charges and would therefore have to languish in jail. It was a savvy response, casting himself into the role of victim, but he was not finished. Evans, inserting a side issue, uses the countersuit to declare that Kirkham's claim on the £200 bond had already been nonsuited.

In short, Evans's suit is another example of the Welsh scrivener's legal savvy. The £200 bond was nonsuited in the court of common law, and now Evans beat Kirkham to the bench in equity. Before Kirkham could think that he still might have a remedy in Chancery, Evans went on the offensive. Because they were in Chancery, Evans used equity rather than common law pleadings. It is only good gamesmanship in equity to claim to be the victim of malicious litigation. It is really the only way Evans could get a hearing in Chancery. Evans is, after all, praying for a writ of *subpoena* against Kirkham, and vitriol may fairly be termed the language of equity.

Kirkham's answer clearly indicates the sincerity of his claims. However, now on the defensive, Kirkham can do little more than iterate his claim that Evans and Hawkins once denied him access to a dining room above the playhouse. In the context of Evans's declaration of malicious prosecution, Kirkham's answer seems paltry indeed. Evans does not stop there, however. His pleading opens all the doors through which Kirkham may claim a wrong. Evans is evidently looking for *res judicata* on all possible actions against him. According to Evans, Kirkham first offered "to quit the place [the playhouse]." It was Kirkham who "caused the apparels, properties, and goods belonging to the co-partners, sharers and masters of the Queen's Majesty's Children of her Revels (for so it was often called) to be indifferently [ap]praised, and upon such praisement the same was divided, and so praised and divided that the praisers were at [Kirkham's] own mere appointment . . . which [Kirkham and the partners] took and accepted and seemed fully satisfied."

Evans avers that Kirkham "said he would deal no more with [the playhouse], 'for,' quoth he, 'it is a base thing.'" Therefore, according to Evans, it was Kirkham who sought to breach the contract he now seeks to prosecute under. Finally, according to Evans, Kirkham "delivered up their commission, which he had under the Great Seal, authorizing them to play, and discharged divers of the partners and poets." This seems likely. Given that Evans held only the lease in the eyes of the law, Kirkham and the partners to the Articles of Agreement would be the natural parties to release the contract workers in the playhouse venture. Evans's Chancery suit is more than likely a preemptive legal strike against Kirkham by the more knowledgeable Evans. The Welshman is closing a legal opening Kirkham could have used in his attempt to squeeze money from the Blackfriars' purse.

Kirkham was a legal novice. Earlier, in 1595, he discovered that he had been duped by his own great-uncle Robert Wood. Wood had promised Kirkham £20 if he would not take him to court over a contested will. Kirkham accepted, but Wood never paid. When Robert Wood died, his son Roger refused to acknowledge the verbal agreement, and Kirkham never collected the £20. One commentator has rightfully observed, "The naivity that could have failed to see this coming is astonishing."[93] In a legal contest with Evans, therefore, Kirkham was clearly out of his depth.

That Kirkham was poorly equipped to tie up the legal loose ends of the Blackfriars' business affairs may further be seen in his earlier, 1609 Chancery case, *Kirkham and Kendall v. Daniell*. John Gerrard had purchased Samuel Daniel's right to a £100 bond that Kirkham and Kendall gave the poet five years earlier in 1604. Gerrard had acquired Letters of Attorney from the poet to take Kirkham along with Kendall's widow to court over the bond. The bond was to ensure the payment of the £10 annuity Daniel had earned by virtue of gaining royal favor for the enterprise. In the 1609 suit Kirkham, rather naively, claims to have paid all amounts owing under the bond but that Daniel had failed to return the paper obligation, selling it instead to Gerrard. Gerrard brought action against the bond in the Court of King's Bench, and Kirkham countersued in Chancery for relief. Although the result of the suit is nowhere recorded, the outcome can be reasonably guessed. Gerrard had an uncanceled bond duly subscribed. It is doubtful that Kirkham and Kendall's widow could deny the obligation. The likely outcome was a payment to Gerrard and the return of the twice-paid bond to Kirkham and Anne Kendall.

Evans's Final Legal Fiction

Kirkham clearly saw that Evans had outmaneuvered him in 1612. Even during the pleadings of *Evans v. Kirkham,* Kirkham filed another action in an attempt to race Evans to a judgment. In *Kirkham v. Pauton et al.,* Kirkham went before Chancery to call the lease transfer itself into question. Kirkham argued that he had not been consulted regarding Evans's return of the lease to Burbage. Because he had not agreed to return the lease, Kirkham claimed that he still owned a portion of the Blackfriars income. As such, the King's Men owed him a share of their proceeds retroactively to 1608 and for the remainder of the original lease's twenty-one-year limit. It was Keysar's 1610 argument all over again.

2 : TRICKS AND QUILLETS AT A PLAYHOUSE

The history of the parties since 1608 requires a momentary aside in order to understand the complexion of Kirkham's suit. Hawkins had died in 1610. His widow, Evans's daughter Margaret (whom Kirkham calls Anne), had married Edward Pauton. Rastell and Kendall were both dead. This left only Evans on one side and Kirkham on the other side of the 1602 and 1604 agreements. Pauton apparently had little love for the theatre and refers to "such trash as appertained to plays, interludes and players" and alludes to the complainant, Kirkham, as "damnified in such business." He did not, however, fail to see the wisdom of claiming a portion of the money from it.

Kirkham was playing his last card in 1612. The suit against Pauton is in essence an attempt to get around Evans in Chancery. Kirkham gambled that the use Evans gave to Hawkins could be exploited. He began by claiming, as he must, that he had paid for the right to one half of the lease. He claimed that he and his partners Kendall and Rastell disbursed £400 in furtherance of the project and for this Evans gave them one half interest in the property to be divided between them three ways with a right of survivorship. With Kendall and Rastell dead, Kirkham claimed that he owned the full moiety as the survivor. Kirkham argued that the trust (or use) Evans gave to Hawkins was for the benefit of the partnership. He claimed that their agreement allowed the partners to require Hawkins to reassure the lease whenever they requested it be done.

His pleading is likely enough. When Evans aliened the lease to avoid having Star Chamber confiscate it over the Clifton affair, he would certainly have made verbal assurances to the syndicate. They would have demanded such assurances. It is not too much to imagine that one such assurance would include the transfer of the lease itself to the partners if they insisted. Of course, the partners would be informed of the financial dangers and legal complexities of such insistence (that is, such a transfer would run afoul of the Burbage agreement and thus would cancel the lease). Kirkham claimed that Mrs. Evans stole the lease from Hawkins, her son-in-law, and returned it to the Burbage syndicate against Hawkins's will. The lease agreements, therefore, had never been extinguished according to Kirkham. He averred that he was thereby owed the moiety of the lease for the full twenty-one years it was to have run. He prayed the court to render a writ of *subpoena* against the defendants for the lease.

Burbage and Heminges replied that they were unaware of any agreements regarding the lease passing between Evans and Kirkham. Evans joined them in asserting that the profits that were to arise under the lease were never conceived to flow from the value of the property itself. The profits came from the activity of play-acting on the premises. Upon that, then, they demur. Pauton, however, claimed that all of Kirkham's allegations were true but for one detail. He claimed that the entire lease was made over to Hawkins with no part of it attaching to Kirkham and the partnership. Therefore Pauton, as administrator of his wife's estate, claimed that he was entitled to all proceeds from the lease without the need to split them with Kirkham.

The difficulty arises from Evans's creation of the use in Hawkins. Because of the secrecy required—the fact that it needed to be kept from the cognizance of the law—the partners knew of the trust but could do nothing to enforce their rights under it. In a perfect world, they should have all been made parties to the lease. However, Burbage's stipulation to the contrary prevented that. The Star Chamber decree forced Evans to hide forever the truth of the transfer. Both Kirkham and Pauton—plaintiff and defendant—each claimed a right under Evans's transfer. They succeeded in proving that the transfer occurred because the physical lease was in Hawkins's keeping before it had been returned to Burbage. Each man demonstrated that the transfer of the lease injured him. In fairness, in equity, they should probably have been compensated. And Evans could well have been the malefactor the court seized upon for their relief.

Evans, clever to the last, extricated himself one last time. It was Evans's view of the proceedings that influenced the final decision. A use transfer may be created orally and, because it was in Evans's case, the court found that "the said conveyance was never perfected and sealed." It was therefore unrecognizable in law—Evans had made it so ten years earlier to avoid the Star Chamber edict. And so, like a conjurer, Evans waves an arm and the entire transaction that undoubtedly existed—the transfer that allowed the Blackfriars enterprise to flourish for six years—disappears from sight. Without it, the court has no trouble disposing of the case. Kirkham did not pay rent under the original lease after 1608, thereby demonstrating his willingness to see it voided. The £400 Kirkham claimed that he, Rastell, and Kendall put into the enterprise is found to be monies expended for "erecting a company of players and for playing apparel and other things touching plays." It was not held to be money paid for the lease or any part of it. Because the transfer was never enrolled, and because the lease was not reassured under the partnership—all owing to the operation of the use transfer—the court held "that the matter of the plaintiff's Bill be clearly and absolutely dismissed out of this Court." And with that, Evans wins his final victory in the legal history of the second Blackfriars syndicate.

The use transfer was therefore employed with effect in both the Swan and Blackfriars ventures. The transfers surrounding the Globe property, while not constituting a use, were based upon transfers that share features and goals in common with the use. The image of the use, its complexities and peccadilloes, formed an important and protean image for playwrights during this period. The next chapter will examine the varied poetic applications of this altogether prosaic form of property transfer. What should be noted is that this legal maneuver was more than a matter of passing legal interest to poets of the day. It was an integral part of the playhouse world they inhabited, part of their lives and livelihood.

3
Thy Love's Use Their Treasure

THE USE WAS A CONTROVERSIAL SUBJECT IN TUDOR ENGLAND, lectured over at the Inns of Court, and dear to the hearts of many property owners. Henry Evans made good use of its slippery nature, and Shakespeare mentions the use specifically in two plays, *The Merchant of Venice* and *Antony and Cleopatra*. The law is also given significant mention in plays by Jonson, Middleton, and Massinger, which suggests the importance of the law as an image in the vocabulary of Renaissance dramatists. In its simplest form, the legal doctrine regarding use allows the owner of property to transfer that property to a second person, who is responsible for holding legal title to that property while it is enjoyed by yet a third person. The second person, who has charge of what is the equivalent of legal title, is called the *feoffee to uses*. The third person, who is entitled to the beneficial enjoyment of the property, is called the *cestui que use*. This third person is said to have the *use* of the property.

As an example of how the use works, I may own a valuable tract of land, which I entrust to the care of a friend either because he may keep it safer than I could or because I have no immediate need for it. This is a simple transfer. If I intend my friend to keep the land as his own, I have either created a gift or sold him the land. If, however, I transfer the land to my friend with the stipulation that, although he may hold it on paper, it is to be used by the University Polo Club, I have created a use. My friend is *feoffee to uses* and the University Polo Club is the *cestui que use*. My friend holds the equivalent of legal title to the property. The University Polo Club has the exclusive enjoyment of the property. I have no more interest in the property. This type of transfer may be written "A to B for the use of C."

The use law, however, as will be demonstrated in Jonson's works most specifically, could give rise to fraud. If, for example, I find myself in court being sued and I do not want my valuable land to remain part of my property for fear the court may order it sold to satisfy the judgment, I may decide to transfer the property to my friend while I retain the use of the property for myself. This was what Henry Evans did with the Blackfriars lease. In this case I still hold and enjoy the property, but it is in my friend's name and safe from the court. This is generally written "A to B for the use of A." In this instance, such a transaction would be fraudulent; however, an "A to B for the use of A" transaction could also be entered into both legally and honestly in a different situation. By the sixteenth century, much of England was legally held in use in one form or another, and many playwrights of the period seized upon this legal transaction for the drama they saw in it.

Shakespeare may have understood the implications of the use rather well. Images from various knotty legal issues certainly punctuate a number of his plays. His application of the law, as will be discussed, indicates some familiarity with its workings, at least on a rudimentary level. Shakespeare's application of the law, however, is no better informed (and in many cases it is worse) than that of his contemporary dramatists. Whatever Shakespeare's interest in and knowledge of the use might have been, an examination of how Shakespeare used the law within his plays is rewarding, independent of inquiry into Shakespeare's prowess as a lawyer, if any.[1]

The Merchant of Venice

The first instance of the use in Shakespeare's dramatic work is to be found in *The Merchant of Venice*. In the courtroom scene, after Shylock's bond is forfeited and Antonio is given the opportunity to choose the penalty Shylock must pay, Antonio addresses himself to the court:

> So please my lord the duke and all the court
> To quit the fine for one half of his goods,
> I am content; so he will let me have
> The other half *in use,* to render it
> Upon his death unto the gentleman
> That lately stole his daughter.[2]

The first problem encountered with this speech has been the meaning of "use." The word "use" is applied earlier in the play, especially at 1.3, to mean "usury" or "interest on loaned money." This is clearly not the meaning of "use" in this context. Antonio is applying a more sophisticated meaning to "use" than has yet been seen in the play. Antonio's intention is to take, as *feoffee to uses,* half of Shylock's property in use to Shylock, and to hold that property in trust for Lorenzo and Jessica. The problem with the interpretation of this speech comes less from the concept of use as from the words that follow, in particular "to render."

This "to render" has caused several scholars to take a wrong turning. As competent a scholar as Jan Lawson Hinley has read this passage recently thus: "Antonio, who can have no way of knowing that his ships are not truly lost, has neatly recouped his losses and gained new capital to put in use (an apparent gaining of Shylock's vocabulary along with his money)."[3] Hinley may be following Marc Shell:

> What the bankrupt Antonio will now have to use is exactly equal to what Shylock will have to use. Both users say "I am content" . . . Antonio and Shylock are matched as two gelded users of money . . . Other conditions in Antonio's merciful offer to Shylock include Antonio's right "to render [the sum that Antonio will use] / Upon [Shylock's] death unto the gentleman / That lately stole his daughter."[4]

There have been several other glosses of the use as it is employed in this quotation. Kenneth Myrick, in his Signet Classic edition of *The Merchant of Venice,* glosses this "use" as "in trust," which is correct, but he adds "to the use of his business." It is unclear whether he means by "his" to follow Shell and Hinley's argument that the use implies "to use in Antonio's business," which is probably incorrect, or "to use in Shylock's business," which may be correct. J. R. Brown offers a more precise and complete gloss in his Arden Shakespeare edition:

> in use in trust. This does not imply that Antonio would give or receive interest; he probably means to administer this half of the estate, giving the legitimate profits to Shylock until his death, when the property would become Lorenzo's (cf. Halliwell). However, the terms are not clear: they could mean that Antonio would enjoy the revenue (so Johnson), or Lorenzo (so Clarendon).[5]

It is unlikely that Lorenzo and Jessica will be the *cestuis que use* in light of Nerissa's line in 5.1, "There do I give to you and Jessica / From the rich Jew, a special deed of gift, / After his death, of all he dies possessed of." Surely, if they were to derive immediate benefit from the use, as Clarendon would seem to argue, that would be the first news to tell them. It is equally clear that Antonio cannot derive the profits from the property in question, as Johnson, Hinley, and Shell argue, because the purpose of a use, as has been discussed, was to separate legal title from beneficial enjoyment. Because Antonio is asking for the legal title, which is clear because an "A to A for the use of B" transaction was as unknown as it was unnecessary in a use conveyance,[6] it follows logically that either Shylock or Jessica is to enjoy the property until Shylock's death. With no evidence that Jessica is to enjoy the use, it is reasonable to assume that Shylock is to be the *cestui que use*. Antonio is to act as a mere trustee of the property for the future benefit of Lorenzo and Jessica. The unfortunately imprecise "to render" has been interpreted to mean "to deliver what I have not used." The correct interpretation would be "for the purpose of delivering the property intact." Hence, the shorthand formula for this transfer would be written "S to A for the use of S, the residue to L and J upon S's death."[7]

The use creates a perfect settlement of the Jew's affairs. Antonio is able to secure one-half of Shylock's property for his friend by a simple oral agreement requested in open court. The bargain is struck and no more need be done. Furthermore, the use is dramatically contrasted with the deed of gift which Shylock must "record . . . / Here in the court" (4.1.387–88). This relatively cumbersome transfer requires Portia to order, "Clerk, draw a deed of gift" (4.1.394). It further requires Shylock to sign it. The formality of signing the document is shown to be more cumbersome than the creation of the use because, when the Jew becomes ill in court, he must request: "Send the deed after me, / And I will sign it" (4.1.395–96). Finally, the deed will not be enforceable unless Shylock does sign it. The Duke is required to admonish him to "do it" (4.1.397). The point to be derived from this examination is the relative ease Antonio has securing one-half of Shylock's property in use as opposed to the demonstrable difficulty of securing the other half by deed of gift.

It becomes evident, moreover, that the use enhances our understanding of the play by affording us additional insight into the character of both Shylock and Antonio. Because no money changes hands in the use transfer Antonio requests, there is no "valuable consideration" for creation of the use in *The Merchant of Venice*. Shylock is placed in the position of having to transfer his property for "good consideration." The use arising out of "good consideration" is created for the consideration of marriage or for the consideration that arises out of natural love and affection, or for both marriage and natural love and affection.

As with any transfer of property today, Renaissance law also focused upon the legal question of "consideration" (that is, a determination of the sound reason for the transference of property). The doctrine of consideration, then as now, recognizes two forms. The first form is "valuable consideration," which indicates the tender of money or other valuable goods in exchange for the item desired. The second form is "good consideration," which indicates that there is some good reason for making the transfer, a reason occasioned by some event other than the exchange of money or valuable goods. Without consideration, the use was said to "result back" or return to the original grantor. The theory behind this reasoning was that there must be both proof of the conveyance and a sound reason to make the conveyance of property in order to avoid fraud. The payment of money and the advent of marriage were recognized early as consideration. By the middle of the sixteenth century "natural love and affection" was also held sufficient to create "good consideration" for the use.[8]

It is unlikely that Shylock possesses any love or affection for "the gentleman that lately stole his daughter" (4.1.383–85) or for Jessica, who, Shylock says, "is damned for it" (3.1.30). However, the use is binding insofar as it can be cast, by virtue of a legal fiction, to resemble a transfer occasioned by the marriage of his daughter. The use, therefore, acts as a legal testament to Shylock's love for his children even though the actual emotion is lacking (at least for the time being). We know that Shylock must honor the use. The same man who vowed "I'll have my bond" will likewise honor his own legal obligation. He is constrained to honor the written law as merchant and as Jew. His character will allow no other conclusion. The legal fiction of the use, therefore, is employed to underscore this elemental aspect of Shylock's character.

Furthermore, after Portia's moving plea for mercy, Antonio is given the opportunity to exercise mercy: mercy the Jew denied him. Alice Benston describes Antonio's opportunity thus: "[T]he Duke ... exhibits the ... merciful spirit of his state by pardoning Shylock from a death sentence; ... Portia interrupts to make it clear that the Duke cannot dispose of Antonio's award ... [and allows] Antonio to be the one to stipulate the conditions of the pardon."[9] Antonio's reaction is merciful. Not only does he manage to reunite Shylock and Jessica, at least legally, but he also manages to unite the old Jew with his new son-in-law on the same terms. In addition, Antonio manages this union of Shylock's family while leaving Shylock possessed of all his property for life. The use, seen in this light, becomes Shakespeare's legal equivalent of mercy.

Shakespeare's interest in the use law *circa* 1596 is interesting, for although the use had been around for centuries it had recently been closely scrutinized in governmental and legal circles. It was, in fact, a relatively popular subject among the lawyers and students of the Inns of Court. A brief history of the use law seems appropriate at this juncture to place the dramatic interest into its proper latter-sixteenth-century perspective.

Relatively early in the history of common law, at least as far back as the Domesday book, according to Pollock and Maitland,[10] landowners found it desirable in certain instances to separate title to property from the actual enjoyment of that property. A. W. B. Simpson describes one instance in the following example from the fifteenth century:

> The friars of the Order of St. Francis found it convenient that property should be held by others to their use. Thereby they could, as St. Francis had enjoined, achieve both individual and corporate poverty. Like horses, which used but did not own their stables, the friars used, but did not own, the buildings they occupied.[11]

A committee of aldermen, who acted as the legal titleholders, held the title to the Franciscan buildings. The original committee of aldermen could, as they grew older, nominate new aldermen to replace them as titleholders. This created a perpetual *feoffee to uses* and obviated the problem of disposing of the land when the *feoffee to uses* died.

One problem that landholders had with the use in the fifteenth century was that the *cestui que use* did not have a property right recognized at common law. Persons creating a use clearly relied on the honesty of their *feoffees to uses*. If the *feoffee to uses* decided to raise capital, there was nothing to restrain him from selling the property entrusted to him.[12] By the end of the fifteenth century, however, the Chancellors developed consistent principles regarding the duty owed to the *cestui que use* by the *feoffee to uses*. These principles, combined with the willingness on the part of Chancery to intervene on behalf of *cestuis que use,* rendered the use a defensible property recognized in the court.

In 1535 the Statute of Uses was enacted under Henry VIII. This statute applied only to real property and was therefore directed against landowners. The possession of real property under a claim of freehold estate, known as seisin, passed to the *cestui que use* under the statute. The statute created a problem insofar as it failed to divest the *feoffee to uses* of the right to convey the land. In effect, the Statute of Uses created a tension between the *cestui que use* and the *feoffee to uses* by allowing each the right to sell the property without the approval of the other. The statute was so significant (and so controversial) that, according to E. W. Ives, "[It was] one of the few statutes with the distinction of having fomented an armed rebellion; when the rebels rose against Henry VIII in 1536, they demanded not only the abandonment of the king's religious changes, but the abandonment of the statute as well."[13]

The statute caused such a stir in the Inns of Court throughout the Tudor reign that we find Sir Francis Bacon presenting two readings on it in 1600, sixty-four years after its promulgation. The confusion over the statute is perfectly illustrated by Bacon. Although Bacon referred to the statute as "the most perfectly and exactly conceived and penned of any law in the book,"[14] he went on to say in the same presentation that nobody really knew how to interpret the statute because "it hath been by the humour of the time perverted in exposition."[15] According to Simpson, the statute was unmanageable:

> In the first place the statute contain[ed] gross errors both of commission and omission, and in the second place new devices for its evasion were developed which the draftsmen could not possibly have envisaged ... [T]he abolition of the power of devise produced ... violent political opposition.[16]

The main problem with the statute, as Bacon pointed out in his reading before Gray's Inn, was the uncertainty about who would be affected. Bacon referred to the Statute of Uses as "a law whereupon the inheritances of this realm are tossed at this day, as upon a sea, in such sort that it is hard to say which bark will sink, and which will get to the haven: that is to say what assurances will stand good, and what will not."[17] Bacon's position is interesting when one considers that it was Bacon who argued the leading case on uses, *Chudleigh's Case,* in 1595, five years before that same nobleman, in a telling *volte face,* admitted in his reading before Gray's Inn that he did not know how the statute would affect English landholders. Bacon's comments seem to indicate that the Statute of Uses was subject to numerous interpretations even after a half-century of litigation. The foremost legal minds of Shakespeare's time, men no less than Bacon, Coke,[18] and Hale, wrote about and debated the relative merits and demerits of the use, and their debates were followed with great interest.[19] The attention drawn to the Statute of Uses made uses a well-known topic among law students and persons owning property in sixteenth- and seventeenth-century England.

It seems likely, therefore, that Shakespeare and his colleagues would have been reasonably familiar with the doctrine of the use. As a dramatist, Shakespeare would have appreciated the tension caused by the controversy over the use. It is highly suggestive to consider the timing of *Chudleigh's Case.* It involved the leading legal thinkers of Shakespeare's day, Francis Bacon and Edward Coke. Coke reported *Chudleigh's Case* in 1595; the date of *The Merchant of Venice,* the first Shakespearean play specifically to mention the use, is probably 1596–97. Comparing the timing of the controversy with the writing of *Antony and Cleopatra* further strengthens the link between Shakespeare and the use controversy. Bacon delivered his double reading on the Statute of Uses at Gray's Inn during the Lent vacation of 1600. *Antony and Cleopatra* was written sometime between 1605 and 1607.

By the time we reach the use in *The Merchant of Venice,* however, the plot is nearly completed. In fact, Shylock has only two more lines after Antonio mentions the use. The pound-of-flesh tale has already reached its climax, and all that is left is denouement. What the use does, in essence, is to make that denouement an absolute resolution. Because Shylock's moiety is left in the care of Antonio for the benefit of Lorenzo and Jessica, a legally enlightened audience would understand that all is well. Shylock has no chance of escaping his legally binding fate the way Antonio escaped. The use provides the unraveling of all the troubles experienced by Antonio, Lorenzo, and Jessica without changing Shylock's financial well being. In essence, the use in *The Merchant of Venice* restores harmony.

ANTONY AND CLEOPATRA

The second dramatic application of the concept of use in Shakespeare, which is found in *Antony and Cleopatra,* is more sophisticated, subtle, and thematic than the character-based usage of the law to be found in *The Merchant of Venice*. Antony, called back to Rome, tries to reassure Cleopatra that he still loves her:

> Hear me queen:
> The strong necessity of time commands
> Our services awhile; but my full heart
> Remains *in use* with you.
> (1.3.41–44) [emphasis supplied]

It is not anachronistic for Shakespeare to put the concept of the use into Antony's vocabulary. Although Shakespeare probably means us to understand the use as the English common law use, the concept has precursors in the Roman law; the concepts of *usus* and *fidei commissa* are analogues to what Shakespeare understood as the use. The transfer contemplated in *Antony and Cleopatra* is easier to understand than the transfer contemplated in *The Merchant of Venice* because the conveyance is to be understood as a metaphor. Cleopatra is to be the *cestui que use* of Antony's heart. Antony is saying that, although he is leaving and must have legal title to his heart, Cleopatra will enjoy the profit of its love while he is away. He expresses himself at the end of the same scene in much the same vein: "I hence fleeting here remain with thee" (1.3.105). Unlike the speech in *Merchant,* there is little scholarly debate over this speech. The gloss provided in the Signet Classic edition by Barbara Everett is representative: "in use: for you to possess."[20] There has been no deeper scrutiny of this particular line, which is unfortunate because this single legal metaphor sums up the dramatic tension within the character of Antony and within the play itself.

In the first scene of the play Philo says, "Sir, sometimes, when he is not Antony, / He comes too short of that great property /

Which still should go with Antony" (1.1.57–59). The word "property" is normally glossed here to mean "quality." But Shakespeare may have intended a double entendre on the meaning of "property." Antony has a certain quality, to be sure, but he is also a property, a thing to be owned by Antony, by Cleopatra, by Fulvia, by Octavia, by Caesar. The image of Antony as property is underscored later by Cleopatra's "Antony will be himself"; Anthony Brennan asks, "Is Cleopatra referring to the peerless Antony who loves her, Fulvia's Antony, Caesar's Antony, [or] Antony as actor playing at being Antony the lover to hide his quintessential Roman soldier's heart?"[21] With so many vying for him, Antony has no choice but to parcel himself out. As such, it makes sense to leave his love, in the form of his metaphorical heart, in use to Cleopatra while he returns to Rome to thwart a rebellion. Cleopatra, owning the equitable estate, would be entitled to reap the profit or harvest from that estate. In one of Cleopatra's most famous lines she uses just such an image of enjoying the harvest from Antony: "For his bounty, / There was no winter in't: an autumn 'twas / That grew the more by reaping" (5.2.86–88). Here, as in *The Merchant of Venice,* the use not only provides a clue for the legally enlightened auditor concerning character but it also demonstrates in legal terms the dramatic situation.

In *Antony and Cleopatra,* as in *The Merchant of Venice,* the use underscores the plot. The tension Antony feels between Egypt and Rome, and the pivotal image of the use in describing that tension, is made clear in the repartee between Antony and Cleopatra in act one:

> CLEOPATRA. I would I had thy inches; thou shouldst know
> There were a heart in Egypt.
> ANTONY. Hear me, queen:
> The strong necessity of time commands
> Our services awhile; but my full heart
> Remains *in use* with you. Our Italy
> Shines o'er with civil swords; Sextus Pompeius
> Makes his approach to the port of Rome;
> Equality of two domestic powers
> Breed scrupulous faction.
> (1.3.40–48) [emphasis supplied]

Antony is a man in the middle. His full heart, both metaphorically and by poetic placement within the line, lies between Egypt and Rome. Strong necessity pushes him toward Rome to quell the rebellion of Sextus Pompeius against the triumvirs. The use allows him to remain, at least in his heart, in Egypt.

This image of Antony, wavering between Rome and Egypt, is made emphatic by the context of the quoted passage. Cleopatra has interpreted his leaving to mean that he is taking his love back to Fulvia, who, she does not realize, is already dead: "What, says the married woman you may go? / Would she had never given you leave come! / Let her not say 'tis I that keep you here. / I have no power upon you; hers you are" (1.3.20–23). Because she has power to give leave to Antony's comings and goings, Fulvia has been like Rome. Cleopatra, throughout the play, is Egypt. The tension between these two females in Antony's life, therefore, represents the tension between Rome and Egypt over Antony. This is the essential tension that drives the plot. Antony's solution to this tension throughout the play is to leave his heart to the use of Egypt while his arms go to Rome.

We have been informed already that there is no *feoffee to uses*. The audience learned of Fulvia's death in 1.2, but Cleopatra is unaware of the fact at the time Antony makes the metaphoric use transfer; only after the conveyance, a mere eleven lines later, does Antony inform Cleopatra of Fulvia's death. Without a Fulvia to balance Cleopatra's property interest in the use, Antony's conveyance must be read allegorically in this instance, "Antony to Rome for the use of Egypt." When in act two Cleopatra learns of Antony's marriage to Octavia the conveyance becomes a perfect metaphor *ex post facto*. These legal waters, therefore, are not nearly as muddy as would initially appear. The tension between Egypt and Rome in Antony is never in question.

The messenger in 2.5 announces Antony's marriage in terms of a legally drafted union: "He's bound unto Octavia." The legal jargon is reminiscent of the earlier legal arrangement between Antony and Cleopatra. Antony has, in effect, enfeoffed Octavia; he has transferred legal title to his new wife. Because his property (e.g., Antony's heart/self) is encumbered by the use granted to Cleopatra, Antony has only his name to give to Octavia, and the metaphor is perfected. Octavia/Rome is the *feoffee to uses* of Antony while Cleopatra/Egypt is the *cestui que use*: Antony to Rome for the use of Egypt. The results of the transaction are foreshadowed in the relevant passage: "Equality of two domestic powers [not only Pompey and the triumvirs but also a wife and a mistress in separate domiciles, each having a claim on Antony] / Breed scrupulous faction" (1.3.47–48).

In the decade that elapsed between Shakespeare's application of the use in *The Merchant of Venice* and in *Antony and Cleopatra,* he appears to have developed a greater understanding of it and appreciation of its possibilities. *The Merchant of Venice* demonstrates the early appreciation of the use as a complement to character, an appreciation he maintained in *Antony and Cleopatra.* But because the use appears so late in *Merchant,* its dramatic effect is mostly limited to helping tie up the loose ends. In *Antony and Cleopatra* the use is moved to a significantly earlier portion of the play, and, although the use is mentioned only in passing, in its earlier position it foreshadows the main action of the play. In essence, the doctrine of the use in *Merchant* acts as a final resolution to the main action whereas the doctrine of the use in *Antony and Cleopatra* is a microcosmic legal rendering of the main conflict. Shakespeare's growing awareness of the dramatic possibilities of the use doctrine indicates his disinterest in the law *qua* law. There can be no doubt that Shakespeare's interest in the law, unlike a lawyer's interest, was almost exclusively in how the law could be used for dramatic effect.

Bartholomew Fair

The Statute of Uses was largely abused in the century that followed its enactment. Put simply, the Statute of Uses created a confusion over who actually owned the property in question; *cestuis que use* were deemed seized (that is, given legal cognizance of their rights in the property), but *feoffees to uses* could also claim that the transfer of property was an absolute gift. Hence, a conveyance "A to B for the use of C" could be thwarted if B, the *feoffee to uses,* claimed that A had given him the property without mentioning C. Because, as demonstrated in both *The Merchant of Venice* and *Antony and Cleopatra,* the use could be raised orally, there was often no proof as to the complexion of the conveyance.[22]

This type of cozening by the *feoffee to uses* is precisely the point of Dame Purecraft's admission to the disguised Quarlous in Jonson's *Bartholomew Fair.* She makes a clean breast of her hypocrisy and inculpates her suitor and spiritual leader:

> Our elder, Zeal-of-the-Land, would have had me . . . making himself rich by being made *feoffee in trust* to deceased Brethren, and coz'ning their heirs by swearing the absolute gift of their inheritance.
>
> (5.2.62–66)

This is the last abomination Purecraft relates in her speech, a speech in which she lists a graduated scale of holy transgressions practiced by her.[23] She accuses herself of having traded upon her widowhood in order to extort "feasts and gifts" from her suitors; she has also stolen alms and engaged in bawdry. But her tutor and leader has advanced to misappropriating property entrusted to him in use to another. The implication is that Zeal-of-the-Land's trespass is most heinous. The further implication is that this sort of cozening was common enough to be recognized by the popular audience of the Hope.[24]

Act five of *Bartholomew Fair* features the unmasking of all the disguised characters. Quarlous poses as Trouble-all; Overdo as a porter; Win and Mrs. Overdo as prostitutes; Leatherhead as Lantern. Purecraft is, along with Zeal-of-the-Land, a Puritan, which Jonson seems to suggest represents a form of cozener who needs not strike a posture. And, even as the puppet Dionysius exposes his lack of gender, so are they all exposed. The use was also viewed, as has been discussed, as a form of disguise whereby the *feoffee to uses* could cozen the *cestui que use* by assuming the posture of legatee. While the use, referred to in *Bartholomew Fair* as a trust, is mentioned only by the way, its placement in the play and relation to the action of unmasking in the fifth act represents a significant, albeit minor image. Less central to the structure of Jonson's play than it is in either of Shakespeare's, the use nevertheless exposes a vital trait in Zeal-of-the-Land Busy. Furthermore, the off-handed presentation of the legal doctrine demonstrates its currency in the language and imagination of Jonson's 1613 audience.[25]

The Devil is an Ass

Jonson, like Shakespeare, relies upon the use in more than one play to underscore a variety of themes. In his play, *The Devil is an Ass*, a conveyance in trust is used to avert a misappropriation of property by unscrupulous would-be *feoffees to uses*. Unscrupulous property holders not wishing to follow the rules of descent could create a use and will the beneficial interest to whomsoever they wished. In this way the property holder could exercise control over testamentary conveyance he would not otherwise have, and the devolution of property could be made at the pleasure of the landholder. Likewise, a young bride (or widow) with property could devise her property to a third party, a trusted uncle or brother, for example, and retain the use of that property. This would often occur prior to marrying in order to keep a fortune-hunting bridegroom from seizing her property. Such legal tricks have tremendous dramatic possibilities. The use could therefore be made to operate as a clever and wholly believable *deus ex machina*.

Jonson creates such an effect in *The Devil is an Ass*. In this work, Jonson creates a world of crafty intriguers and confidence tricksters. He presents Fitzdotterel as a perfect target for Merecraft. He is wealthy, landed, and foolish. Our first view of Fitzdotterel depicts him wishing he might see a Devil in order to get the foul fiend to show him hidden treasure.[26] Merecraft, the projector, proposes a scheme to drain all the bogs and fens of England and set Fitzdotterel up as the Duke of Drowned-Land. Before that scheme can come to fruition, however, Fitzdotterel discovers that Wittipol, an Inns of Court man, has made untoward advances toward Mrs. Fitzdotterel, his cloistered wife. He seeks satisfaction on the field of honor, and Merecraft rapidly devises another scheme to cozen Fitzdotterel out of his lands.

The proposed duel is, of course, illegal. The illegality prompts Jonson to call upon the use law. Because a person convicted of treason (or, in Jonson's play, any high crime such as dueling) would forfeit his property to the Crown, the common practice arose that a person contemplating treason would transfer his property to a blameless third party and would himself retain the use of that property. If the malefactor were subsequently convicted of his crimes, his family would not lose the property because, technically, it did not belong to him. This is precisely the intention of Jonson's duello-cozening sequence. By tricking Fitzdotterel into undertaking a conveyance in use, Merecraft hopes ultimately to convert that use into a gift through fraudulent means.

Everill, Merecraft's champion posing as the Master of Dependences, suggests in his invented role that, whenever one is about to undertake a duel, "We . . . advise the party, if he be / A man of means, and havings, that forthwith, / He settle his estate."[27] Merecraft encourages Fitzdotterel to "ha' your deed drawn presently, / And leave blank to put in your feoffees, / One, two, or more, as you see cause" (3.5.59–61). Everill is later sent to the lawyer, Justice Eitherside, to, as Fitzdotterel says, "get the feoffement drawn, with a letter of attorney, / For livery and seisin!"[28]

Merecraft becomes concerned that, because Everill has gone to have the document drawn up, Everill will be named as feoffee. He cautions Fitzdotterel:

> He's one, sir, has no state, and a man knows not
> How such a trust may tempt him.
>
> (4.5.22–23)

Merecraft is obviously alluding to the same sort of cozening by *feoffees to uses* that Purecraft suggests in *Bartholomew Fair*. When Everill returns with the deed just three lines later, he cautions Fitzdotterel about Merecraft:

> Sir Paul Eitherside willed me gi' you caution
> Whom you did make feoffee: for 'tis the trust
> O' your whole state: and though my cousin here
> Be a worthy gentleman, yet his valour has
> At the tall board been questioned; and we hold
> Any man so impeached, of doubtful honesty!
>
> (4.5.28–33)

The use-law-cozening plot is thereby established, but Jonson is too fine a plot deviser to take the straight path to discovery of the trick.

In the next scene, when Fitzdotterel falls in love with Wittipol, who is disguised as the Spanish lady, Merecraft believes Wittipol can be cajoled into convincing Fitzdotterel to have Merecraft named feoffee:

> We have another leg strained, for this Dotterel.
> He has a quarrel to carry, and has caused
> A deed of feoffment, of his whole estate,
> To be drawn yonder; he has't within: and you,
> Only, he means to make feoffee . . .
> Now, you know, 'tis of no validity
> In your name, as you stand; therefore advise him
> To put in me.[29]

When Fitzdotterel approaches the Spanish lady with the proposition, he does so with coy innuendo:

> [Y]ou must not know it: yet, you must too.
> For the trust of it, and the fame indeed,
> Which else were lost me. I would use your name
> But in a feoffment: make my whole estate
> Over unto you ...
> [L]et me put you in, dear madam,
> I may be fairly killed.
>
> (4.7.4–8, 13–14)

Fitzdotterel seems to be implying in this last line that, if he were killed in the duel, the property would become vested in the Spanish lady. Such is certainly not the case. The most likely occurrence would be that the property put in use would result back to the grantor's heir, Mrs. Fitzdotterel,[30] and not to the Spanish lady (as *feoffee to uses*) in the event of the death of the *cestui que use,* which would almost certainly be Fitzdotterel himself in this instance. The shorthand for the proposed transfer would be "F to SL to the use of F."

The character of the conveyance is unquestionably a use. As has been discussed, persons contemplating treason or felonies often created a use in order to keep the use of their lands if they were found guilty and their lands forfeited to the Crown. The duel Fitzdotterel contemplates is most certainly against the law. Merecraft alludes to the king's edict of February 1614 and the proclamation of March 1616—the year the play was first performed—which outlawed dueling. He says, "[T]he State, now, sees / That great necessity of [the office of Master of Dependences], as after all / Their writing, and their speaking, against duels, / They have erected it ... And such as trespass 'gainst the rule of court, / Are to be fined."[31] The law against dueling was clear, and Fitzdotterel is well advised to avert confiscation of his lands through reliance upon a use conveyance.[32]

Wittipol, still disguised as the Spanish lady, nominates Manly, his friend and another Inns of Court man, to act as *feoffee to uses.* Plutarchus, the apprentice attorney to Justice Eitherside, demonstrates his own foolish nature when the conveyance is physically made. As Manly takes charge of the lands, Plutarchus, who actually draws up the conveyance, asks, "You do deliver this, sir, as your deed. / To the use of Master Manly?" (4.7.42–43).

Plutarchus's father, Gilthead, has extended credit to Fitzdotterel, and the young clerk is obviously shocked to see his father's security being transferred. In his astonishment, he fails to use his legal terms technically. Instead, he uses the word "deed" to mean "performed action" as well as "document of ownership." And he seems to assume that the property will be misappropriated by Manly, who does not have the property *in use,* being the *feoffee to uses,* but who may certainly convert it to his use by swearing the absolute gift of the estate.

Immediately after the transfer is perfected, Wittipol unmasks. Fitzdotterel sees that he has been duped and demands the return of his deed. Wittipol refuses and says that the estate "shall be kept for your wife's good, / Who will know best how to use it" (4.7.68–69). Clarkson and Warren wonder whether changing the *cestui que use* from Fitzdotterel to his wife was "to be accomplished by the simple expedient of blackmailing Fitzdotterel[, or,] if the deed was absolute instead of in trust, how was the imputation of fraud to be overcome?"[33] They dismiss their own questions too simply: "Regardless of how much Jonson may have known about conveyances in trust, he was too much a master of the drama to overburden his play with unessential technical details beyond creating the appropriate dramatic impression."[34] But a simple bit of stage business uncomplicates all. If while Wittipol is speaking he takes Plutarchus' pen and scribbles on the document, the audience could imagine he is either filling in the other blank—remembering the feoffee was left blank, and therefore so might the *cestui que use*—or he is simply adding "Mrs." in front of the name "Fitzdotterel" already on the document. In either case, the problem of fraud such an act raises in a real-world context should not trouble the reader for the simple fact that no one in the world of the play raises it.

The use in this case is pressed into service as an answer to the evils practiced upon Mrs. Fitzdotterel and to save Fitzdotterel from himself, a *legis ex machina* if you will. Earlier in the play, Mrs. Fitzdotterel tells Wittipol as Manly secretly listens that,

> I am a woman . . . matched to a mass of folly;
> That every day makes haste to his own ruin;
> The wealthy portion, that I brought him, spent;
> And (through my friends' neglect) no jointure made me.

My fortunes standing in this precipice,
'Tis counsel that I want, and honest aids:
And in this name, I need you, for a friend!
(4.6.18, 20–26)

Because the portion she brought into the marriage has been spent by her prodigal husband, and because she did not have a jointure (the property provision for the wife, which was made before marriage in order to secure the wife of property in the event of her husband's death), Mrs. Fitzdotterel is quite absolutely at the mercy of her foolish husband's financial whims. This is the crucial moment of the play when Wittipol desists in his amorous advances toward the married woman and determines to rescue her from her plight. Within thirty lines of Mrs. Fitzdotterel's lamentation, Merecraft enters with the news of Fitzdotterel's decision to make the Spanish lady *feoffee to uses,* which provides Wittipol with the device for saving the woman he has pursued and come to respect.

In the next scene the conveyance is made. Mrs. Fitzdotterel is made *cestui que use* of her husband's estate, giving her the equivalent of the jointure she failed to receive at marriage. Merecraft's plot to cozen Fitzdotterel is quashed. Despite Merecraft's ploy to have Fitzdotterel deemed *non compos mentis* in act five,[35] the conveyance in use holds. Because it holds, Fitzdotterel is saved from the covey of cozeners who have attempted to cheat him out of his estate with promises of bizarre moneymaking projects. Fitzdotterel is, by his own realization, "A cuckold, an ass, and my wife's ward; / Likely to lose my land."[36] And, ironically, through the use conveyance, which subjugates his right to his land to Mrs. Fitzdotterel's,[37] he becomes the Duke of Drowned-Land he has aspired to be. Fitzdotterel recognizes this fact himself when he laments, "Let me alone, I would enjoy myself, / And be the Duke o' Drowned-Land you ha' made me" (4.7.82–83); and again at 5.8.159, "My land is drowned indeed."

The Staple of News

In Jonson's *Staple of News* (1626), the conveyance to Picklock in use to Pennyboy Junior is central to the theme of the play and to the main action of the final act. Although Eugene Waith has characterized act five as having "somewhat the quality of a coda,"[38] Anthony Parr has commented pointedly that "the formal impact in stage terms of Picklock's 'fresh cheat' should not be underestimated."[39] The "fresh cheat," of course, takes the form of Picklock, the *feoffee to uses,* trying to cozen Pennyboy Canter out of the use (referred to in this and all of Jonson's plays as a trust) which Pennyboy Canter gave to him to the use of Pennyboy Junior in a "Canter to Picklock for the use of Junior" conveyance. The image of this use pervades the structure and theme of the play throughout, albeit in an often understated manner. The gallimaufry of images in the play—allegorical, political, legal, and even culinary—makes difficult any attempt at image tracing. Furthermore, Jonson's skill and delight in layering his imagery renders any such tracing discretely lamellar. But, perhaps most especially with the writings of Jonson, an examination of the laminae of his imagery renders profoundly satisfying results.

The Staple of News is most generally considered among Jonson's least effective plays.[40] This may be due in part to a misunderstanding of the use as it operates within the play. Even Anthony Parr, whose edition of the play seeks to resurrect *The Staple of News* from its relative obscurity, fails to discuss how the underlying legal pact between Pennyboy Canter and his lawyer, Picklock, functions within the main themes of the play.

The images from the *dramatis personae,* wherein characters named Mortgage, Statute, Band, and Wax are listed, and in the Induction, 14–22, where the Prologue and Mirth analogize watching the play to sitting in judgment in court, insist upon the legally enlightened attentions of its audience. Jonson's *Staple of News* toys with the third type of cheat perpetuated under the conveyance in use. In this cheat, property holders found that it was possible to avoid feudal dues by creating a use. Royal feudal incidents, such as relief and wardship, were levied against persons who died seized (that is, in legal possession) of a freehold estate (that is, a right of title to land, an estate in realty of uncertain or indeterminate duration). Uses, wherein one man held title while another held beneficial enjoyment of the land, could be used to deny the feudal lord his dues. It was this form of cheating that Henry VIII sought to thwart through his Statute of Uses. Because such feudal dues were payable only upon the death of the titleholder, they could be escaped by creating a perpetual *feoffee to uses* as did the Franciscans. What the Franciscans did for legitimate purposes could, therefore, be turned to illegitimate avoidance in the hands of unscrupulous property holders.

The opening repartee of *The Staple of News* lays the groundwork for the image of a conveyance of real property. In 1.1 Pennyboy Junior, having just reached his majority, exclaims, "Look to me, wit, and look to my wit, land" (1.1.3). Pennyboy Junior will in fact need to look to his wit in act five to recover his land. Act one continues with like imagery; the prodigal Junior sees himself as "the lord of mine own ground ... an heir" (1.1.21, 32). The Fashioner who calls upon him to deliver his new clothes suggests that he dare not come too early for fear "your worship might have pleaded nonage / If you had got 'em on ere I could make / Just affidavit of time" (1.2.7–9). Pennyboy Junior rewards his jest by exclaiming, "I'll make thee a copyholder," and promising to do it "when I have sealed the lease of my custom."[41] Most significantly, Pennyboy Junior goes on to say that, "for now / I'll sue out no man's livery but mine own."[42]

The legal phrase, sue out, is properly used. To sue out a writ by a ward in chivalry who reaches majority indicates that the ward, Pennyboy Junior, will make a legal and proper plea to the court to obtain delivery of the possession of his lands out of the hands of his guardian. The image of asking a guardian with a fiduciary interest to honor his obligation is here introduced. In a law-abiding world, with an eye to both justice and equity, the ward should receive his inheritance from his guardian.

But such is not the world of *The Staple of News*. Later in the first act, when Pennyboy Junior congratulates himself that his father was "a right, kind-natured man / To die so opportunely" (1.6.15–16) and leave him in possession of all of his estate, Picklock, the lawyer, responds in words that prove situationally ironic. Says the lawyer:

> And to settle
> All things so well, compounded for your wardship
> The week afore, and left your state entire
> Without any charge upon't.
>
> (1.6.16–19)

The irony, of course, is that the settling of the estate has been by way of a use, with Picklock as the *feoffee to uses*. The settling of the estate in this manner has indeed been done well from Picklock's point of view. At the Staple, Cymbal sees through Picklock's ulterior motivation. At 3.1.9–11 he says:

> He will have a trick
> To open us a gap by a trap door
> When [the young prodigal and his train] least dream on't.

Almost immediately afterward, Picklock identifies his major trait and, in doing so, hints at his plan to convert his status from *feoffee to uses* to legatee:

> I am Vertumnus,
> On every change or chance, upon occasion,
> A true chameleon. I can colour for't.
>   (3.1.34–36)

The conveyance in use does not come into complete light until the final act. Once Pennyboy Canter has tested his son and found him wanting, he determines to retrieve the land that he has put in use to him through Picklock. Pennyboy Junior learns, however, "that your father / And Picklock are fall'n out, the man o'law . . . And a great suit is like to be between 'em" (5.1.51–52, 54). Thomas, the barber, details the reason for the lawsuit:

> Picklock denies the feoffment and the trust
> Your father says he made of the whole estate
> Unto him, as respecting his mortality,
> When he first laid this late device to try you.
>   (5.1.55–58)

One difficulty with this pronouncement, as Clarkson and Warren note,[43] is that, while Picklock does deny that the feoffment was given *in trust,* he does not deny that the *feoffment,* the gift of the land, was given. The incorrect terminology need not trouble the reader, however. Thomas, the barber, has characteristically delivered exaggeration and half-truth for news; as the newest clerk at the Staple, inflation of what he has heard but barely understood has been his vocation; as a barber, canard has furnished his avocation. He has obviously heard that Picklock has denied the trust and denied he was given the land as *feoffee* and simply substituted the abstract noun for the agent noun in reporting it to Pennyboy Junior. This interpretation is entirely in keeping with the mass misinformation that the Staple has disseminated throughout the play. Indeed, this news is characterized by Thomas as "the last hum that [the Office of the Staple of News] made" before it vanished.[44]

Jonson transforms the loquacious pronouncement of the barber in Pennyboy Junior's mouth to the simple question, "Has Picklock then a trust?" (5.1.59) Thomas humorously answers, "I cannot tell," indicating that the barber-newsmonger knows all of the staple of news reasonably well but none of its meaning. In the important action that follows, Pennyboy Junior hides Thomas behind the arras and tricks Picklock into admitting privately that the land was conveyed as a use. The lawyer (trying to "commit father and son / And make my profits out of both; commence / A suit with the old man for his whole estate / And go to law with the son's credit, undo / Both, both with their own money"[45]) pretends to side with Pennyboy Junior's claim to the land:

> PICKLOCK. Your father's . . . fall'n out with me for being yours
> And calls me knave, and traitor to his trust.[46]
> JUNIOR. Had you a trust then?
> PICKLOCK. Sir, I had somewhat will keep you still lord
> Of all the estate.
>
> 5.1.63, 69–70, 78–80)

When asked where the deed is, Picklock says, "It is a thing of greater consequence / Than to be borne about in a black box / Like a Low Country *vorloffe* or Welsh brief,"[47] and sends for it to be brought to them. Pennyboy Junior secretly sends his own messenger to intercept the all-important document, and, while they wait for it, tries to persuade Picklock to admit the conveyance in use. Picklock, believing himself safely alone with Pennyboy Junior, admits:

> [T]rust you unto my *trust,*
> 'Tis that that shall secure you, an absolute deed.
> And I confess, *it was in trust for you,*
> Lest anything might have happened mortal to him.[48]

The character of the use conveyance is now completely spelled out, "Canter to Picklock for the use of Junior, the remainder to Junior on Canter's death." Picklock proposes to claim the absolute gift of the land ("that that shall secure you") from Pennyboy Canter.

Picklock's trick, however, is to keep the absolute deed for himself. He suggests that he must sue the old man in his own name and use the young man's money to go to court with:

> I am not able to wage law with him,
> Yet must maintain the thing as mine own right—
> Still for your good—and therefore must be bold
> To use your credit for monies.
>
> (5.1.117–20)

When Pennyboy Canter arrives six lines later, Picklock begins his scheme. In the confrontation that ensues, Canter declares the character of the use:

> CANTER. Will you restore the trust yet?
> PICKLOCK. ... What trust? Where does't appear? I have your deed.
> Doth your deed specify any trust? Is't not
> A perfect act, and absolute in law,
> Sealed and delivered before witnesses,
> The day and date emergent?
>
> (5.2.4, 6–10)

As has been demonstrated, because the use was raised orally, an unscrupulous *feoffee to uses* could always claim the conveyance was a gift, "a perfect act." But also there must be consideration for the transfer, either valuable consideration or good consideration. Pennyboy Canter asks what consideration was given when he asks, "But what conference, / What oaths and vows preceded?" (5.2.10–11). Because he knows Picklock cannot prove any money changed hands, and valuable consideration cannot therefore be proved, he asks what good consideration occasioned the transfer. His allusion to "oaths and vows" glances at a marriage, which was the most common form of good consideration.

Picklock, however, responds that the good consideration arises from Pennyboy Canter's guilty conscience, and that he gave the estate to Picklock to keep it out of the hands of his prodigal son; he says,

> As I remember,
> You told me you had got a grown estate
> By griping means, sinisterly ... and were
> Ev'n weary of it. If the parties lived
> From whom you had wrested it, ... you could be glad
> To part with all for satisfaction.

> But since they'd yielded to humanity,
> And that just heaven had sent you for punishment—
> You did acknowledge it—this riotous heir,
> That would bring all to beggary in the end
> And daily sowed consumption where he went—
> . . . .
> After a long, mature deliberation
> You could not think where better to place it.
>
> (5.2.12–22, 24–25)

But Pennyboy Junior, in an attempt to deal rightly by his father, exclaims, "Unto me / He hath confessed the trust" (5.2.45–46).

Picklock believes he is safe. His oral pronouncement was not overheard, he believes. He demands, "I must have witness. / Where is your witness? You can produce witness? . . . I live by law . . . I must have witness, and of your producing, / Ere this can come to hearing, and it must / Be heard on oath and witness" (5.2.56–57, 61, 65–67). Pennyboy Junior then produces the concealed Thomas as his witness, who begins his loquacious pronouncement with "Sir, he said / It was a trust," (5.2.70–71) before he becomes superfluous. Pennyboy Junior interrupts to add that Picklock planned to bring a suit "which he was to maintain in his own name / But for my use" (5.2.79–80). Junior presents a double entendre that resonates differently between layman and lawyer in the audience.

But even the witness to Picklock's admission might not be enough. So long as Picklock has the deed in his possession he has *prima facie* evidence of a transfer. With only their word against his as to the character of the transfer, whether *with livery of seisin* or *in use,* he claims he will argue that they are collusive, interested parties fraudulently bringing the suit: "I'll prove yours maintenance and combination, / And sue you all" (5.2.92–93). The use, when in the wrong hands, is once again demonstrated to be almost impossible to prove, even when witnesses testify to its character.

Pennyboy Junior's device to intercept the deed Picklock sent for proves to be the lawyer's undoing. With the physical possession of the deed once again in the hands of the Pennyboys, Picklock laments, "I am lost. A plot! I scent it . . . Plague o'your trust. / I am trussed up among you."[49] Pennyboy Junior's "act of piety and affection" reconciles father and son and successfully underscores the action of divesting misers and prodigals of wealth put to the wrong use.[50]

The action of the fifth act of *The Staple of News,* far from being an afterthought or coda, is thematic and well anticipated in the preceding acts. Throughout the play wealth has been allegorized in the person of Pecunia, hemmed in and protected by the allegorized figures of legal documents and accoutrements, Mortgage, Statute, Band, and Wax. There is an allegorical sequence at 4.3 that reflects Picklock's attempt to cheat the Pennyboys of their estate. The miser, Pennyboy Senior, enters the Apollo to discover Broker, whom he left in charge of Pecunia's well-being, drunk asleep. Says he, "What through sleep and sack / My *trust* is wronged, but I am still awake / To wait upon your grace."[51] The allegory that ensues demonstrates the necessity of holding the legal documents in order to hold the property. Pennyboy Senior asks Statute, Band, and Wax to return home with him while his prodigal nephew entertains Pecunia (4.3.18–19). The jeering that follows allegorically demonstrates what happens in a use conveyance.

Pennyboy Senior, who has failed to keep his "instruments" at home, "bound back to back" with their "legs[52] turned in or writhed about—or else displayed,"[53] but has rather let them walk abroad with Pecunia, discovers that he has lost all. Madrigal bluntly tells him as much, "You have now no money." This is precisely the problem that arises in the fifth act. By conveying the legal instrument along with the property it secures (as one must do with a use conveyance) one stands an excellent chance of losing both. Pennyboy Senior's final realization is typical of the losing party in such a conveyance: "I am cheated, robbed, jeered by confederacy." The difference between this conveyance and the conveyance in act five is that the property had been entrusted to Broker for the use of Pennyboy Junior, but, while the drunken *feoffee to uses* slumbered, the Statute of Uses worked to deem the *cestui que use* seized of the property. It is, after all, the character of Statute who first informs Pennyboy Senior, when he asks the allegorized legal documents to return with him, that, "Truly we will not" (4.3.20). The jeering by Pecunia, Statute, Band, and Wax thematically rejects the miser's misuse of his property. And the use itself comes to represent the same sort of ephemeral written work that characterizes the Staple's product in the world Jonson creates.[54]

The image of the use ultimately comes to underscore what Robert Knoll calls "Jonson's teleological doctrine of moderation."[55] Knoll sums up the received attitude toward Jonson's philosophy as it is expressed in *The Staple of News* when he says:

> When men are rational, they reduce money to its proper place. They begin to be wise when they see that money is only one of the world's goods. Jonson does not preach poverty and mortification of the flesh, nor does he deny that money is desirable; he knows that "*Merit* will keepe no house, nor pay no house rent" (2.4.62). He contends that one should neither prostrate oneself before the world, nor treat it with contempt; one must act between these extremes.[56]

The use in *The Staple of News* is an ideal image of the *via media* Jonson espouses. Covetousness is exposed in the *feoffee to uses,* Picklock; niggardliness in one grantor, Pennyboy Senior; prodigality in the *cestui que use,* Pennyboy Junior; and moderation in the other grantor, Pennyboy Canter.[57] Pennyboy Junior's trick to retrieve the land put in use acts to redeem him in his father's eyes. Pennyboy Canter's restoration of Pennyboy Senior's money, which was converted to the *cestui que use* (Pennyboy Junior) by the Statute of Uses, acts to restore the miser to his senses and sensibilities (5.6.31–37). On one level of imagery, then, the use in *The Staple of News* acts to underscore Jonson's main themes: the wrong use of wealth, bastardization of language, and the self-exposure of selfishness.

A Trick to Catch the Old One

Thomas Middleton, even though himself an Inns of Court man, seems to have a looser grasp of the workings of a trust conveyance than did either Shakespeare or Jonson. He understands, for example, that being able to create a use makes a man a good lawyer.[58] This is a truism rather than an application of a legal concept, however. But he did understand the concept well enough to use it at a pivotal point in *A Trick to Catch the Old One* (c. 1606) as an image to demonstrate both Lucre's ravenous character and Witgood's improved sense of legal matters.

As the play opens, Witgood has just been cozened out of his land by his unscrupulous uncle, Lucre.[59] Says Witgood:

> But where's Long-acre? in my uncle's conscience, which is three years' voyage about; he that sets out upon his conscience never

finds the way home again—he is either swallowed in the quicksand of law-quillets,[60] or splits upon the piles of a *præmunire;* yet these old fox-brained ox-browed uncles have still defences for their avarice.[61]

Lucre's ploy to shark up Witgood's land was both straightforward and simple. The prodigal Witgood mortgaged his estate to his uncle for the ready cash he needed to continue his rioting. Lucre then merely called for the mortgage to be paid, and, when it was not, took possession of the property by calling the note.[62] The object of the trick referred to in the title of the play is for Witgood to retrieve his lands by reclaiming the mortgage Lucre holds. Lucre well understands, as apparently does Middleton, that only by holding the papers does Lucre hold the land. Says Lucre:

> [G]ive him his due—marry, that's his mortgage; but that I never mean to give him. I'll make him rich enough in words.
> (2.1.167–69)

But when Witgood springs the trap, Lucre believes his nephew might lose the rich widow. Lucre means to cozen her money from Witgood; at 4.1.74–76 he sees there is no choice but to return the mortgage to Witgood in order to make him a man of substance worthy of the widow. He affirms:

> Widow, believe it, I vow by my best bliss, Before these gentlemen, I will give in The mortgage to my nephew instantly, Before I sleep or eat.

To this point in the play, Lucre labors under the delusion that his nephew is not aware that he has been cheated.[63] He delivers the mortgage to Witgood in front of witnesses and, with a flourish, says:

> Here nephew [*giving paper*], before these kind gentlemen I deliver in your mortgage, my promise to the widow; see, 'tis done.
> (4.2.36–38)

At line 43, however, Lucre pulls his nephew aside and admonishes him as to the character of the transfer. He tells Witgood that he has given him the mortgage merely "to blind the widow and the world" (4.2.53). He fully expects to have the land back once the widow has married Witgood. Says Lucre, "When you are full possessed, / 'Tis nothing to return it" (4.2.56–57). Witgood, of course, has no intention of returning the mortgage, which has been delivered to him freely and in front of witnesses. The transfer is, after all, the goal of the titular trick. But Lucre introduces a potential dilemma.

When Witgood exclaims that the return of the mortgage is "a thing quickly done" (4.2.58), Lucre responds, "Well said! you know I give it you but in trust" (4.2.59). To an audience familiar with the vagaries of a use conveyance, this verbal addition to what seemed to be a conveyance of an absolute gift before witnesses has the potential of taking on a far different character. Significantly, Witgood seems to understand that a conveyance in trust represents a potential for cozenage. As already discussed, a *feoffee to uses* may, at nearly any time, claim that the property is his own, and, likewise, under the Statute of Uses the *cestui que use* was deemed seized of the land. Middleton does not make clear whether Witgood imagines that Lucre is intending to deliver the property to him in a "L to L for the use of W" conveyance, which would indicate a misunderstanding of the law,[64] or a "L to W for the use of L" conveyance, which would give Witgood the mere title to the property. The latter interpretation would fulfill Lucre's promise to "make him rich enough in words," while keeping Lucre in actual control and ownership of the property under the relevant statute.

The question is mooted almost at once, however. After Lucre has made his *sub rosa* pronouncement that he has given the document in trust only, Witgood embarrasses the old man by speaking loudly enough for all the witnesses to hear, and the following, highly humorous exchange occurs:

> WITGOOD. Pray let me understand you rightly, uncle: You give it me but in trust?
> LUCRE. No.
> WITGOOD. That is, you trust me with it.
> LUCRE. True, true.[65]

The humor, without further textual explanation, can work only if the audience understands the underlying quibble raised by the tension between *trust* (to have confidence in) and *trust* (a legal conveyance in use). Witgood demonstrates how very far he has come from the beginning of the play. He is no longer the dupe. Witgood, who was earlier cheated of his lands through the simplest of deceptions, is now both clever and wary enough to appreciate the fine distinctions of a relatively complicated legal scheme used to deprive even rather cautious men of land. It is at this moment that Witgood fully lives up to his name.

The use, as has been demonstrated in another context, might have been raised by the oral addendum to the transfer,[66] and Witgood seems to sense it. His response to the trick is characteristically humorous. Middleton, never one to pass up a play on words, places a homophonic pun in Witgood's mouth relative to the question of trusts and trusting:

> [*Aside*] But if ever I trust you with it again, would
> I might be trussed up for my labor!
> (4.2.64–65)

Lucre, in his attempt to further his riches by entrusting his nephew with the lands in question, demonstrates a quality of his greed that blinds him to his own gulling.[67] He has delivered the mortgage into Witgood's possession in front of witnesses and failed in his attempt to place a string on the transfer by casting it in the form of a use. Witgood sees the potential for trouble in the use conveyance, and thwarts Lucre of his opportunity to retain the property. Again, despite the argument that a nice understanding of the law would be required to appreciate the significance of this theatrical sequence, Middleton seems to have thought his audience equal to it.

A NEW WAY TO PAY OLD DEBTS

When Massinger reworked *A Trick to Catch the Old One* in his *A New Way to Pay Old Debts* (c. 1621),[68] he retained the image of the use conveyance in an altered form. The riotous nephew, Wellborn, has been cheated of his land by his uncle, Overreach. Overreach's instrument, Marrall, attempting to curry favor with Wellborn, whom he believes will soon be richly wed, tells the nephew to challenge the uncle's right in the land. Marrall tells Wellborn not to accede to securing the thousand pounds Overreach has given to Wellborn:

> [H]e's in your debt
> Ten times the sum, upon the sale of your land.

> I had a hand in't (I speak it to my shame)
> When you were defeated of it . . .
> Then urge him to produce
> The deed in which you pass'd it over to him,
> Which I know he'll have about him . . .
> I'll instruct you further
> As I wait on your worship.[69]

When Wellborn accosts his Uncle Overreach on the matter, Overreach protests that he had the land by sale and purchase (5.1.160). He offers to open the box containing the reputed deed to the land. Wellborn claims that the land was conveyed in use, which Overreach unscrupulously converted, as *feoffee to uses,* to an absolute gift. When Overreach insists that there is a "deed that does confirm it mine,"[70] Wellborn retorts,

> I do acknowledge none; I ne'er pass'd o'er
> Any such land. I grant for a year or two
> You had it *in trust,* which if you do discharge,
> Surrend'ring the possession, you shall ease
> Yourself, and me, of chargeable suits in law.
> (5.1.166–70) [emphasis supplied]

Overreach then opens the box containing the deed and discovers that the writing, signatures, and sealing wax that make the deed binding have disappeared, owing to the machinations of Marrall—who used "certain minerals incorporated in the ink and wax."[71] Thus the villainous uncle is undone. Neill suggests part of the thematic significance of the passage when he says, "The forms and bonds of communal society, which for Overreach were vacuous nothings, prove immutably solid, while his own omnipotent bond becomes literally 'nothing,' 'void.'"[72] Neill's discussion suggests the significance of the use in Massinger's play which is equally relevant to Jonson's *The Staple of News:* "By the same token the chronicles of honor, which in Overreach's eyes were so much historical dust, prove indestructible, while his own 'deed' turns to dust before his eyes":

> What prodigy is this, what subtle devil
> Hath raz'd out the inscription, the wax
> Turn'd into dust! the rest of my deeds whole,
> As when they were deliver'd! and this only
> Made nothing.

In both plays the use conveyance becomes, at least upon one level, an image of the ephemeral, legalistic foil to the everlasting values of fair dealing and familial love. The use conveyance creates an untidy ending to the argument. The play ends without deciding who owns the land, whether Wellborn or Meg, Overreach's daughter. The good Lovell tentatively resolves the matter by saying,

> And for your land, Master Wellborn,
> Be it good, or ill in law, I'll be an umpire
> Between you, and this, th'undoubted heir
> Of Sir Giles Overreach.
>
> (5.1.383–86)

The denouement, therefore, is patently couched in terms of a legal decision. However, the foiled ending of the story provided by this use conveyance, in contradistinction, *exempli gratia,* to its use in *The Merchant of Venice* to bring about accord, is more directly relevant to the thematic redemption of Wellborn.

Unlike Middleton's Witgood, who had a reputation for rioting but is in actuality an honorable young man, Massinger's Wellborn has fallen into depravity with his failed fortunes.[73] By the end of the play he sees that he must reclaim himself from his riotous past:

> [T]here is something else
> Besides the repossession of my land
> And payment of my debts, that I must practise.
> I had a reputation, but 'twas lost
> In my loose courses; and, till I redeem it
> Some noble way, I am but half made up.
>
> (5.1.389–94)

It is significant to the moral vision of the play, therefore, to keep in question Wellborn's reinstatement into society. The doubtful outcome of his pursuit of honor in war is therefore reflected in the doubtful outcome of Lovell's decision concerning who owns the land: the daughter of the *feoffee to uses* or the *cestui que use.*

The image of the use, therefore, spans the drama of the Renaissance from at least 1596, the *terminus post quem* for *The Merchant of Venice,* to at least 1633, when *A New Way to Pay Old Debts* was published. In those thirty-seven years it was used to many different ends. It provided an image of divided loyalties in

Antony and Cleopatra, of proper familial oversight in *The Merchant of Venice* and *The Devil is an Ass,* of ephemeral values in *A Trick to Catch the Old One, A New Way to Pay Old Debts,* and *The Staple of News.* It provided the opportunity for bawdy jokes in Sonnet 20, *The Phoenix,* and *Epicoene.* It exposes the essential character traits of Shylock, Antony, Zeal-of-the-Land Busy, Picklock, the three Pennyboys, Lucre, and Overreach. And it provides an opportunity for self-sacrifice for Antonio, Pennyboy Junior, and Wittipol. Furthermore, the use reunites Shylock with his daughter, Pennyboy Canter with Pennyboy Junior, and Fitzdotterel with Mrs. Fitzdotterel. For Shakespeare, it helped develop character and underscore theme. For Middleton, Jonson, and Massinger, it created conflict. It is an apt image in Jonson for the misappropriation of language. In every case, the image was obviously aimed at an audience sophisticated in the language of the law. Despite the uncertainty of the law among the scholars and pundits at the Inns of Court, the use provided early modern playwrights with an invaluable theatrical device that should not be underestimated in modern evaluations of the period's drama.

4

I Knew a Wench Married in an Afternoon: Secret Marriages *per verba de præsenti* and *per verba de futuro*

SEVERAL COMMENTATORS ON SHAKESPEARE'S USE OF MARRIAGE law are satisfied to conclude that secret marriages were not common in general and were quite rare among the upper classes, and therefore Shakespeare's plays do not represent normal social practice.[1] This approach, more abortive than perceptive, only succeeds in begging the question. Neither was murder a normal social practice in Shakespeare's England, but it is dramatically interesting. The image of secret marriage, as does the image of murder, allows for highly inventive motifs drawn from the popular imagination that affords the poet an opportunity for metaphoric significance. Murder was clearly uncommon, but the murder of Duncan, and its pointed metaphoric significance when the killer is haunted by a spectral voice crying, "Macbeth does murder sleep," develops a strong sociopsychological resonance that continues to capture the imagination. Similarly, we need to understand the sociopsychological response Shakespeare's audience might have had to secret marriages—a phenomenon in contradistinction to murder for which we have no adequate current social analogy. Different literary treatments of secret unions, when set in their context, have varied effects. For instance, as Duncan's murder is of a different responsive stripe than is Cloten's, so, too, is the secret marriage in *The Duchess of Malfi* distinguishable from any of the marriages in *As You Like It*. Thus it is important to understand the legal perception of and cultural response to secret marriage within Renaissance English society in order to gauge the reaction to it in the drama.

4 : I KNEW A WENCH MARRIED IN AN AFTERNOON

The primary difficulty in treating the law of marriage in Renaissance England as it pertains to dramatic literature has been the inability of commentators to marshal the viewpoints that survive on the subject. There are some that will insist, for example, that the very word *clandestine* must be narrowly confined to the sorts of secret marriages performed by clergy as found in *Romeo and Juliet*. They argue, very narrowly, that Shakespeare never referred to a *sua sponte* pledge as marriage, preferring the word "betrothal," and will further argue that the seventeenth century jurist Swinburne referred to them only as "spousals." Such commentators are quick to suggest that Shakespeare himself is scrupulous in never using the word marriage when referring to a pre-contract, whether *de præsenti* or *de futuro*—"husband" and "wife" yes, marriage no, they contend.[2] The fussiness of such distinctions should probably strike the reader as ingenious at best. These distinctions grow from the theoretical imperative to pigeonhole and are of modern origin. Truly there would have been a perceived hierarchy of marital attitude even as we have today between a church wedding and a common-law marriage. Nevertheless, the attitude toward secret marriage, at least as it is presented from the stage, was sympathetic.

It is not difficult to understand why literary commentators have found the world of early modern marriage practice and its law perplexing. Applying all of the known facts and opinions relevant to the Renaissance law of secret marriage is analogous to developing a cogent picture of the current societal attitude toward abortion. As with any instance where the cold statement of law is commingled with an emotional topic (especially one with moral implications and Church involvement) the developing vision of the law takes on kaleidoscopic proportions: dozens of individual pieces in flux, recombining into varied designs at once clarifying one aspect and obscuring another.

The varied commentaries require careful navigation. The scholar must discern which treatments of the topic represent dissenting voices,[3] which apply the law correctly, and which are merely commenting upon a confused situation.[4] All of this is necessary in order to decry what is known and what is merely wished for—which gray areas of the law exist in practice and which only in philosophical legal theory.[5] The additional difficulty for the Renaissance dramatic historian lies in discovering which dramatic sequences treat the issue of secret marriage and which do not.

One commentator, for example, inquiring into *The Taming of the Shrew* has perceived a clandestine marriage in Petruchio's wooing of Kate.[6] Kate and Petruchio are certainly not married in the "joint stool" scene, as will become clear in the discussion that follows. They are engaged, to be sure, and that engagement is forced upon the hapless Kate, but the marriage itself takes place later in the church after Petruchio appears in his quixotic outfit and after the banns have been read. They do not engage in a secret *or* a private marriage.[7]

As You Like It

Shakespeare's *As You Like It* offers a simple introduction to the Renaissance view of marriage *per verba de præsenti*. The play opens with an image of a corrupt world. As will become apparent in the discussions to follow, secret marriage plots seem to focus upon a world of overbearing authority. The action of the play concerns a rejection of the strictures of an oppressive society in favor of the freer world of the forest of Arden. In Arden, where there is "no enemy, but Winter and rough weather," a world where one finds one's "sermons in stones and books in the running brooks," lovers fall in love simply and at first sight. Rosalind and Orlando, Touchstone and Audrey, Celia and Oliver each seek marriage at the first available opportunity after meeting. The image of incontinence after contracting a marriage is revealed in Rosalind's description of the love-at-first-sight betrothal of Oliver and Celia:

> [T]here was never anything so sudden . . . For your brother, and my sister, no sooner met, but they look'd: no sooner look'd, but they lov'd: no sooner lov'd, but they sigh'd: no sooner sigh'd but they ask'd one another the reason: no sooner knew the reason, but they sought the remedy: and in these degrees, have they made a pair of stairs to marriage, which they will climb incontinent, or else be incontinent before marriage; they are in the very wrath of love, and they will together. Clubs cannot part them.[8]

This passage hints at the contracting of a *de futuro* contract, which is a special sort of engagement, between the lovers.[9] Rosalind correctly jokes that this type of betrothal may be converted into present matrimony by their incontinent desire to be together. This is true because sexual relations after such a *de fu-*

turo promise converted the promise to marriage. Hart was the first commentator to see in the allusion to the "pair of stairs" an image of wedlock which time has lost.[10]

A second instance of secret marriage, but of a different form, may be found in Touchstone's attempt to marry the country wench, Audrey. This clandestine marriage is a burlesque of the Romeo and Juliet marriage. Romeo and Juliet marry secretly with only Friar Lawrence attending. Likewise Touchstone informs Audrey, "I will marry thee: and to that end, I have been with Sir Oliver Martext, the Vicar of the next village, who hath promis'd to meet me in this place of the Forest, and to couple us" (3.3.38–41). It is significant that Touchstone is at least fulfilling some form of ecclesiastic celebration by including Martext. This is the sort of clandestine marriage, conducted by a cleric, that would—perhaps humorously in the Touchstone context—make the vicar culpable in the Ecclesiastical Commission while leaving the parties to the marriage alone.[11] The informality of the marriage is underscored by Touchstone's question to Martext, "Will you dispatch us here under this tree, or shall we go with you to your chapel?" (3.3.61–62).

Martext insists on some formality, however, when he asks, "Is there none here to give the woman? . . . Truly she must be given or the marriage is not lawful" (3.3.63, 65–66). Though Martext is presented as a bit of a fool, the pronouncement Shakespeare has placed in his mouth is technically correct. Martext does not suggest that the clandestine marriage will not be valid, but merely "not lawful." It will require a further church solemnization. Of course, even were there someone to give Audrey, as, indeed, Jaques immediately volunteers to do, the clandestine nature of the ceremony—lack of banns, insufficient witnesses—also renders the proposed ceremony illicit. Martext, as his name suggests, is not sophisticated in his calling and fails to understand that his presence alone is not enough to create a union *in facie ecclesiæ*. However, in 3.3.76–85 both Jaques and Touchstone do appear to understand what is involved in this sort of union, as the fool's response to Jaques' question reveals:

> JAQUES. And will you, being a man of your breeding, be married under a bush like a beggar? Get you to church, and have a good Priest that can tell you what marriage is, this fellow will but join you together as they join wainscott, then one of you will prove a shrunk panel, and like green timber warp, warp.

TOUCHSTONE. I am not in the mind, but I were better to be married of him than of another, for he is not like to marry me well, and, not being well married, it will be a good excuse for me hereafter to leave my wife.

Touchstone's aim, clearly, is to use the secret marriage as a seduction tactic. Of course, it was precisely this sort of rascality that the injunction to solemnize clandestine marriages was in force to inhibit.[12] The court records are full of cases where men used an irregular marriage merely to seduce an unsuspecting virgin.[13] Touchstone's desires are contrasted with those of Oliver and Celia when he says, "Come, sweet Audrey, we must be married, or we must live in bawdry" (3.3.88–89). His incontinence is wholly libidinous whereas Oliver and Celia's appears to be an outgrowth of mutual affection.

In act five Rosalind controls the action—and in particular the marriage action—when she sets up a conditional *de futuro* contract between Silvius and Phebe. She asks Phebe, who is smitten by the young and lovely Ganymede, "if you do refuse to marry me, You'll give yourself to this most faithful shepherd." To which Phebe responds, "So is the bargain." Rosalind then asks Silvius, "You say that you'll have Phebe if she will," to which Silvius answers, "Though to have her and death were both one thing." The only condition now is that Phebe reject Ganymede. If she does, she has promised to take Silvius, and Silvius has promised to take Phebe if she will take him. Therefore, when Ganymede returns as Rosalind and Phebe cannot marry her the condition is met. Phebe affirms to Silvius, "I will not eat my word, now thou art mine, Thy faith my fancy to thee doth combine" (5.4.152–53).

By far the most interesting secret marriage in the play is that which is contracted on the stage. The marriage *per verba de præsenti* is precisely dramatized in 4.1. The genius of the sequence, however, is that Rosalind's disguise creates a brilliant *coup de théâtre* in its legalistic dramatic irony:

> ROSALIND (AS GANYMEDE). Come, sister, you shall be the priest and marry us.
> Give me your hand, Orlando: What do you say, sister?
> ORLANDO. Pray thee, marry us.
> CELIA (AS ALIENA). I cannot say the words.
> ROSALIND. You must begin, "Will you, Orlando . . . "
> CELIA. Go to. Will you, Orlando, have to wife this Rosalind?

ORLANDO. I will.
ROSALIND. Aye, but when?
ORLANDO. Why now, as fast as she can marry us.
ROSALIND. Then you must say, "I take thee, Rosalind, for wife."
ORLANDO. I take thee, Rosalind, for wife.
ROSALIND. I might ask you for your commission, But I do take thee, Orlando, for my husband. There's a girl goes before the priest, and certainly a woman's thought runs before her actions.

(4.1.118–35)

Rosalind, who directs the action of the play throughout—planning the disguises, buying the sheepcote, manipulating most of the other characters—here manages to have her unwitting lover marry her.

The action evolves organically. Rosalind, as Ganymede, has earlier instructed Orlando to think of her as Rosalind. Ostensibly "he" is to cure him of his love. Secretly Rosalind is testing the strength of his love. The courtship game proceeds to its logical end, to wit, the marriage game. With Celia, posing as Aliena, playing the priest and the forest as their cathedral, they begin the ceremony. In proper ceremonial form, Orlando responds, "I will," to the priest/Aliena/Celia's question. "I will," however, is the very problematic promise with which the courts were even then, in 1599, grappling. Was the phrase "I will," they asked, sufficient in a secret marriage to create either a present or future contract. "I will" sounded very much to the judges like a promise to do something in the future. However, "I will" could also be taken to mean "I *will* marry you now and *will* furthermore be a proper spouse to you from this point onward." "I will" is a sticky phrase from a purely legal perspective. Rosalind appears to understand the difficulty of "I will." Once Orlando makes his confession that he would marry Rosalind "now, as fast as she can marry us," Rosalind seizes her opportunity.

The form of words Rosalind instructs Orlando to say is precisely correct for the formation of a *sponsalia per verba de præsenti*. She has assured herself a witness to the promise in Celia. She toys with asking for his commission, or warrant, the license required to marry, and in so doing Shakespeare could be quibbling on the Ecclesiastical Commission whose job it was to enforce solemnization of such contracts.[14] But, abandoning the coy request for a commission, she responds with the appropriate words required to create a mutuality of consent *per verba de præsenti*.

Her next comment, "there's a girl goes before the priest," resonates on several levels. As Ganymede, she is flouting the impetuosity of females. As an actor in the marriage game, she is commenting upon having cut Celia/Aliena out of her part as priest. But as Rosalind, she refers to her having married her beloved before they could get themselves in front of the proper ecclesiastical authority.

The genius of the sequence, however, comes in the form of some fairly nice legalistic questions. The law states that two persons of proper age may marry if they are single, consenting, not impaired by Levitical sanctions, and if they cast their promises in proper form. The sequence under consideration asks whether this still holds true when one of the persons is disguised. Orlando wants to marry Rosalind, says he marries Rosalind, and says it to Rosalind, but he believes he is speaking to Ganymede. The question in law then is whether there is a mutuality of consent in this form of mistake. Rosalind knows who she is and who Orlando is. There is no problem seeing her words of present consent as binding—but only if there is mutuality. What of the man who speaks words of present consent to his intended without recognizing her?[15] Here, indeed, is proper fodder for a mooting.

The final scene depicts the dramatized solemnization of the various weddings. Hymen's blessing is most instructive in viewing Shakespeare's attitude toward the various marriage pacts:

> Here's eight that must take hands,
> To join in Hymen's bands
> If truth holds true contents.
> You and you no cross shall part;
> You and you are heart in heart:
> You to his love must accord,
> Or have a woman to your lord.
> You and you are sure together,
> As the Winter to foul weather.
>
> (5.4.130–38)

The imperative mood of the first line quoted suggests that these contracted parties have no choice now but to solemnize their contracts. The only certain identification as to whom Hymen is addressing is Phebe, who alone can be described as taking a woman for her lord. At lines 193–96 in this same sequence, Jaques refers to the four couples and does so in a particular order. That order is generally agreed to be first Rosalind and Orlando followed by Celia and Oliver with Phebe and Silvius next and Touchstone and Audrey last. I suggest that Hymen follows the same order in this sequence. The placement of Phebe/Silvius at the third position is compelling.

It is important to note, from the perspective of Rosalind's marriage *per verba de præsenti,* that the first benediction (You and you no cross shall part) presupposes a fait accompli, while the second and fourth benedictions are cast in the present tense as if being presently conferred. This would appear to be the moment when the *de futuro* contracts of both Celia/Oliver and Touchstone/Audrey are converted into present matrimony. Only the admonition aimed at Phebe ("You to his love must accord / Or have a woman to your lord") is placed in the conditional precisely as Phebe's *de futuro* contract was created as a condition to Phebe rejecting "Ganymede."

If we may cautiously assume that the first benediction is directed at Rosalind and Orlando, then it is possible that the *de præsenti* union of act four is here merely being ratified while the *de futuro* agreements of Oliver and Celia, Touchstone and Audrey are actually being translated into matrimony. There can be no question that Hymen's presence is meant to signal matrimony. The action is clearly described as a wedding several times.[16] But the presence of Hymen and reference to Juno indicate a pagan, pastoral ritual, and not the ecclesiastical solemnization of a Christian society.[17]

The vision of the play seems to focus upon the corruption of society. The play is filled with images of usurpation and a need to escape. The society led by Duke Frederick, filled as it is with human blood sport, fraternal betrayal, and avuncular banishment, has lost its ability to sanctify. Shakespeare balances this world against the natural world, which is characterized by images of marriage, pagan deities, and contentment. This natural world is itself an image of sanctification.

Not to overburden a light romantic pastoral, however, one must hasten to remember that the play is a romp, not a sermon. Taken within the more obvious context of the play, the secret marriages of *As You Like It* serve to move the romantic plot rapidly and humorously along. The only *de præsenti* marriage in the play is accomplished by yet another of Rosalind's clever tricks, underscoring the elemental nature of her character. In her trick, she manages to attain her heart's desire, albeit in such a clandestine manner as not to let even her husband in on the trick. In a play where characters' hearts are tripped up with wrestler's heels, where love springs up as quickly as one can sigh and ask the reason, a marriage formulation as simple as a philosophy that can find "good in every thing" succinctly demonstrates the natural innocence of the forest of Arden and of the lovers who haunt it.

Shakespeare's use of marriage *per verba de præsenti* in this play seems to indicate that it was an uncomplicated, natural pact. The law itself during the sixteenth and seventeenth centuries, however, was far from benign. An examination into the history of marriage law demonstrates the complications that Shakespeare chose to ignore in the forest of Arden, complications he would later employ to great dramatic advantage.

During the Renaissance, and for centuries before, marriage was considered a civil contract, much as it is still viewed today. The civil nature of the contract allows the Justice of the Peace as well as the cleric to perform the ceremony. The question of sacrament in marriage, those questions of "*holiness,*" according to Blackstone, were "left entirely to the ecclesiastical law."[18] Blackstone's commentary, written a century and a half later, is illuminating:

> [T]he parties must not only be willing, and able, to contract, but actually must contract themselves in due form of law, to make it a good civil marriage. Any contract made, *per verba de præsenti,* or in words of the present tense, ... was before the late act[19] deemed a valid marriage to many purposes; and the parties might be compelled in the spiritual courts to celebrate it *in facie ecclesiæ* ... it being said that pope Innocent the third[20] was the first who ordained the celebration of marriage in the church; before which it was totally a civil contract. And, in the times of the grand rebellion, all marriages were performed by the justices of the peace; and these marriages were declared valid, without fresh solemnization, by statute 12 Car.II. c.33.[21]

Because a valid contract is nothing more than a meeting of minds both willing and able to enter into a binding agreement, provided that the appropriate form is employed in so doing, early marriages could be extremely informal affairs. Despite Blackstone's suggestion to the contrary, the civil law touching the marriage contract was based, *de jure* if not *de facto,* upon the Church's definition of a valid marriage.[22]

During the twelfth century, the two seminal works on canon law, Gratian's *Concordia discordantium canonum,* also known as the *Decretum Gratiani,* and Peter Lombard's *Sententiarum libri,* book IV, diverged on the issue of how the marriage contract was formed. According to Gratian and the Bolognese school, a lawful marriage required only the consent of the parties; this was called the *desponsatio.* However, according to the *Decretum Gratiani,* "Sciendum est quod conjugium desponsatione initiatur, commixione perficitur."[23] That is, the marriage was not perfected (made indissoluble) until coitus consummated the union. A man, therefore, could enter into a consensual marriage and, before engaging in a sexual union, enter into a second consensual marriage, perfect it by the *commixitio sexuum,* and thereby have the second marriage held valid and the first rendered unenforceable.

The formulation espoused by Peter Lombard refined the Gratianic system by bifurcating the notion of *desponsatio.* One form of *desponsatio,* which actually served to meliorate the Gratianic formulation, was created by what Lombard termed *verba de futuro,* or words of future consent. The system presented by Lombard was not precisely like Gratian's *desponsatio.* Gratian deemed mutual consent the formative force of a marriage and the sexual consummation merely the perfection of an already existing union. The system set out in the *Sententiarum libri,* on the other hand, saw in the consent *per verba de futuro* merely the promise to form a marriage, often through coitus, at some later date. The result, however, was the same; the sexual union created an indissoluble marriage. The other form of *desponsatio* was the license created by words of present consent, called marriage *per verba de præsenti.* According to Helmholz,

> Drawing its inspiration, or at least its most important example, from the marriage between Joseph and the Virgin Mary, [the theory of marriage *per verba de præsenti*] held that the present consent alone created a perfect marriage and an indissoluble bond. Consent, not coitus, makes a marriage valid.[24]

Pope Alexander III favored Peter Lombard's formulation that words of present consent alone created the indissoluble marriage bond. So, while public ceremony, including the publication of banns and a clerical blessing, was required to *sanctify* the marriage, the private exchange of words agreeing to be married constituted all that was required to create a valid, enforceable marriage. This ruling favored the concept that there are only three necessary parties to a marriage: wife, husband, and God. Failure to seek sanctification of a marriage, though both reprehensible and open to ecclesiastical censure, did not invalidate the secret marriage made in the sight of God.[25]

Secret marriages appear to have been extremely popular in pre-Reformation England, owing most probably to their ease of creation. A surviving record from York exemplifies the simplicity of this type of marriage. A saddler named John Beke and his beloved, Marjory, married one another while sitting on a bench one day.[26] Their marriage was perfected by casting the verb "to accept or take"—*accipio*—in the present tense. At the conclusion of her brief speech on the sidebench, "at the third hour after the ninth and shortly after May Day," Marjory had become wife to John Beke, saddler. Eighty-nine secret marriages representing some seventy percent of the Ely case load were the subject of litigation heard in Ely between March 1374 and March 1382.[27] Helmholz notes that all but three of the forty-one marriages found in the Canterbury deposition book of 1411–20 were created *per verba de præsenti*.

Helmholz has noted marriages occurring in a wide variety of locations. The variety alone lends support to the simplicity of the act. Helmholz notes marriages occurring in locations as diverse as a Blacksmith's shop[28] and in a field;[29] on the King's Highway[30] and in a bed.[31] The sites range from a kitchen[32] to two in gardens.[33] Marriages are also noted in a grove,[34] under an oak tree,[35] in a storehouse,[36] under an ash tree,[37] in a tavern,[38] and near a hedge.[39] The practice was not limited to the pre-Reformation, however. Furnivall cites a number of instances where marriages *per verba de præsenti* were contracted in locations ranging from barns to highways during the reign of Elizabeth I.[40] And Houlbrooke, while demonstrating a decline in matrimonial contract litigation during the Tudor period, succeeds in proving a continued popularity of the informal marriage and its continued validity in court.[41]

The Gentleman Usher

The early ideal of secret marriage in Renaissance drama tended to depict such marriages as a natural, nearly-pagan-yet-Christian-sanctified celebration. It is no wonder, then, that Shakespeare chose to set his secret marriages in the forest of Arden. In fact, as has been seen, actual marriages *per verba de præsenti* were often if not usually conducted in sylvan, pristine settings. It is not then surprising to find the earlier playwrights setting their secret marriages in woodlands and glades.

Chapman, for example, in *The Gentleman Usher* presents another such forest-haunted marriage and a *sua sponte* marriage in reaction to a corrupt society. Two young lovers must hide their love because Vincentio's father, Duke Alphonso, wishes to marry Margaret himself. Margaret's lament regarding Alphonso's abuse of power,

> But is there no mean to dissolve that power
> And to prevent all further wrong to us
> Which it may work by forcing marriage rites
> Betwixt me and the duke?

is answered immediately by Vincentio:

> No mean but one,
> And that is closely to be married first.

Margaret's response to Vincentio's remedy reflects the attitude toward such private ceremonies throughout the drama of the period:

> May not we now
> Our contract make and marry before heaven?
> Are not the laws of God and Nature more
> Than formal laws of men? Are outward rites
> More virtuous than the very substance is
> Of holy nuptuals solemniz'd within?
> Or shall laws made to curb the common world,
> That would not be contain'd in form without them,
> Hurt them that are a law unto themselves?
> My princely love, 'tis not a priest shall let us,
> But since th'eternal acts of our pure souls
> Knit us with God, the soul of all the world,
> He shall be priest to us, and with such rites
> As we can here devise we will express
> And strongly ratify our hearts' true vows
> Which no external violence shall dissolve.[42]

The next thirty-eight lines dramatize the exchange of vows in a less artistic, more melodramatic fashion than Shakespeare employs in *As You Like It*. But the work is done nonetheless, and the sequence ends with Vincentio declaring, "It is enough, and binds as much as marriage."

Chapman's bawdy, broadly satiric tragicomedy sacrifices character complexity and a good plot for spectacle. Two full acts are devoted to plays within the play—masques and anti-masques. There is very little action or intrigue. The play is, therefore, adequately suited to the Children of the Chapel, who probably performed it around 1602 at Blackfriars. The secret marriage adequately underscores the main plot, which focuses upon inner strengths, especially strength derived from God as it is represented in Strozzo, pitted against the treachery of the powerful, represented by Mendice.

Little is made of Vincentio and Margaret's spousal. The plot could develop as it does if the lovers did no more than merely exchange love tokens with no actual *sponsalia* taking place. The image of the union, however, demonstrates the inner value of their love. This is especially true in view of Margaret's declaration that the laws of God and Nature are more powerful than the formal laws of men. As such, it helps underscore Margaret's self-mutilation in act five. Alphonso rejects the scarred Margaret, being able to see only the public face, while Vincentio, who sees her inner, God-granted beauty, reaffirms his love of her. This admittedly simplistic reading is influenced by the simplistic vision with which Chapman imbues his play.

Of particular interest to our study of the image of secret marriage is Chapman's identification of it as a mixture of God's law and Natural law in opposition to the formal laws of men. As discussed, the Christian world had no trouble viewing the act as a marriage of true minds before God's all-seeing majesty. But once again, as in *As You Like It,* the introduction of the pagan vision of marriage as a law of Nature arrests the attention. Margaret, like Rosalind before her, seems to view the proposed union as one blessed not only by a Judeo-Christian God but also by Nature herself. As becomes apparent time after time in the image of the secret marriage, the ceremony is far more than a private contract between two people evading a strict society. It is an acceptance of an alternate, benevolent, quasi-pagan yet somehow heavenly social order.

The ease of creation in a marriage *per verba de præsenti*, its simplicity in execution (especially as dramatized in the period), began to grow complex after the period of Chapman's play. Though theoretically, any single man and woman of age and mental capacity would, by simply saying "I take you for my spouse," become legally married. Problems grew out of such promises, of course, and the complications of secret marriage occupied the attention of the courts and began to intrude into the period drama.

In the first place, proving the contract existed was a problem. This is often the case in such parole (that is, oral) contracts. The courts were obliged to ask a number of sticky, ultimately insoluble questions: Did the parties agree to marry, and, if words to that effect were exchanged, were those words legally sufficient to create the contract of marriage? The problem was still plaguing jurists in the seventeenth century. Swinburne lamented that

> so very little (very often) is the odds betwixt the form of words of these two Contracts, that the best Learned are at great variance, whether such Words make Spousals *de futuro* or *de præsenti* . . . some words are so untoward, that it is a question whether they make any kind of Spousals at all; and contrariwise, some words so flexible that they may easily be stretched to make either the one or the other.[43]

In the second place, clandestine marriages came to be regarded, at least officially, as illegal and immoral. We find that, with the dawning of the Jacobean period, the pristine nature of secret marriage in drama grows dark. Playwrights continue to see such unions as sanctified and even beatified, but the contracts *per verba de præsenti* and *per verba de futuro* become the targets of petty, slanderous, and mean-spirited attack usually from some figure of authority. Questions of sexual relations, pregnancy, and incontinence intrude. And this intrusion ushers in a new, more deeply philosophical vision of secret marriage in the drama.

The sudden dramatic interest in carnality within such unions indicates a growing awareness of the realities behind the law. Under James, courts had begun to look into these very issues of sexual relations following promised marriage. Dramatists were quick to see the dramatic potential of copulation as the defining force in marriage. The church law initially accepted Peter Lombard's definition of marriage occurring when the words were said. But by the time of James greater emphasis began to be given Gratian. Coitus became an issue in marriage. Dramatists seized upon the concept that coitus, so often viewed in their society as loathsome carnality, now became the defining act of holy union. Their drama followed (and commented upon) this developing legal understanding.

The law governing secret wedlock began to enter the bridal chamber, so to speak, and courts began to peek under the marriage sheets. Where sexual relations could be proved to have followed a promise *per verba de præsenti* or *futuro* the issue of marriage became *res ipsa loquitur* (that is, the act of sex was seen to be confirmation of the foregoing marriage).[44] The irrebuttable presumption in cases of copulation following a promise was that a marriage had taken place, and the question of the character of the original promise, whether *de futuro* or *de præsenti,* was mooted.[45]

However, where conjugal intimacy was denied or unproved, decisions on cases often relied upon a swearing match with one party denying that words were exchanged (or that the proper words were exchanged) while the other swore they were.[46] The precise wording of promises, then, became pivotal to the outcome of many cases. Often evidence was given at these hearings from witnesses to the exchange, who could testify as to the character of the actual words spoken.[47] But it remains clear that uncelebrated marriage contracts such as these were frowned upon and that clandestine and private lay marriages were expected by both ecclesiastical and civil authorities to be solemnized in a church service.[48]

Indeed, evidence exists that even witnesses to such extra-ecclesiastical marriages (as in the case of Celia witnessing the marriage of Rosalind and Orlando) were themselves subject to ecclesiastical punishment.[49] It cannot be too greatly emphasized, however, that many—perhaps even most—of the cases concerning secret nuptials focused upon proof of marriage rather than ecclesiastical censure of the secret spousal even where ample proof of the Church's disapproval of such union is apparent.[50] The great peculiarity of consensual marriage, at least as it is usually described in the legal literature, is that it is both a valid and enforceable contract, a perfected union, while at the same time failing to be an entirely licit marriage. The *sub silentio* conclusion in law, therefore, is that a *de præsenti* or a *de futuro* union, without solemnization, is tantamount to a legally binding venial sin. This conclusion only gained force under James.

As mentioned earlier, the marriage between Kate and Petruchio is not a secret marriage. The instance of Friar Lawrence marrying Romeo and Juliet quietly in his cell is a more apt example of a clandestine marriage carried out by a cleric, a type of marriage that is attested in documentary evidence from Shakespeare's time.[51] There are also examples to be found in Furnivall of Elizabethan private lay marriages in which a couple is joined in a home or a field using all of the appropriate solemnities but without a priest to speak the words. These marriages are distinct from mere Petruchio/Kate–type betrothals that occurred in the home, which are more in the manner of our modern understanding of an engagement. And it is with this understanding that we begin to discern the difficulties inherent in an examination of Renaissance secret marriage law. The dramatists of the period, we will see, employed a real genius in manipulating the law to their dramatic needs. To understand these manipulations, however, we must first understand the labyrinthine concerns surrounding Renaissance marriage law.

The fine lines separating Kate/Petruchio engagement-style betrothals from marriages *per verba de futuro* are not at all distinct. The obvious case of betrothal is in agreeing to marry on a certain date and asking that the banns be read in church. This is a simple engagement. The first step into obscurity is in agreeing to marry each other but failing to set the date or ask the banns; this is an agreement of future consent, or *de futuro*. It may not be broken but by mutual consent or some significant intervening cause such as adultery or a subsequent marriage *per verba de præsenti,* either privately or publicly contracted.[52]

The next step into obscurity concerns the couple who agree that marriage would be most agreeable wherein one believes that the context of the comment means that the other intends to marry at a future date, but this is not the understanding of that other party. If, in any of these three foregoing cases, the couple engages in coitus, the church condemns them for their incontinence but regards them as married. The state, taking its cue from the church, regards them as married by the act though their marital property rights, dower, and children's status would remain an open question. The state and church can therefore force the couple into church to solemnize the pact. The public solemnity would act for the church as proper sanctification and for the state as proper notice.

In the next case of obscurity, a couple discovers themselves in a secluded setting and, giving way to the romantic or hormonal impulse (or in an attempt to circumvent parental disapproval), vow there in the quiet of their matrimonial bower that they do, there and then, take the other as spouse. This is a marriage of present consent, or *per verba de præsenti*. In the eyes of both church and state—and most importantly in the eyes of God—the couple is married. They may not afterward decide not to be married. They may not marry someone else.[53] If this couple engages in coitus, the church again is affronted by their lack of ceremonial sanctification, and, because the state has an interest in recording such marriages, the couple may again be forced into church or before a Justice of the Peace to solemnize the pact. Legal problems arise when one of the two later decides not to be married or a parent intervenes to have one of the two marry someone else. That is when the couple goes to court to prove or disprove that the union occurred under the proper form of promise.

There is one further fly in the ointment of such contracts. An ardent lover may contract marriage by saying, "I take you here and now as spouse and will solemnize our marriage in church Sunday next." This is a marriage *per verba de præsenti* combined with a *futurarum Nuptiarum*. It has all of the effect of a *de præsenti* marriage and includes a proper affirmation, from the vantage of civil and ecclesiastical authority, of the need for solemnization *de futuro*.[54] If coitus follows the promise, whether *de futuro* or *de præsenti,* there is no question of fornication.[55] The word or even intimation of it is not to be found in any of the court records I have viewed except in a case where one of the contracting parties engaged in fornication with a third party. Carnal copulation after contracting is in the civil world a question of recordation—a perfection of the contract[56]—and in the ecclesiastic court of reprehensible incontinence, but not fornication.[57]

Despite arguments to the contrary, evidence is not wanting that secret marriages transcended the lower classes. Edward IV married Elizabeth on a May morning in 1464 by slipping away from Stony Stratford and secretly journeying to Grafton Regis. There he was married, perhaps at a forest retreat known as the Hermitage, a short walk from Grafton manor house, and returned later in the day as if from a hunting expedition. He was married with only his bride, a priest, the bride's mother, two gentlewomen, and a singer in attendance.[58] The marriages of Ralegh, Essex, the Earl of Leicester, Lady Rich (Sidney's "Stella") and Charles Blount, and Lady Arbella Stuart provide support for secret marriages in the highest court circles. Lady Catherine Grey's secret marriage of 1563, which produced two children, struck too closely to Elizabeth's throne. The Privy Council annulled it for lack of recordation when the witnesses and priest (doubtlessly suborned by the ruler) failed to bear witness to the marriage.

John Donne secretly married Anne More. Within Shakespeare's life, one need not stretch too far to see the possibility of some sort of *sponsalia* passing between the poet and Anne Hathaway before the recorded solemnization, which would explain the otherwise suspiciously early birth of their first child.[59] Additionally, evidence has been provided that Shakespeare's aunt, Agnes Arden, was married *per verba de præsenti* on or before 17 July 1550, even though the church solemnization did not occur until three months later on 15 October 1550.[60] Thomas Russell, who would later oversee Shakespeare's will, engaged in a *de præsenti* union with a widow—one Anne Digges. This took place in 1600. Russell and Digges cohabited as man and wife for three years while settling the widow's annuity. Under the terms of the annuity, her rights would be forfeit if Digges remarried. The widow struck a deal with her son from the previous marriage to release his inheritance early if in return he would reimburse her for the lost annuity. Once the finances were worked out, Russell and Digges solemnized their union in 1603. The union thus recorded, the annuity—which had operated during the three years of informal cohabitation—ceased.[61] Shakespeare certainly knew of such contracts and their effect as marriage. He also appreciated the swiftness and informality of such spousals, for he has Biondello quip in *The Taming of the Shrew*, "I knew a wench married in an afternoon as she went to the garden for parsley to stuff a rabbit" (4.4.99–101).[62]

It is not at all surprising that dramatists of the period would turn to secret marriage for their material. As has been seen, the latter Elizabethan dramatic view of secret marriage tended to favor a sylvan, bucolic setting. As the Jacobean period dawned and the church became increasingly paranoid, a social stigma began to attach to the secrecy behind such marriages. The stigma was reinforced in the courts and, as we shall see, protested from the stage.

In examining the court records from the period in question, one is immediately struck by the increase in marriage litigation.[63] Because of the heightened suspicion of recusancy in the period covering 1582–1602, the courts, and significantly the Ecclesiastical Commission, began to pry into marriages of a questionable nature. According to Carlson,

> [T]he surviving records from 1582–1602 stand out from their predecessors... [I]n the period from 1599 until the death of Elizabeth cases concerning clandestine or other irregular marriages became a standard feature of each meeting of the commission. Until that time, the commissioners had punished the clergy who participated in such ceremonies but had not bothered with the principals... Throughout 1602, the act books of the commission were filled with folio after folio of long lists of couples presented for secret marriages.[64]

The 1599 date is important, for, beyond being the date cited by Carlson as the most significant period of debate over secret marriages, it is also the year that produced *As You Like It,* the first play of the period to use secret marriage as a significant and recurring metaphor.

After 1603, plays depicting secret marriage take on a hard edge. The general tenor of innocence in secret marriages found in pre-1604 plays is darkened considerably. In 1604, when the English Church enacted the *canons,* and the ecclesiastical laws were codified, a great deal of debate ensued over construction of the laws. As the new statutes were to be applied to the laity as well as the clergy, questions arose whether the new laws would take precedence to parliamentary statutes and what, if any, role the *ius commune* would play.[65] With the Church asserting its right to enforce its existing laws—including marriage laws—more strictly, it is not surprising to find a number of plays rebelling against institutional control over what many believed to be a private contract.

MEASURE FOR MEASURE

The most celebrated, certainly the most hotly contested, example of secret marriages arising in Renaissance dramatic literature involves the unsolemnized unions found in Shakespeare's *Measure for Measure* (*circa* 1604). To be sure, the moral vision of the play is anything but clear; furthermore, the legal status of secret marriage yielded many peculiar, contradictory, and often pedantic decisions based upon exceedingly nice linguistic distinctions. So, when the conundra of the play are combined with the riddles inherent in the law, it is little wonder that commentators betray their frustration in articles more strident than analytic.

One writer created an entire argument premised upon the remarkable foundation that

> By excising from their context certain . . . comments made by Swinburne in *A Treatise of Spousals* and by relating them to Angelo's contract together with a little rearrangement of the so called internal evidence it should not be very difficult to interpret Angelo's contract as *de præsenti* and Claudio's as *de futuro*.[66]

Every lawyer and journalist knows that manipulation of fact can yield almost any conclusion, but such manipulation is neither probative nor particularly helpful. Birje-Patil's hostility toward a legal analysis of the play is betrayed early in his article when he scoffs at what he calls attempts to convey "the impression that *Measure for Measure* is simply a dramatized version of certain social conflicts stemming from the contemporary debate about 'spousals.'"[67] He suggests that such an examination treats dramatic expressions "as if they were petrified pieces of legal deadwood."[68]

Margaret Scott's article reflects the same tendency to reject a legal reading of the play when she suggests that such approaches are merely vain attempts "prompted, I suspect, by the beguiling prospect of exactitude."[69] She is of course ignoring the myriad subtleties of the law, which, like literature, constantly resist exactitude. Her naïve approach to the inherent legal complexities in *Measure for Measure* leads her to state further, "It seems that questions [regarding the marriage contracts] can be readily decided by reference to . . . the *Encyclopædia Britannica*." She dismisses the whole issue as one concerning "story-book law . . . the like of which has never been enacted in England"[70] and from the discussion of which "nothing of great value has emerged."[71] Scott's argument continues by suggesting that Lord Bacon would have been the only legally minded audience member at the play capable of understanding marriage law.

Scott then engages in a *volte face* nearly two-thirds through her rebuttal of the legal approach when she says, "[I]t is difficult to escape the conclusion that Shakespeare ... remind[s] us that English Protestant law [is] inevitably shaping our responses."[72] Notwithstanding Scott's early hostility toward a legal examination of *Measure for Measure,* she seems to call for just such an examination in the latter portion of her discussion. Margaret Loftus Ranald presents the far saner, more scholarly approach when she concludes,

> If we are to understand Shakespeare's plays fully, we must recover as much as possible of his views of marriage. To do that, we must endeavor to recover the Elizabethan and Jacobean milieu that helped shape his thought and dramaturgy, even if the search leads into the labyrinthine passages of canon and civil law.[73]

And, in his excellent treatment of marriage contracts in *Measure for Measure,* Wentersdorf goes so far as to say,

> To recognize that there were widely differing viewpoints on matters of morality and that Shakespeare's work was intended to mirror the ambiguities of his time may not immediately clear up the confusion regarding the action in *Measure for Measure.* It may, however, save us from the temptation to give up on the problem.[74]

To view the marriage contracts of *Measure for Measure* in their proper light, one must first look to Shakespeare's source materials. In Whetstone's *Promos and Cassandra,* the Claudio character, named Andrugio, has a sexual liaison with a young woman, and both are sentenced to punishment. In Cinthio's *Epitia* the same character, here named Vico, rapes a virgin and is sentenced. Neither Andrugio nor Vico is married to the woman with whom he couples. Promos and Juriste, the Angelo characters of their respective works, promise to free the brother character (Andrugio or Vico) if the sister character (named Cassandra in Whetstone's work and Epitia in Cinthio's) will allow herself to be seduced just as Angelo importunes Isabella. In both cases the sister is promised marriage in return for the act.

In both stories, the Angelo character forswears the promised marriage, sends out a sentence of execution for the brother, and is ultimately forced by a higher authority—the emperor or the king—to marry the wronged sister. There is no Mariana character pining for an Angelo. The Vincentio character, an emperor or a king, is merely a *deus ex machina* for the happy resolution of difficulties. The question of marriage comes up only as a method of averting the sister's shame and is therefore of secondary or no importance in the sources.

Two early conclusions present themselves at this level of inquiry. First, in order to introduce a popular disguised-Duke plot to his new play, Shakespeare had to redefine the sovereign's role. In choosing to unite the sister character with the sovereign, Shakespeare had to shift the balanced marriages from the union of Promos/Juriste and Cassandra/Epitia. The idea of Isabella marrying Angelo is repugnant. Shakespeare needed to create a new character for the malefactor to marry, hence Mariana in her moated grange. Second, although Andrugio and Vico were of little interest to the earlier writers, Shakespeare is obviously attempting to exculpate Claudio in order to make his crime less clear than Andrugio's simple fornication or Vico's heinous rape. Isabella, in pleading for her brother, must appear to be pleading for one worthy of mercy in order to make her, in turn, clearly worthy to be Vincentio's bride.[75]

The problem of creating a character in Mariana with a claim on Angelo as strong as that of Cassandra on Promos or Epitia on Juriste—one that would succeed in marrying off the rapacious ruler and creating a comic ending while remaining relatively true to the source material—was solved with Shakespeare's invention of a *sponsalia* between Angelo and Mariana and combining it with the bed trick. The promise created a binding contract which, when perfected through the sexual liaison, created a marriage. Thus, where Promos and Juriste promise marriage to the sister then forswear themselves after copulation, Angelo promised marriage to Mariana, whom he beds by mistake, creating the same conclusion based upon the same premise by way of a more clever piece of dramaturgy. This secret marriage is then balanced against the other secret marriage in the play, that of Claudio and Juliet, which serves to mitigate Claudio's guilt in the eyes of the audience if not in the eyes of Claudio, Juliet, or Isabella. This much is at least tenable from a purely dramaturgical point of view, but it does little to answer the nagging questions concerning the nature of the contracts and the ultimate meaning behind the use of secret marriages in the structure of *Measure for Measure*.

Because of the complexity of the marriage contracts and their individual relationships to the structure and characters of the play, it is prudent to begin with an individual analysis of each and then move on to a discussion of how they interrelate in the play. The first contract, between Claudio and Juliet, is introduced in 1.2. In explaining the reasons for his arrest to Lucio, Claudio says:

> Thus it stands with me: upon a true contract
> I got possession of Julietta's bed:
> You know the lady; she is fast my wife,
> Save that we do the denunciation lack
> Of outward order: this we came not to,
> Only for propagation of a dower
> Remaining in the coffer of her friends,
> From whom we thought it meet to hide our love
> Till time had made them for us. But it chances
> The stealth of our most mutual entertainment
> With character too gross is writ on Juliet.
> *LUCIO.* With child, perhaps?
> *CLAUDIO.* Unhappily, even so.
> And the new deputy now for the duke—
> Whether it be the fault and glimpse of newness,
> Or whether that the body public be
> A horse whereon the governor doth ride,
> Who, newly in the seat, that it may know
> He can command, lets it straight feel the spur;
> Whether the tyranny be in his place,
> Or in his eminence that fills it up,
> I stagger in:—but this new governor
> Awakes me all the enrolled penalties
> Which have, like unscour'd armour, hung by the wall
> So long that nineteen zodiacs have gone round
> And none of them been worn; and, for a name,
> Now puts the drowsy and neglected act
> Freshly on me: 'tis surely for a name.

Wentersdorf wonders if a "question might be raised as to whether Claudio is speaking the truth when he alleges the existence of a matrimonial contract" (140). He uses the negative evidence of Juliet's not referring to a pre-contract as confirmation that such a contract does not exist. Although much of Wentersdorf's discussion of clandestine contracts is sober and persuasive, this particular reading is strained.

Three initial points from this dialogue are worthy of notice, though one must be careful not to fall into the trap of making too much of them as they stand alone. First, Claudio is adamant that his marriage is lawful, created "upon a true contract." Second, Claudio has no doubt that Juliet is—and Claudio uses the present tense—his wife even though the marriage still has not been solemnized. Third, Claudio believes that Angelo behaves tyrannically when he imposes a sentence of death upon him for the act of impregnating his wife. Claudio is unequivocal on each of these points, and the lines that Shakespeare places in his mouth at this early moment in the play seem to underscore the playwright's intention of making this marriage a *de facto* union in the audience's mind.

A fourth point, one that has never been treated as far as I am able to discern, is of utmost importance in this interchange. The very fact that the marriage is secret lies at the heart of the play's vision. Too many commentators have ignored or glossed over the importance of the secrecy itself as the driving motivation in the play's action. Yet, Claudio's lines clearly demonstrate that secrecy was the point Shakespeare attempted to fix in his audience's mind during this interchange. Claudio and Juliet, for the dowry held by Juliet's friends, chose to keep the marriage secret. It is certainly the first Claudio's friend, Lucio, has heard about it, and Lucio is the play's gossipmonger. The secrecy is so important to Shakespeare that he finds it necessary to invent both a shipwreck and a drowned brother in order to give the lost dowry verisimilitude and through it the need for the secret union. If the marriage was, indeed, a perfect secret—and Claudio's description of their mutual entertainment having been maintained in "stealth" is suggestive—then we have a greater ability to understand why the act is being treated as fornication. The state has not been put on notice that these two people are married and legally entitled to enjoy sexual relations.[76] Despite arguments to the contrary,[77] contemporary attitudes[78] and extant case law[79] indicate that consummating a secret marriage was not only tolerated, at least in society and the common law courts, but relatively common.[80] The couple's secrecy, therefore, gives us insight into the state's condemnation and possibly even into Isabella's repudiation of Claudio's act.[81] Their secret marriage is never mentioned again onstage, rendering its character virtually impossible to identify, save that it is secret. That secrecy is the motive force behind the varied reactions to Juliet's pregnancy. In contrast to the legal or ecclesiastical attitude toward unsolemnized marriage, the clandestine nature of the marriage—the question of secrecy itself—is of utmost importance to understanding the opening of the play. The only answer to be given in regard to this contract, therefore, whether *de præsenti* or *de futuro,* is that such distinction is unrecoverable from the evidence as presented, but the sexual act has converted either promise into present matrimony.

Despite some extremely ingenious arguments given in favor of a *de præsenti* contract[82] and some fairly unpersuasive approaches favoring a *de futuro* interpretation,[83] a "true contract" is a proper description of both. The further information that the contract gave Claudio "possession of Julietta's bed" could mean either that the *de præsenti* nature of the contract gave him the right of consummation or that the *de futuro* nature of the contract was thereby translated into matrimony. In either case Juliet would properly be identified as "fast [Claudio's] wife." The denunciation they lack of outward order is also ambiguous because either type of secret union would want the public solemnization to which Claudio refers.

The guilt Claudio feels in this scene, like that represented in Juliet's confession scene at 2.3 (and the fact that no one in the play claims that either is guiltless—factors that have caused many commentators needless trouble), is their personal recognition of the ecclesiastical shame of incontinence, not of a secular, criminal guiltiness.[84] This private shame is combined with the publicly perceived guilt of fornication that their secrecy has created in the eye of man and society.[85] Indeed, Claudio feels at the same time both that he is wrong and that Angelo is tyrannous. The distinct possibility exists that the interpretive problem with Claudio's feelings of guilt springs from a misreading of 1.2. Claudio's feelings of personal guilt, which so many analysts have fixed upon, are confined to one brief speech in which he says he is restrained because of

> too much liberty, my Lucio, liberty:
> As surfeit is the father of much fast,
> So every scope by the immoderate use

> Turns to restraint. Our natures do pursue,
> Like rats that ravin down their proper bane,
> A thirsty evil; and when we drink we die.

Wentersdorf says of this passage that "[u]nless these lines are spoken ironically, a possible but unlikely interpretation, Claudio seems here to regard his offence as an evil" (139). While Wentersdorf's reading of the play is cogent and sound, it founds itself upon a reading of Claudio as both a liar and a coward. Frightened he certainly is and possibly a liar, and an actor's performance choice could bear out Wentersdorf's interpretation. Literature is, of course, open to varied interpretations as valid as Wentersdorf's. Reading Claudio as an honest man, however, and worthy of his sister's plea for clemency reveals new texture to the character of both Claudio and the contract at issue. Far from "unlikely" then, Claudio's "rats that ravin down their proper bane" speech may indeed be ironic if not sardonic.

Except for this one statement, Claudio's lines in 1.2 center upon Angelo's mistreatment of him. Claudio is quite angry with Angelo and makes many references to him as "the demigod authority," "the fault and glimpse of newness," tyranny which is either "in his place, Or in his eminence that fills it up," and "the strict deputy." In his comment that "still, 'tis just," we are left to wonder what Claudio means by "just." Several commentators have seen Claudio's remark as an acknowledgement of his guilt.[86] But we must look to the vision of the play. Justice is not a wholly positive concept in the body of Shakespeare's work. Mercy must season justice. In the world of *Measure for Measure*, justice is tantamount to blameworthy strictness.[87] Claudio's explanation of the marriage contract tends to indicate that that contract is an exculpating factor in Claudio's mind, placed as it is between his comment on the justice of his censure and his plea to have Isabella speak in his defense.

Claudio's diatribe upon "too much liberty" would appear then to be a condemnation of Viennese society more than a personal acceptance of sin. The subject of the speech is, after all, cast in the first person plural. Claudio does not refer to his personal license but to "every scope." The statement, read in this light, is Claudio's angry denunciation of a libertine society that has created the need for enforcement of old morality codes so strict that even those who merely appear to transgress, such as he, are caught in the general censure. Claudio's next comment serves to underscore his resistance to the idea that he has transgressed. When Lucio guesses that he has been restrained for "Lechery," Claudio does not respond in the affirmative, but he rather says, "Call it so." Claudio, apparently, is unwilling to call it so himself.

The second marriage contract, that between Angelo and Mariana, is both a clearer and a more obscure case. The contract is clearer in that more is said about it during the course of the play. It is more obscure because we cannot tell from the context which references to the contract are to be taken at face value, which are lies told by Angelo to extract himself from an awkward situation, which are Vincentio's modifications of the law to expedite an equitable conclusion, and which are Mariana and Isabella's misinterpretations of the contract based upon the Duke's representations. The relevant passages concerning the second contract are found at 3.1.221–32, 234–39 (Duke as friar to Isabella):

> [Mariana] should this Angelo have married; was affianced to her by oath, and the nuptial appointed; between which time of the contract and limit of the solemnity, her brother Frederick was wrecked at sea, having in that perished vessel the dowry of his sister. But mark you how heavily this befell to the poor gentlewoman. There she lost a noble and renowned brother, in his love toward her ever most kind and natural; with him, the portion and sinew of her fortune, her marriage-dowry; with both, her combinate husband, this well-seeming Angelo . . . Left her in tears, and dried not one of them with his comfort; swallowed his vows whole, pretending in her discoveries of dishonor; in few, bestowed her on her own lamentation, which she yet wears for his sake; and he, a marble to her tears, is washed with them, but relents not.

And at 4.1.72 (Duke as friar to Mariana):

> [Angelo] is your husband on a pre-contract:

And at 4.2.165–68 (Duke as friar to Provost):

> Claudio, whom here you have warrant to execute, is in no greater forfeit to the law than Angelo who hath sentenced him.

And at 5.1. 201–13, 216–30:

> DUKE. You say your husband?
> MARIANA. Why, just, my lord, and that is Angelo,
> Who thinks he knows that he ne'er knew my body,
> But knows he thinks that he knows Isabel's.
> ANGELO. This is a strange abuse. Let's see thy face.
> MARIANA. My husband bids me; now I will unmask.
> This is that face, thou cruel Angelo,
> Which once thou swor'st was worth the looking on;
> This is the hand which, with a vow'd contract,
> Was fast belock'd in thine; this is the body
> That took away the match from Isabel,
> And did supply thee at thy garden-house
> In her imagin'd person.
> . . . .
>
> ANGELO. My lord, I must confess I know this woman;
> And five years since there was some speech of marriage
> Betwixt myself and her; which was broke off,
> Partly for that her promised proportions
> Came short of composition, but in chief
> For that her reputation was disvalued
> In levity: since which time of five years
> I never spake with her, saw her, nor heard from her,
> Upon my faith and honor.
> MARIANA. Noble Prince,
> As there comes light from heaven and words from breath,
> As there is sense in truth and truth in virtue,
> I am affianced this man's wife as strongly
> As words could make up vows; and, my good lord,
> But Tuesday night last gone in's garden-house
> He knew me as a wife.

And at 5.1.379–82:

> DUKE. Come hither, Mariana.
> Say, wast thou e'er contracted to this woman?
> ANGELO. I was, my lord.
> DUKE. Go take her hence, and marry her instantly.
> Do you the office, friar.

And at 5.1.423–30 (Duke to Mariana):

> It is your husband mock'd you with a husband.
> Consenting to the safeguard of your honour,
> I thought your marriage fit; else imputation,
> For that he knew you, might reproach your life

And choke your good to come. For his possessions,
Although by confiscation they are ours,
We do instate and widow you withal,
To buy a better husband.

The knotty problems arising from the foregoing evidence will probably never be entirely solved from a purely legal point of view. There is every reason to believe Shakespeare included just enough law in the discussion of this contract to satisfy the requirement of the plot; but an examination of the legal evidence presented does, indeed, point in only one distinct direction for the plot to follow.

The analysts who have commented that the type of contract is irrecoverable,[88] irrelevant,[89] or *de præsenti*[90] are wrong. Only Schanzer has looked in the right direction. The evidence that Angelo was "affianced to her by oath," that they were affianced by a "vow'd contract," and that Mariana was "affianced this man's wife as strongly / As words could make up vows" points directly to a spousal confirmed by oath. Swinburne's §XVI treats this type of contract, called *jurata sponsalia,* at length. Because a *de præsenti* marriage is a *de facto* union, and confirmation of it by oath did not take place, the contract in question is a *de futuro* spousal. Swinburne is most clear on this distinction in law.[91]

Acceptance of this contract as *jurata sponsalia* opens up an intriguing debate over several interesting questions in law raised in the play. These questions follow Swinburne's examination nearly point-by-point. First, such a contract may not be broken unilaterally (¶5), as Angelo has attempted to do. Shakespeare makes the unilateral nature of the breach patent through the now-famous image of Mariana in the moated grange. Attempting to dissolve such a contract takes the Lord's name in vain (¶3). However, such a contract may be dissolved unilaterally by the innocent party if the other party commits adultery (¶5), as Angelo falsely accuses Mariana. Hence, Angelo is contracted to Mariana.

Contrariwise, several incidents militate in favor of Angelo's position. If, for instance, the dowry lost at sea had been a condition of the contract—which is never clearly stated; Angelo refers only to "her promised proportions" (5.1.219), which is open to interpretation—then the breaking of that condition would invalidate the precontract.[92] Further, there is a reference that the date of solemnization had been set.[93] When that day passed without solemnization, the *de futuro* contract was in breach and became a nullity.[94] Therefore, if Mariana were dishonest or if the dowry had been a condition of the contract, Angelo was free to allow the contract to lapse without guilt. But, because both seem to be trumped-up charges,[95] Angelo is at fault for allowing the prescribed day for solemnization to pass; although Mariana, as the innocent party, is free to marry elsewhere, Angelo is punishable *propter læsionem fidei*.[96] The issue, however, is far from clear as Mariana's five-year wait may have caused her suit to have grown stale.[97] It is, however, at least tenable that Angelo is still obliged to marry Mariana. He breached the contract dishonestly. She has remained true to her obligation when it lies in her, as innocent party, to dissolve the agreement to marry if she so desires.

Positing, then, that a contract may still exist between Angelo and Mariana, albeit a contract grown stale and riddled with allegations of misconduct sufficient to nullify it, one of Isabella's lines comes into a clearer focus. In 3.1 the Duke-as-Friar places the bed-trick in the context of a triple benefit. He argues that it will save Claudio, retain Isabella's chastity, and, finally, advantage Mariana by compelling Angelo "to her recompense." At least on one level the sense of Isabella's response, "I trust it will grow to a most prosperous perfection," is a precise, legalistic expression involving the execution of the contract.[98]

Although it seems from the foregoing discussion that there is at least some ability to discover the type of marriage contracts found in *Measure for Measure,* such is not the case. All that can be said definitively about the character of the contracts is that the contract that exists between Claudio and Juliet is a perfect, or "true," contract and the contract between Angelo and Mariana, while almost certainly a *jurata sponsalia,* may or may not still be enforceable, though it may in equity be perfectible. Claudio and Juliet view the first contract as creating a valid marriage. There is evidence in 5.1 that the duke also comes to accept the irregular marriage as valid and binding. The second contract is viewed by everyone involved as valid, at least in equity, with the significant exception of Angelo, who has done his best to dissolve the contract with allegations of "levity" and failure of dower. The question most commentators focus upon is what type of contracts are involved. Though there is no question, and should be no question, that secret marriage contracts do exist, the question that has been avoided in previous discussions is what these contracts tell us about the play's vision.

Measure for Measure features a world grown lax. Morality has given way to license and the world has turned upside-down. In an attempt to restore moral order, a secular ruler disguises himself as a cleric. A religious zealot is left to enforce the secular laws. A young novice is asked to plead for her brother on a temporal offense and does so by calling for Christian mercy (2.2.72–79). It is therefore not surprising that a number of articles have divided upon the question of whether to treat the play from a biblical or humanistic perspective. The play seems to invite both approaches simultaneously. As such, the law of secret marriage, which is viewed differently depending upon whether it is being treated in an ecclesiastical or temporal context, seems a perfect image and plot device for this play.

No matter what source one examines, the same conclusion emerges: two forms of marriage (a common law/humanistic marriage and a canon law/sacred marriage) are created in the single act of matrimony. Although the Ecclesiastical Commission vigorously asserted the church's plenary authority over marriage in the time of James, the ancient understanding of marriage as a private contract arising from the *ius commune* remained strong in the popular imagination. Vincentio is leader of both views in the play. Just as canon law was subordinated to common law under the post-Reformation English monarch so too is Vienna's religious code subordinated to Vincentio's sovereign need to enforce morality. In *Measure for Measure,* Vincentio, the secular ruler in religious garb, argues for the humanistic approach. Although he appears to be a holy man, taking confession and admonishing Juliet for her "sin," he is also the secular judge of men, championing, in the guise of friar, the common law, *de facto* marriages of Claudio and Juliet, Angelo and Mariana. Mariana embraces this common-law view of marriage. Isabella initially reviles but later accepts it.

The religious man in the garb of the secular ruler, as first portrayed by Angelo, is portrayed as harsh, fanatical, even hypocritical in disguising his own human desires. Later, the religious man as secular ruler, now portrayed by the undisguised Vincentio (emerging from his clerical habit), punishes the wicked, represented by Lucio, redeems the fallen and wronged, Angelo and Mariana, Claudio and Juliet, and purposes marriage to the balanced, mature religious life, represented by Isabella.[99] The balance of the secular and religious aspects of the play may also be represented in the religious solemnization of the Angelo–Mariana marriage contract. In each case the vision seems to be of a merciful, secular enforcement of the state's overly harsh religious moral code.

The secret marriage contracts, therefore, though their exact nature is only partially recoverable from the text, are ideally viewed as images of an enforceable temporal marriage pact. Viewed from a secular point of view, the bed-trick is not blameworthy. The precontract does, indeed, "extenuate the forehand sin" to a degree that allows the secular ruler in religious garb to say truthfully, "To bring you thus together, 'tis no sin, / Sith that the justice of your title to him / Doth flourish the deceit" (4.1.73–75). Viewed from this perspective, the bed-trick does not make the duke/friar a well-meaning bawd.[100] There is, in fact, a wealth of surviving evidence to indicate that the law had cognizance of couples who entered lightly into *de futuro* marriage contracts, forgot their promises, later lay together, and were thereby created husband and wife.[101] The strong presumption in law favored matrimony where carnal copulation was involved, despite a great number of foreseeable protestations.[102] The central issue of the bed-trick, then, revolves around the mystery of matrimony.[103] The Renaissance concept of the creation of husband and wife through an act that might otherwise be viewed as damnable fornication—a miracle that founds itself in the mystery of a temporal legal formulation which creates a spiritual unity with God—is found very plainly expressed in Swinburne's §V.3. He states in regard to contracting unperfected, *de futuro* spousals:

> [I]t is a greater matter to contract matrimony than spousals, for by lawful marriage the knot is made for ever indissoluble; but [*de futuro*] spousals are many ways subject to overthrow and dissolution. Marriage was ordained by God in *Paradise,* spousals long after by man: by marriage the man and woman are made one flesh, so are they not by only spousals. To be short, marriage is that great mystery representing that spiritual marriage betwixt Christ and his Church; but spousals are utterly destitute of this mystical effect.[104]

Angelo is ordered to solemnize his marriage with Mariana in 5.1, but the solemnization is more to keep Mariana from slanderous imputation and give her marital rights in Angelo's property than it is to give an ecclesiastical blessing to the union.[105] Lucio is dragged away to prison until his marriage to Kate Keepdown, the punk who bore his child, is solemnized. This marriage smacks of ecclesiastical censure, which often took the form of excommunication, apprehension, and imprisonment for persons secretly married who refused to solemnize their vows. Lucio, of course, has never suggested a precontract with Kate Keepdown although he has admitted to having forsworn the child before the duke to avoid being ordered to marry her (4.3.179–84). Vincentio takes Isabella away at the end of the play obviously intending to propose marriage. Only Claudio and Juliet, the couple who began the chain of events with their contract, are not specifically ordered to solemnize their nuptial. At 5.1.531 Vincentio skirts the issue of solemnization by saying simply, "She, Claudio, that you wrong'd, look you restore."

The quibble on the word "restore" creates an interesting question regarding solemnization. To see this verb as an injunction to solemnize the marriage requires the scholar to use the rare definition found in the O.E.D., "(7) to compensate or recompense for an injury," which cites examples from 1330 and 1461. The more obvious reading of the verb may be taken from the other readings found in the O.E.D., which suggest placing her in her former position, indicating that no future ceremony is required since she is already his wife on a true contract. This reading is further supported by the legal rendering of the word restore, *restitutio in integrum,* which requires "annulling a change in the legal condition produced by an omission [i.e. solemnization], and restoring the parties to their previous situation or legal relations."[106] The possibility exists that Vincentio's pronouncement serves as a public, civil ratification of the *de præsenti* contract and no further solemnization is required.

Measure for Measure is, among many other approaches, a play about appearances. The play deals with Vincentio's apparent absence, Angelo's apparent virtue, Isabella's apparent cloistering, Claudio and Juliet's apparent sin, Mariana's apparent hopelessness, Claudio's apparent death, the statutory law's apparent justice. In such a play, the image of the secret marriage fits in quite well. It allows Claudio and Juliet to appear guilty without actually being so (or at least not completely so). It allows Angelo to appear guiltless to a world that asks him more than once to search his conscience for a sin like Claudio's in himself, and it then allows him to appear guiltless to himself. To him, Claudio and Juliet appear to be fornicators. In fact, Claudio and Juliet are less guilty than Angelo, who is in almost precisely the same circumstance as Claudio. Claudio hid his marriage for a dowry; Angelo canceled his for one. Claudio lay with his wife lovingly; Angelo lay with his wife lustfully. Claudio has remained true to his private marriage vow, appears to have wronged Juliet, and is condemned to die; Angelo has forsworn a private marriage vow, ruined Mariana's reputation in doing so, yet to Vienna appears as the model of "ample grace and honour." To Vincentio, Angelo's fault is greater than Claudio's. He tells the Provost as much when he says, "Claudio, whom here you have warrant to execute, is in no greater forfeit to the law than Angelo who hath sentenced him." Angelo, in fact, is in greater forfeit of the law. He intended a damnable fornication upon Isabella. He is saved only by a precontract and a switch of bedfellows that transforms apparent— and intended—fornication into *de facto* matrimony. The marriage contracts work this resolution.

THE MISERIES OF ENFORCED MARRIAGE

Instead of bringing about a tragicomic resolution, as in *Measure for Measure,* the marriage contract *per verba de præsenti* engenders tragic calamity in George Wilkins's *The Miseries of Enforced Marriage* (1606). The play is a melodramatic mixture of a Shakespearean-styled Green World in Yorkshire, where the *de præsenti* marriage occurs, and a Middletonian London, full of parasitic, cozening gallants and clever servants. The play tends to make the most of the worst excesses of both genres. Nevertheless, *Miseries* presents a socioreligious vision of secret marriage that is both forceful and specific.

The play opens with the waggish gallants, Ilford, Wentloe, and Bartley, meeting Scarborrow in the Yorkshire home of Sir John Harcop. Ilford jokes that Scarborrow is there at Harcop's request in order to be married to "some pittifull peece of his Workmanship, a Daughter I meane" (lines 67–68).[107] Scarborrow's rejoinder, "I haue bin guest here since last night" (line 74), is significant in demonstrating how rapidly secret marriages could take place. Ilford's quip, "Why, and that is time enough to make vp a dozen marriages, as marriages are made vp now adayes" (lines 75–76), underscores the point. The play hinges upon the difference between marriage for love and marriage for social position. Ilford's humorous estimation of fathers using their daughters to capture rich sons-in-law is, in Ilford's view, entirely dependent upon being able to force the young prospect into a *de præsenti* marriage:

> Where the young puppet [the daughter], hauing the Lesson before from the old Fox, giue the sonne halfe a dozen warme kisses, which after her fathers oths, takes such Impression in thee, thou straight [c]alst by Iesu Mistris, I loue you: —When shee has the wit to aske, but sir, will you marry me, and thou in thy Cox-sparrow humor replyest, I (before God) as I am a Gentleman wil I, which the Father ouer-hearing, leaps in, takes you at your word, . . . he will haue you contracted straight, and for a need makes the priest of himself. (lines 105–13)

Scarborrow responds that he is no such cynic and compares maids to angels and wives to sovereigns. His monetary quibble on angels and sovereigns is clearly intended to turn Ilford's misogynistic cynicism against itself by arguing the true value as opposed to monetary value of women. Scarborrow makes clear his belief that marriage must be founded upon love rather than gain.

When Scarborrow is left alone with Clare Harcop, the shy courtier draws on a stratagem reminiscent of Ganymede's first encounter with Orlando. He asks Clare, "What ist a Clockc [*sic*]?" to open their conversation. When she responds that she has no watch and so cannot tell, Shakespeare's play is further echoed when Scarborrow teases Clare, "You are not to keepe sheepe." In their love prate, it becomes apparent that Clare is drawn from the impudent-woman mold favored by Jacobean audiences and is therefore to be viewed with favor by the audience. Their talk of marriage begins less than thirty lines after they have begun to speak:

> SCARBORROW. Your father sayes I shall marry you.
> CLARE. And I say God forbid, Sir: I am a great deale to young.
> SCARBORROW. I loue thee by my troth.
> . . . . .
>   thou art my Clare,
> Accept my hart, and prooue as Chast, as fayre.
> CLARE. O God, you are too hot in your gifts, shoulde I accept them, we should haue you plead nonage, some halfe a year hence: sue for reuersement, & say the deed was done vnder age.

SCARBORROW. Prethee do not Iest?
CLARE. No (God is my record) I speak in earnest: & desire to know Whether ye meane to marry me, yea or no.
SCARBORROW. This hand thus takes thee as my louing wife.
CLARE. For better, for worse.
SCARBORROW. I, till death vs depart loue.
CLARE. Why then I thanke you Sir, and now I am like to haue that I long lookt for: A Husband. How soone from our owne tongues is the word sed, Captiues our maiden-freedome to a head.
SCARBORROW. Clare your [sic] are now mine.

(lines 227–49)

Scarborrow then lists what he believes and expects a wife to be and concludes by saying, "If such a wife you can prepare to be, *Clare* I am yours: and you are fit for me" (lines 265–66). Clare responds by listing what she believes and expects a husband to be and concludes by saying,

> Those betwixt whom a faith and troth is giuen,
> Death onely parts, since they are knit by heauen:
> If such a husband you intend to be,
> I am your Clare, and you are fit for me.

(lines 279–82)

Clare admonishes Scarborrow that "Men neuer giue their faith, and promise marriage, But heauen records their oth" (lines 285–56).[108] They are thereby married. When Harcop returns to them, Scarborrow informs him, "Your daughters made my wife, and I your sonne" (line 294). Harcop knows that such a marriage requires a mutuality of promise and so asks, "And both agreed so," to which they both answer, "We are Sir" (lines 295–96). There is no chance to consummate the marriage. There is no talk of solemnizing their vows until scene four. Immediately after this interchange, the Butler enters from London to inform Scarborrow that his guardian, Lord Falconbridge, has called for him to attend him.

In London, Falconbridge forces Scarborrow to marry Katherine, his niece. Despite Scarborrow's initial argument that he is too young and later admission, "I haue no hands to take her to my wife," Falconbridge threatens Scarborrow with destitution and the wasting of his ancestral estate if he does not marry the niece. Scarborrow is forced to choose between his free marriage for love and the enforced marriage for wealth. Scarborrow's argument in this sequence is repeated time and again throughout the play, that "I haue done so much, that if I wed not [Clare] / My marriage makes me an Adulterer / In which blacke sheets, I wallow all my life / My babes being Bastards, and a whore my wife" (lines 429–32).[109] Scarborrow sums up the motive force in the play when he says:

> O but good vnckle could I command my loue,
> Or cancell oaths out of heauens brazen booke,
> Ingrost by Gods own finger, then you might speake.
> . . . .
> were oaths but puffes,
> Men might forsweare themselues, but I do know,
> Tho sinne being past with vs, the acts forgot,
> The poore soule grones, and she forgets it not.
> . . . .
> O tis to miserable:
> That I a Gentleman should be thus torne
> From mine owne right, and forct to be forsworne.
> (lines 458–71)

Scarborrow, Clare, and the audience view the *de præsenti* marriage as a binding tie.

There is ample evidence that the secret union could be easily dissolved. Wilkins has made clear the fact that the couple has not consummated. Of course, consummation is not required to create a legally binding contract when words of the present tense are exchanged. Nevertheless, the lack of physical union is important insofar as it informs the audience that Clare is still a worthy bride, *virgo intacta,* for a future suitor. It also removes the possible argument that Scarborrow might have been trifling with a young virgin, using the promise as a seduction ploy.

Second, as the marriage was entirely private, passing between the principals without a witness, they could easily argue that the words, or that the proper words, were never said. In fact, if one examines the sequence in question, the actual form of the words employed between Clare and Scarborrow is open to attack on the grounds that they never actually say "I take you as my spouse." They premise their vows upon conditions—*if* such a wife you prepare to be, *if* such a husband you intend to be, I am yours. Scarborrow only begins his vow, "By heauen," before Clare admonishes him not to take his vow lightly. Harcop then intrudes upon the scene before Scarborrow has formulated an actual, present tense vow and before Clare has promised anything of marriage. Nevertheless, the couple believes they have so spoken and inform Harcop that they have mutually agreed. Their actual words, however, are imperfect.[110]

Third, we learn that Scarborrow may legally plead nonage in order to avoid the contract. At line 326 we learn he is seventeen. We learn at line 780 that Clare is sixteen. This is an instance where reference to Swinburne is unhelpful. Swinburne's §VII.1 treats questions of nonage as applying to children of fourteen, twenty-two, eighteen, twenty, or twenty-five, depending upon the authority consulted. Swinburne opts, at §VII.2, for *Impuberes,* or that age when the individual has the corporal ability to perform the act of generation. Wilkins's text probably refers to the fact that Scarborrow is underage because he is still, and for three years to come will be, under the guardianship of Falconbridge. Falconbridge has plenary power over him until he reaches the age of twenty-one, when Scarborrow may plead for his livery.[111] Scarborrow may, therefore, as Clare suggests, plead nonage. In law, Scarborrow does not have the right to marry without his guardian's consent. If he does so marry, he forfeits his estate to his guardian's pleasure. There is no question, however, that Scarborrow and Clare believe that the higher authority of heaven views them as indissolubly married despite the temporal register's failure to record it or the technicalities of wardship.[112]

In a creditable stroke of invention, Wilkins, who scrupulously (albeit imprecisely) depicted the private union with Clare, leaves the public marriage with Katherine to be reported by the parasites, Wentloe and Bartley. The obvious intention is to focus upon the private love match and subordinate the public enforced match. The public marriage is set in the negative light of informing parasites of a new victim. It is less a celebratory halloo than it is a rancorous hue and cry after newly created wealth. The negative features of the reported public marriage are amplified when Scarborrow must tell Clare of this marriage in a guilty, impersonal letter. The letter arrives in Yorkshire while the Harcops are entertaining Scarborrow's younger brothers, Thomas, who has come from the Inns of Court, and John. Harcop's references to the marriage between Scarborrow and Clare help to illuminate the peculiarity of *de præsenti* unions.

Although the passages cited are apparently intended to make no mistake that the marriage is complete, and Scarborrow from that point refers to Clare as his wife, Harcop uses the future tense in scene four when discussing the wedding. Harcop refers to Scarborrow as the man who "ere long shall be my sonne, By wedding this young girle" (lines 661–62). Harcop is almost certainly referring to the solemnization, for he says a few lines later that, when Scarborrow returns, he and Clare will be "at noone ith Church, at night betweene the sheets" (line 709). Nevertheless, Scarborrow has already identified himself as Harcop's son. A tension is thereby created between what constitutes the marriage in the characters' minds, the personal vow or the public solemnization. By depicting the private marriage and only reporting the public ceremony, Wilkins succeeds in leaving the distinct impression that Clare is Scarborrow's wife in fact and Katherine is Scarborrow's wife in law. Once this uneasy dichotomy is established, he is able to explore the surrealistic tensions that drive the plot.

These tensions can cause a great deal of trouble for the scholar not familiar with the socio-religious aspects of Renaissance marriage law; aspects which, as has been suggested, blurred the line between theology and legality.[113] Clare's reaction to the letter reporting Scarborrow's marriage to Katherine is contorted by a variety of social and personal responses. After a confused, injured, and wholly human reaction to the betrayal, she realizes the social stigma attached to being so forsworn. Vincentio saw fit to solemnize the marriage between Angelo and Mariana to avoid Mariana's shame in *Measure for Measure,* Clare begins to see the vision of this type of shame befalling her:

> He was contracted mine, yet he vniust
> Hath married to another: whats my estate then?
> A wretched maid, not fit for any man,
> For being vnited his with plighted faiths,
> Who euer sues to me commits a sinne,
> Besiedgeth me, and who shal marry me:
> Is like my selfe, liues in Adultery, (O God).
>
> (lines 812–18)

Clare's choice, therefore, is not a happy one. Even in the eyes of legal scholars, Clare's choice is between a vow of single life and an adulterous marriage. Swinburne's opinion of this situation is illuminating:

> A Man and a Woman are first secretly, yet truly and before God contracted, either of them mutually giving their full and perfect Consent thereunto; Afterwards the Man is publickly contracted to another Woman; The former Woman practiseth all good means as well by Suit as otherwise, to recover him for Husband, but prevaileth not for want of sufficient proof; In this Case whether may she with safe Conscience Marry another Husband? It seemeth that she may, for having endeavoured to the utmost of her power, nor able to continue any longer; It were not only against Law, but against Reason and Equity, that she should be bound to an *impossibility;* and therefore of two Evils (whereof the one is inevitable) the less is to be chosen, that is to say, it is better for her to marry than to burn in the Fire of Lust and Concupiscence.
>
> (§XIV.13)

She foresees that her father will force her to marry elsewhere (lines 834–36), but cannot bring herself to accept adultery.

Ultimately, however, Clare's decision is phrased in terms of benefiting Scarborrow rather than avoiding personal shame. Her choice to commit suicide, she reasons, will free Scarborrow of his continued sin of adultery:

> whilst I liue
> He doth but steale those pleasures he enioyes,
> Is an Adulterer in his married armes,
> And neuer goes to his defiled bed,
> But God writes sin vpon the Teasters hed.
> Ile be a Wife now, helpe to saue his soule
> Tho I haue lost his body, giue a slake
> To his iniquities, and with one sinne
> Done by this hand, ende many done by him.
>
> (lines 859–67)

She is, in fact, correct. Swinburne presents the other side of the argument quoted above by asserting that a spouse so contracted will never truly be free to remarry until the first spouse is dead (§XIV.14).

The argument could certainly be made that Wilkins is criticizing secret marriage, which is responsible for the subsequent ills of the play. It taints an otherwise prosperous, subsequent match; it brings about Clare's suicide and Scarborrow's self-destructive lifestyle. Wilkins's title, however, and depiction of Falconbridge's final repentance point directly at the blameworthy, enforced church marriage to Katherine. Indeed, the near-tragic ending depicts Scarborrow preparing to murder his "bastard" children, "whore" wife, and the Oxford Divine, Doctor Baxter, who united them. Although news of Falconbridge's death and his acceptance of all blame prevents a final catastrophe, the Divine is given a stern reprimand for his conduct in solemnizing the adulterous union. One expects at this point an impassioned argument, á la *Romeo and Juliet,* that the quiet sanctity of marriage is best left to private protestations of love passed between lovers and the ears of God. The many references in the play to the records of marriage kept by heaven certainly seem to point toward that conclusion. But such is not the case.

Perhaps the weakest point of this weak play is to be found in the ultimate conclusions concerning marriage. Although the play seems to present a dichotomy between the loving secret marriage and the mercenary public union, and favors the former, the conclusion abandons that vision. Scarborrow could be persuaded that the long-suffering Katherine has earned his love. However, the peripeteia comes instead with the news that Falconbridge—in a poor figuring of the sacrificial lamb motif—has taken the sin on himself in his death and given everyone ample monetary recompense for the troubles he has caused. The denouement, therefore, seems to accept the cynical view expressed by Ilford that one should marry for money and find love after.

The Atheist's Tragedy

In his treatment of *The Atheist's Tragedy* (1607–1611), Robert Ornstein reflects the received opinion of Tourneur's work when he comments upon its "wooden characters and its heavy-handed moralism."[114] Of the stilted characterizations that plague the work, D'Amville alone seems the only persona to capture much scholarly attention. This myopic vision of the play—along with the ever-surfacing fantasy that it is a companion piece to Middleton's *Revenger's Tragedy*—is largely responsible for removing focus from the actual movement in the play. Scholars such as Ornstein have satisfied themselves with the assertion of the play's "painfully obvious and labored moralism" and resisted knocking out their own brains trying to analyze the work.

Although the play is rather seriously flawed, and although the flaws are to be found in the insistent didactic tone of the play, one must not be too quick to dismiss it as mere polemic. Tourneur has presented us with a sincere attempt to dramatize a view of morality in the popular mode of the theatre of his period. Witness the murder of Montferrers, coshed on the moors at night after a fight between torchbearers has thrown him into blackness; the arras scene wherein the duplicitous Levidulcia is caught by her husband with not one but two paramours in her chambers; or the final catastrophe of D'Amville, beating out his own brains with a headsman's axe at the moment of his supreme triumph. If these and the other sequences are overwrought, at least they are not entirely moralistic. As obvious as their moral vision may be, they are also demonstrably spectacular and dramatic.

The Atheist's Tragedy further gives us our only clear figuring of a *de futuro* spousal in Renaissance drama. As Castabella prepares to say her farewells to Charlemont, she kisses him and desires "that we should breathe but one contracted life" (1.2.91). Toward that end Charlemont has arranged for Languebeau Snuff to act as "witness to the contract of our vows, / Which my return by marriage shall confirm." Charlemont's dichotomy here between "contract" and "marriage" indicates that he intends them to promise to marry at a future date. Further, Snuff's opening remark to the pair indicates that he, too, believes that they intend now merely to promise to marry when Charlemont returns from the wars. Says Snuff:

> I salute you in the spirit of copulation. I am already informed of your matrimonial purposes and will be a testimony to the integrity of your promises.
> (1.2.99–104)

The construction of the sequence indicates the actual *de futuro* vows occurred offstage before the sequence began. We are, however, given every reason to suspect that Charlemont and Castabella believe they have contracted to marry upon Charlemont's return.

Tourneur's selection of a *de futuro* union is in perfect keeping with his moral vision. Castabella, being only promised in marriage, does not sin in the eyes of heaven by her subsequent, forced marriage to Rousard.[115] So unlike Wilkins's Scarborrow from *Miseries,* or Middleton's Isabella from *The Witch,* who each live adulterously with forced mates, Castabella has merely, albeit unwittingly, dissolved her *de futuro* contract with Charlemont by marrying Rousard. Rousard, being the wrong match, however, in the eyes of Tourneur if not of heaven, falls mysteriously ill in his courting scene, 1.3. His illness grows upon him in the 2.1 wedding scene, and in 2.3 he is significantly too sick to consummate the union. Sebastian, though himself a libertine, is not so lascivious that he could not earlier see the wedding of his brother to Castabella as "but a rape to force a wench to marry, since it forces her to lie with him she would not" (1.4.129–31). Rousard himself comes to recognize that,

> A gen'ral weakness did surprise my health
> The very day I married Castabella,
> As if my sickness were a punishment
> That did arrest me for some injury
> I then committed.
>
> (3.4.64–68)

And, as should probably come as an incident worthy of notice to Renaissance scholars, Rousard has the distinction of being one of the extremely few characters in Renaissance tragedy (excluding histories) to die a natural death during the course of his play.

The *de futuro* marriage of Charlemont and Castabella allows Tourneur to play with his dichotomies of good and evil: Charlemont/Castabella against D'Amville. From his opening lines, D'Amville associates man with beast while Charlemont, bound for the wars, sees man as ennobled and valorous. Charlemont it is who represents virtue in his vows before heaven to marry Castabella. D'Amville's youngest son, Sebastian, sums up his father's state when he verifies the proverb, "The nearer the church the further from God" (1.4.140–41). Because the *de futuro* contract of marriage is conducted away from a church, it must be (given the proverb) nearer to the God D'Amville denies. To D'Amville, Nature is represented in the natural order, the bestial world, and the Machiavellian world of temporal laws. His son's wedding to Castabella is, after all, in a church we are probably intended to view as paradoxically worldly and far from God. The last act, where D'Amville is raised to the pinnacle of his worldly hopes, takes place in a court of secular law. Conversely, the lovers obviously view Nature as the natural, moral law that flows from heaven that can recognize lovers vowing secret marriage to one another.

In essence, therefore, the *de futuro* contract allows us to see the lovers pledge their intentions before heaven while inhabiting a

Godless society. The contract, though binding, does not rise to the level of matrimony that a *de præsenti* union would, and its dissolution at the moment Castabella marries Rousard allows the same emotional effect of the forced marriages in the *de præsenti* plays without a taint of sin besmirching the virgin. The divine vengeance directed at Rousard is probably meant as both a scourge to the atheistic father, whose whole hopes have rested in his sons, and retribution against Rousard for unwittingly tampering with the holy vows made before heaven. This interpretation should probably account for a retribution against Languebeau Snuff, who witnesses the contract and does nothing to enforce it later, but Tourneur seems content with boxing the bawd puritan's ears and sending him back to his tallow shop. And, in the final analysis, owing to the special nature of the *de futuro* contract and heaven's punishment of Rousard for violating the sacred vows, Castabella is allowed to remain both virginal and sinless, thus presenting the perfect match for the valorous and sinless Charlemont. Charlemont obviously, and correctly, fails to view himself as married to Castabella by virtue of their earlier vows. In his next-to-final line in the play he vows:

> I will tempt
> My stars no longer, nor protract my time
> Of marriage. When those nuptial rites are done
> I will perform my kinsmen's funerals.

Thus, in a bizarre Dante-esque visioning of a tragicomedy, Tourneur manages to end his play with both a wedding and a funeral.

The Duchess of Malfi

Perhaps the most troubling *de præsenti* play, however, is Webster's *The Duchess of Malfi* (1612–1614). As much as *Measure for Measure*, Webster's play has enjoyed a wealth of critical attention focused upon its image of marriage. Like *Measure for Measure*, much of the commentary is premised upon a misconception of the law as it applies to the culture, which causes mistaken assumptions concerning the vision of the play.[116] But, in contrast to *Measure for Measure*, *The Duchess of Malfi* allows one to see into the cultural attitudes concerning private unions as those attitudes found their way onto the seventeenth-century stage.

As should come as no surprise, *The Duchess of Malfi* explores the tensions between the public and the private world. Unlike the world of *As You Like It,* however, there is no physical escape into an Edenic Arden. Rather, there is only the private person and the public persona. Further, the public world is allegorically bifurcated between the Duchess's brothers. Ferdinand, the Duchess's twin, represents public, worldly order. The Cardinal obviously figures the institution of the Church.

Accepting that the brothers represent two forms of the public world, we are better able to view the vision of the *de præsenti* marriage in the play. The public world, secular and religious, conspires to dissuade the Duchess from remarriage. Their argument denounces privacy:

> FERDINAND. Your darkest actions: nay, your privat'st thoughts,
> Will come to light.
> CARDINAL. You may flatter yourself,
> And take your own choice: privately be married
> Under the eaves of night—
> FERDINAND. . . . Such weddings may more properly be said
> To be executed, than celebrated.
> CARDINAL. The marriage night
> Is the entrance into some prison.
> (1.2.235–38, 241–43)

The brothers thus expound the institutional views of the law, civil and canon. The temporal vision is concerned with recordation—"celebration" announces, "execution" merely creates. The moral vision is concerned with concupiscence, as when a properly formed marriage fails to occur before coitus—the proper formation of which may be assured only through ecclesiastic cognizance. The brothers' ulterior motivations, of course, are to control the Duchess, but they do so in exactly the manner that the canon lawyers strove to control the individual, through arguments of law.

Immediately after this interchange, only 20 lines after the brothers depart, the Duchess calls Antonio into her chamber and there woos and weds him. The verbal exchange from line 280 to the end of the scene presents a marriage *per verba de præsenti*. The Duchess describes it as such at line 392. The implicit *mise en scéne* and context, however, are worth exploring.

The wooing begins with the Duchess in control, literally and figuratively dictating her will to Antonio. She does so in terms of doing good deeds (lines 301–3). Antonio's is concerned with children (lines 317–22). There is a strong sense of tenderness as a ring is exchanged (lines 322–32) and Antonio kneels before his sovereign only to rise again before his wife. Antonio is throughout concerned that his actions might be mistaken for ambition; the Duchess fears being thought lecherous. She disdains "vain ceremony" and claims him with a widow's half blush, calling him her "gentle love" and drawing a circle of security around their private love, saying "All discord, without this circumference, / Is only to be pitied, and not fear'd" (1.2.384–5). He, in turn, vows to be the "constant sanctuary" of her good name. The private exchange completed, the Duchess calls forth Cariola, the secret witness to the secret vows, and exclaims against the public institution she subverts, "What can the Church force more? . . . How can the Church build faster? / We now are man and wife, and 'tis the Church / That must but echo this" (1.2.401, 404–6). And she is correct. Proper words said by legally capable persons, the exchange of a ring, hand-fasting, and a witness have created a marriage before heaven. But more importantly the context of sweetness, the genuine fear they express of being thought lustful or greedy, and the appropriate concern for the other's well-being indicate that this scene is to be accepted with sympathy, even sentiment.

The old view of this sequence was that the Duchess had gone too far and here loses her audience's sympathy.[117] The evolving view is that the Duchess is most sympathetic here.[118] The discomfort expressed by even the modern, sympathetic commentators, comes in attempting to make sense of the ominous note struck at the end of the scene by Cariola:

> Whether the spirit of greatness, or of woman
> Reign most in her, I know not, but it shows
> A fearful madness: I owe her much of pity.
>
> (1.2.417–19)

James Calderwood cites Cariola's ominous expostulation as a commentary upon the Duchess's "dangerously naive" disrespect for external realities.[119] In viewing the Duchess as a libidinous woman, unable to control her personal desires for Antonio, Calderwood fails to take into account the moral disorder of the public, social world of *The Duchess of Malfi*—a disorder that requires privacy for morality.

John Selzer's excellent work on Webster's vision,[120] wherein he demonstrates most convincingly the Duchess's desire to establish a meritocracy and abjure aristocratic mores, treats Cariola's coda as self-revelatory. Says Selzer,

> Cariola hardly qualifies as a moral commentator; for example, her death vividly shows her weakness and establishes her as a contrast to the Duchess' boldness. Her comment is best seen as another indication of her weakness. The comment also reinforces the *importance* of what the Duchess has done, but it establishes no moral fault.[121]

To take nothing away from Selzer's reading, which correctly appreciates the Duchess's secret marriage as a sacred union that is to be approved, there is yet another approach.

If the Duchess and Cariola's death scene teach us anything, it teaches us that the Duchess is a figure of patient sanity in an insane world. Her admission, "I'll tell thee a miracle, / I am not mad yet, to my cause of sorrow" (4.2.24–25), and endurance of the song and dance of the madmen demonstrate her moral superiority. Her mind fixed on the unyielding sacred constants, she is able to withstand her persecution and die in a prayerful attitude with "Mercy" on her lips. In so doing, the Duchess converts Bosola. The Duchess, however, is not a sinner who finds virtue through suffering, but she is rather a piece of virtue who endures this world's horrors through strength derived from integrity and merit. Her marriage, therefore, before God and heaven rather than the corrupted temporal institutions of Church and State, would be regarded as a moral, heavenly match.

Cariola's comment at the end of the wedding scene, therefore, is ironically correct. Such a marriage is, indeed, madness in the world of Malfi. In a world where corruption in the State and Church is absolute, Cariola is a perfect commentator—not a moral commentator, perhaps, but a reliable observer of her world—for she clearly sees the degradation around her Duchess. And she is correct that one who seeks morality and privacy in an immoral and public world is, in that world, mad. It is a form of lawlessness to be virtuous in a culture of vice. The *de præsenti* marriage in *The Duchess of Malfi* becomes for the Duchess and Antonio what the Forest of Arden symbolizes to Rosalind and Orlando. It is their escape into a pristine world, their escape from the horrors of society. Their guiltless, godly marriage is made guilty only by Malfi's depraved society. The depravity is embodied in her brothers, who seek to control their sister's spirit as they seek to control her body, power and mind. In the end they succeed only in taking her life. She remains, even in death, "the Duchess of Malfi still."

THE WITCH

Middleton's "ignorantly-ill-fated" play, *The Witch* (*circa* 1613), presents a number of troubling points regarding our examination of the image of informal marriage in Renaissance drama. First, not nearly enough attention has been leveled at this sprightly play with the problematic though characteristic Middletonian conclusion. The scholarly commentary that does exist typically examines the many fascinating coincidences between Middleton's work and *Macbeth*. The structure of the play, however, has much to recommend it beyond its Shakespearean connections. Most troubling, however, is the image of the marriage between Sebastian and Isabella, which is at one and the same time the central motivating element of the plot and entirely unnecessary to it. Despite the speculative nature of the import of the marriage in *The Witch,* according to Anne Lancashire, "it seems high time that closer attention be paid, along these or similar interpretive lines, to *The Witch.*"[122]

The play begins with Sebastian's marital dilemma. He contracted a *de præsenti* union with Isabella before going off to war,[123] but upon his return he finds Antonio has married Isabella. He disguises himself as one Celio, a servant, and employs the spells of Hecate to keep his wife chaste and free from the adulterous embraces of Antonio. Isabella believes Antonio to be her legitimate husband because Antonio has lied that he saw Sebastian killed in action. Therefore, although Sebastian's wedded condition is central to the main conflict, there would appear to be no reason for Middleton to have chosen to characterize Sebastian and Isabella's marriage as secret. Had they been married in a church, the banns read, and all Ravenna there to witness, Antonio could still return from the wars, lie about Sebastian's death in battle, and marry the unsuspecting Isabella adulterously. The plot could still unfold exactly as it does.

Even the usually secret nature of the *de præsenti* marriage is not here at issue. Antonio, Fernando, Gaspar, and the Governor are all aware of Sebastian's claim upon Isabella. Nevertheless, Middleton appears to believe that the secret character of their marriage has an elemental part to play in the plot. Despite Lancashire's suggestion that Sebastian is not Isabella's husband,[124] the fourth line of the play introduces the *de præsenti* marriage directly. Sebastian says, "She is my wife by contract before heaven / And all the angels, sir." And again at 2.2.222–25:

> SEBASTIAN. Still, she's not mine, that can be no man's else
> Till I be nothing, if religion
> Have the same strength for me as 't has for others:
> Holy vows, witness that our souls were married!

And most vehemently at 4.2.8–20:

> SEBASTIAN. We're registered
> Husband and wife in heaven; though there wants that
> Which often keeps licentious men in awe
> From starting from their wedlocks, the knot public,
> 'Tis in our souls knit fast; and how more precious
> The soul is than the body, so much judge
> The sacred and celestial tie within us
> More than the outward form, which calls but witness
> Here upon earth to what is done in heaven:
> Though I must needs confess the least is honourable;
> As an ambassador sent from a king
> Has honour by th' employment, yet there's greater
> Dwells in the king that sent him; so in this.

But the clandestine nature of Sebastian's marriage, though manifest, is ostensibly unnecessary to the plot. If, therefore, the secret nature of the secret marriage is not at issue, as, for example, it is in *Measure for Measure* or *The Miseries of Enforced Marriage;* and if, furthermore, the same plot could have been explored had the central marriage been originally conducted *in facie ecclesiæ,* one is irresistibly drawn to the conclusion that Middleton is relying upon the image of the *de præsenti* marriage for the positive psychological effect he calculated it would have upon his audience. Here, as in *The Duchess of Malfi,* we are asked to sympathize with a main character that has contracted a private union. But what is most significant is that we are now asked to sympathize with a main character *because* he has contracted a private union.

In Sampson's *The Vow Breaker, or The Fair Maid of Clifton* (1625), the secret union is again central. Again, it is held up to a higher authority even than a celebrated church wedding. Ann Boote's broken *de præsenti* contract with Bateman is punished despite an interceding, fully solemnized public marriage—a mercenary marriage, to be sure, but one following the correct forms. Bateman's ghost ultimately drags her into hell for her perjured love. Unlike Wilkins's *Miseries,* the death of the guiltless partner does not render the vow breaker innocent, and the image of Faustian punishment only underscores again the cultural bias in favor of secret unions conducted before God. Many other plays of the period also employed the secret marriage in a comparatively minor but nevertheless revealing manner. Barton has discerned probable secret unions of various types in *The Taming of the Shrew* (1594, Lucentio and Bianca), *A Midsummer Night's Dream* (1596, Demetrius and Helena), *The Merry Wives of Windsor* (1600, Fenton and Anne Page), and *The Winter's Tale* (1603, Florizel and Perdita), and suggests that the lost play, *Cardenio,* must have turned upon the point of a secret marriage. She finds likely *de futuro* unions in *Love's Labour's Lost* (1595) and *The Historie of Clyomon and Clamydes* of 1570.[125] Other plays that may be readily included in this list are *Tancred and Gismund* (original version written in 1566), Dekker's *The Shoemaker's Holiday* (1599), Middleton's *A Mad World, My Masters* (1606), Beaumont and Fletcher's *A King and No King* (1611), Middleton's *A Chaste Main in Cheapside* (1613), May's *The Heir* (1620), Dekker, Rowley, and Ford's *The Witch of Edmonton* (1621), Dekker's *A Contract Broken Justly Revenged* (1626), Hemming's *The Fatal Contract* (1639), among others. Notwithstanding the reduced importance of the secret marriage in many of these plays, these and many other plays of the period include to some degree a need to understand the functioning of clandestine marriage law in order to understand fully some sequence, image, or theme. We find that these plays tend toward using the image as a convenient dramatic device. Following are examples of the importance of the image in such drama.

A Fair Quarrel

For example, in Middleton and Rowley's *A Fair Quarrel* (*circa* 1615) Fitzallen, kinsman to the Colonel, is identified in the *dramatis personæ* as "secretly married to Jane."[126] The secrecy of Fitzallen and Jane's marriage is central to the action and resolution of the subplot but is used primarily as a plot device. It is important to notice only that the marriage exists in fact, is not known by the principal parties courting Jane, and that the secrecy of Jane's marriage creates difficulty when Jane becomes pregnant. There is little attention paid to the sanctity of the marriage. The usual talk of "marriages written in God's own book" is given little attention. In sum, the clandestine nature of the marriage is useful to *A Fair Quarrel* primarily as a dramatic complication.

The play moves from Russell's soliloquy against Fitzallen as son-in-law to the titular quarrel between the Colonel and Ager. The next plot point in the play (1.1.188 et seq.) concerns the secret marriage. The Colonel suggests that Jane and Fitzallen marry *per verba de præsenti:* "here's witness / Enough if you confirm it now." But Jane confesses the secret marriage has already occurred: "Sir, my voice / Was long since given, since that I gave my hand." The Colonel, looking to be made kinsman to Ager through this marriage and thereby patch up their recent quarrel, says, "Would you had sealed too!" indicating a wish that the marriage be celebrated *in facie ecclesiæ*. Jane informs the Colonel of her father Russell's reticence and asks him to act as intermediary for the young lovers, "To join the hands of two divided friends, / Even these two that would offer willingly / Their own embrace." Both the Colonel and Ager agree to help the lovers win Jane's father. Russell knows a better trick than that, however, and bribes two sergeants to arrest Fitzallen on a trumped-up charge of debt. The arrest sets the Colonel and Ager upon a fresh quarrel that precipitates the remainder of the play's primary action.

There is no doubt that the two lovers are married. Fitzallen is so described in the *dramatis personae*. As Fitzallen is being taken to jail he tells Jane, "To be still thine is all my part to be, / Whether in freedom or captivity" (1.1.372–73). Jane, referring to her lawful pregnancy, tells Fitzallen that "Thou hast too firmly stamped me for thine own / Ever to be rased out: I am not current / In any others hand" (380–82). Russell, however, has other plans for her. In "One Master Chough, a Cornish gentleman" Russell has found "a lad of thousands coming in" (399). Audiences by now must have been inured to this type of plot: the secretly married bride whose unknowing father compels her to marry a wealthy man. Middleton makes short work of the plot, however, and focuses upon the fun of the situation. Jane, playing the part once occupied by Juliet, Clare Harcop, and Margaret, is not required to fend off a serious contender, a Paris, but rather a foolish Cornish wrestler more interested in roaring than wedding. Jane's secret marriage is therefore subordinated to Chough and Trimtram's roaring school fun.

Middleton does, however, continue to reflect the uncertain nature of such marriages. As noted in *Measure for Measure,* a secretly wed couple may at one and the same time defiantly avouch themselves married and still feel guilty. In 2.2 Jane indicates that she is guilty in pregnancy: "The father of my fault would have repaired / His faulty issue" (2.2.61–62). But she then claims that she is properly wed: "'tis not all so ill / As you may yet conceit it: this deed was done / When heaven had witness to the jugal knot; / Only the barren ceremony wants, / Which by an adverse father is abridged" (2.2.84–88). The secret marriage is necessary to allow Jane to bear a child apparently out of wedlock and create the difficulties with the physician and Chough. In the end, Russell is happy to learn that he is a grandfather, even if his grandbaby is (as he believes) a bastard. The final calamity is thereby avoided. We should notice that, for purposes of the plot at least, Jane never really had to be married at all. The secret marriage therefore operates merely to keep Jane on the windy side of morality in the audience's eyes.

In 5.1 Russell is enlightened. Fitzallen tells him, "Sir, this is mine own child, / You could not have found out a fitter father; / Nor is it basely bred, as you imagine, / For we were wedded by the hand of heaven / Ere this work was begun" (353–57). The attitude toward marriage *per verba de præsenti* remains unchanged: heaven remains the witness to the holy rite; children born before the church celebration are rightfully gotten; only the public celebration is wanting. This causes legal tangles, to be sure, but the morality of the act ceases to be an issue. Middleton continues to reflect the attitude of the other playwrights and presumably the general populace: such marriages are both binding and holy. He does not, however, dwell upon the sanctity of the secret union. Indeed, he opens the marriage to a rough joke. Chough comments that the secret wedding probably took place "At Pancridge, I'll lay my life on't" (358). Pancridge, according to

Sugden, "seems to have been often used for hasty and irregular marriages."[127]

A Fair Quarrel demonstrates Middleton's fine sense of plot/ subplot reflection, and the secret union of the subplot doubles Lady Ager's lie in the main plot. In each plot there is a woman seemingly stained: Jane's apparent out-of-wedlock pregnancy and Lady Ager's admission to being a "whore." Lady Ager claims to have been "betrayed to a most sinful hour / By a corrupted soul I put in trust once, / A kinswoman" (2.1.185–87). This parallels the trust Jane places in the physician's sister, Anne. In Lady Ager's lie, the kinswoman acted the part of bawd. In Jane's real predicament Anne betrays her brother's lust and protects Jane. The reversals work well to develop Middleton's themes of holy secrets and kindred's betrayal in both plot lines.

Despite the centrality of the secret marriage to the subplot, however, Middleton seems to have had little interest in inquiring into the complications of the marriage bond itself. Having fully explored the secret marriage plot two years before, in *The Witch*, Middleton was likely unmotivated to cover the same ground again. Rowley certainly had little interest in the more spiritually romantic notions of marriage. Therefore, the secrecy of the marriage is introduced primarily as an aid to the development of the complications when the physician lusts after Jane and Chough is betrothed to the married woman. The audience once again is privy to the truth of the marriage and therefore appreciates the spotless nature of the lovers. It little matters what the other characters in *A Fair Quarrel* might believe. The audience shares the exculpating secret from the first and is therefore freed from morally censuring the play. Middleton's famous amorality triumphs yet again.

A Mad World, My Masters

Middleton uses the secret marriage of Jane and Fitzallen in much the same manner as he uses Bounteous Progress's will in his 1606 *A Mad World, My Masters*. Because we know from the beginning that there is a marriage in *A Fair Quarrel* and a will bequeathing all of Bounteous Progress's wealth to Follywit in *A Mad World, My Masters*, we are not concerned that Jane is pregnant or Follywit is cheating Bounteous Progress out of his money. We are allowed to laugh at the chicanery safe in the knowledge that the deceptions ultimately hurt no one. *A Mad World, My Masters* additionally uses a secret union to spring a joke when Follywit is himself fooled into marrying the "virtuous virgin" Gullman. The entire marriage requires two short lines:

> FOLLYWIT. What, is't a match? If't be, clap hands and lips.
> MOTHER. 'Tis done, there's witness on't.
>
> (4.5.103–4)[128]

The "clapping" of hands and lips might have suggested to Middleton in 1606 the mutuality of consent required by law and perhaps even the "handfasting" so many commentators have fastened upon as a requirement for such marriages. It is, of course, an insufficient marriage in form. No words either *de præsenti* or *de futuro* are spoken. But the technicalities of the law are of little importance to Middleton's moment. Speed is the element in this sequence. The audience could not help but see the humor in the marriage. The guller, Follywit, is ultimately gulled into marrying a punk. He rushes headlong into his folly—with the clap.

After this two-line sequence Follywit routinely refers to Gullman as his wife and her mother as his mother even as Mother calls Follywit son. She does go on to say, "Send for a priest and clap't up within the hour" (4.5.112). The marriage will then be perfected as was Juliet's to Romeo, but that is of little consequence to Middleton at this early stage of his career. The fun has been achieved. Follywit has leapt into marriage as an enthusiastic lemming into the sea. The fact and not the character of the marriage affords Bounteous Progress his mirth in the final scene.

Middleton turns the precipitous wedding into a happy marriage. Gullman brings three hundred pounds with her into the marriage as well as the promise of faithfulness. Progress gives the couple one thousand marks as a present. Follywit is appeased. The clandestine nature of the marriage is hardly important. Middleton uses the hasty marriage as a flash point of humor, a comic device. He ignores entirely all questions of sanctity, secrecy, and public opinion.

King Lear

Another example of the secret marriage used as a mere device, albeit to darker effect, may be found in *King Lear* (*circa* 1605). Shakespeare creates pseudo contracts between Edmund and Regan and Edmund and Goneril. At 5.3.77–78 Regan, already poisoned by her sister, attempts to marry Edmund in a *sua sponte* contract: "Witness the world, that I create thee here / My lord and master." Then at line 81 she calls, "Let the drum strike, and prove my title thine." Albany, in an underappreciated, creditable piece of irony confronts Regan, saying at 84–89, "For your claim, fair [sister], / I bar it in the interest of my wife; / 'Tis she that is subcontracted to this lord, / And I, her husband, contradict your banes [i.e., banns]. / If you will marry, make your love to me, / My lady is bespoke." Moments later Regan is assisted off to die of the poison Goneril has secretly administered. There is no secret marriage here but only *verba de præsenti* marriage talk. There is no mutuality of agreement. Edmund never responds. Albany may or may not be aware of a precontract existing between Edmund and his own wife, Goneril. There may in fact be no precontract. If there were, it would be void on its face because Goneril is already married. That matters little. His line barring Regan's contract is ironic. In essence he sarcastically asserts—in his role as Goneril's husband—Goneril's legal rights under a pre (or what he scathingly terms a "sub") contract to marry Edmund.

The deceived husband is undeceived. Even as Gloucester has learned to see his way feelingly through the world so too does Albany gain insight into his marriage at the moment he has apparently lost his wife. Of course, Goneril's *de facto* marriage to Albany is ample bar to her precontract (if any) to Edmund, but the pith of the sequence lies not so much in the laws of secret marriage as in the force of Albany's realization. Two brief scenes earlier Albany wondered aloud why the war was being waged at all. He now sees the reasons. The subversion of order and the undermining of the law, both natural and statutory, by Lear's daughters suddenly impress themselves upon Albany, the only good man in a camp of malefactors. In this short sequence Albany comes to himself. His ironical subversion of the marriage law underscores the subversions he now recognizes in the actions of Goneril and Regan toward Lear, Gloucester, Edgar, and himself.

In *King Lear* Shakespeare employs an image of secret marriage that he appears to have understood well enough. In this case the image is only that. No one is suddenly married. No one is contracted to be secretly married. Shakespeare merely draws upon a familiar motif in order to develop Albany's character and repeat the theme of subverted rights he has explored throughout the play. If *King Lear* may be viewed in part as a domestic tragedy, a story of the destruction of familial love and filial duty, then we may view Albany's acknowledgment of Goneril's *subcontract* at the end of the play as a balance to Gloucester's libidinous betrayal of his own marriage bed from the play's opening. Significantly, the illegitimate Edmund is central to both sequences of perverted marriage.

As can be seen, the secret marriages in *A Fair Quarrel, A Mad World, My Masters,* and *King Lear* are mostly incidental. Unlike these plays, which use the image primarily as a plot device, other plays, such as *Romeo and Juliet, The Gentleman Usher,* and *As You Like It* employ the image as an important motif but do little to explore its social and moral ambiguities. Yet the main group of titles in this discussion, and especially *Measure for Measure, The Duchess of Malfi,* and *The Miseries of Enforc'd Marriage,* employ the secret marriage as a significant metaphor. Marriage law of the period, therefore, must be understood in all of its complexities in order to appreciate certain colors within these plays. It should not be enough to rely upon the frustrated dismissals of commentators who claim that *sponsalia* law is either unrecoverable or too intricate to be of any use.

A thoroughgoing evaluation of secret marriage imagery in Renaissance drama reveals several conclusions. All characters engaged in secret marriages are sympathetic characters, with the exception of Angelo, who, it may be significantly noted, tried to avoid his *sponsalia* and Edmund/Regan/Goneril, who never actually create one. The privately contracted marriage became such a notable feature of sympathy within plays that by the time we reach Middleton's *The Witch,* a late play of the "secret marriage play" period (roughly 1599–1615), the secret marriage itself has become a virtual short-hand for identifying the sympathetic characters.

To be sure, there was an increasing trend in courts of the period to hold against contested, improperly witnessed marriage contracts. Nevertheless, playwrights of the period appear to have continued to uphold some dimly remembered spirit of the *ius commune* and to conclude that marriage was an *affaire du coeur* shared between wife, husband, and God. Words of proper form had to be employed, of course, and customary ritual often enacted, but seldom is the Institution *qua* Institution celebrated in the period's plays. The drama's anti-Institutional vision of matrimony may indicate that the prevailing popular (or at least theatrical) view of marriage followed the foundations of medieval canon law set out in the works of Gratian and especially Peter Lombard. But the dramatic presentations most clearly indicate the tension between the private and public. This tension may well have presented the non–legally minded audience member with a romantic vision of love triumphing over the corruption of society. But it almost certainly and simultaneously sparked debate among the legally minded audience members over the spirit versus the letter of the law.

Conclusions

MANY OF THE FOREGOING DISCUSSIONS REMAIN OPEN-ENDED. MY lack of positive conclusions regarding the law is calculated. While some "answers" have from time to time been suggested to some of the legal-dramatic problems posed in these explorations, in the end no fully clear solution should be reached in this form of study. The admittedly frustrating reticence to develop exactitudes lies at the heart of my thesis. If the legal motifs, at least some of them, here presented were intended as grist for the pedagogical legal mill, and the Inns of Court students were intended to use these hypothetical situations for their mootings, boltings, and puttings of cases, then the more open to debate and free exchange they remained, the better they suited purpose. At least one reason playgoing was a lure for those "afternoones men" may well have been this very quality of presenting fully realized fact patterns drawn from society for the neophyte lawyer to examine.

The law found in Renaissance drama, while certainly exhibiting the Gordian complexities of societal law, is, I believe, calculated ultimately to appeal to a wide class of audience member. Even today, several centuries past the world of the use and præmunire, when we no longer accept the notion of solitary lovers marrying under a tree, modern audiences accept the legal motives of the drama as probable, or at least reasonable, within the context of the performance. What matters to a modern audience the momentary utterance of Antonio's concerning a use of one-half of Shylock's property? The gist is clear enough: Antonio is winning, Shylock is losing. The modern audience perceives the shift and is satisfied or chagrined (depending upon the individual's perceptions within the context of her own personal sociopolitical receptivity and the modern production's vision). This perception is self-evident, holistic, and organic to the theatrical experience.

How much richer is the experience, then, when the play in question is presented for a group of persons who have at least a passing familiarity with the legal concepts contained therein? And it is passing familiarity that should now be our concern, for it would seem that the law we have examined would have been understood, at least in its general outlines, by a significant number of the audience who had not trained at the Inns of Court. We are not, then, examining knotty peculiarities of legal jetsam, but, rather, we have before us law that was reasonably well understood by the uninitiated. The law under examination is presented here in far more detail, of course, than the average afternoon play fancier of 1598 could reasonably be expected to absorb. However, that same casual playgoer would understand the lay law significance of the images presented—Rosalind's marriage, Antonio's triumph, Claudio's trouble, Scarborrow's villainy. The law would underscore these elements, even if not fully understood by the layman, and would resonate brilliantly within the work for the few audience members who did fully appreciate the significance.

To take a modern example of lay law from popular culture, in the original version of *Invasion of the Body Snatchers,* the romantic lead learns of his former lover's return from Reno, a lover whom he had avoided since her marriage several years before. With no further preamble, and no more explanation, the two begin dating. The screenwriter obviously expected his audience to equate Reno with divorce. Non-lawyers appreciate the relative laxity of Nevada marriage statutes—and Las Vegas weddings and Reno divorces have become common clichés carrying legal significance. One need not have a full knowledge of the statutory workings of Nevada law in order to understand the dramatic significance of an unhappily married woman's visit to Reno. Similarly, one need not take a course in tax law, with all of its vagaries and loopholes and shifting requirements, to appreciate the dramatic image of April 15 in a play set in the states, or a reference to V.A.T. in a British drama.

What is lay law today, commonly appreciated though not fully understood by the common man, is the obscure law of next century. An appreciation of lay law does not require a full or even substantial understanding of law as it is taught to or practiced by lawyers. It requires only a passing interest in the society in which one lives. As society changes, so change the perceptions of lay law. Tomorrow's scholar will be greatly perplexed, when her society has codified and simplified its law on abortion (however it may turn out), when she sifts through our society's laws and debates and the shifting policies concerning the rights of unborn children and the rights of women. We, however, have little difficulty appreciating the competing views even though the actual legal philosophies that drive court decisions concerning abortion elude us. Lay law might best be described as that law that has captured popular attention.

A clever playwright is well advised to reflect his society in his work. Law shapes and defines society, and lay law is the popular understanding of that formative force. The best playwrights will create legal images that will reward further examination, allowing for a passable understanding by the casual observer and an increasingly significant understanding by the increasingly more learned observer. This is precisely the case with the images of law to be found in the Renaissance. When that playwright introduces such legal images to the stage, those images may fairly be termed Playhouse Law.

Several playwrights conversant in the law, either through social connection with lawyers and law students or through actual study of the law, created within their theatrical works legal images that were rich in dramatic significance. Still other playwrights of the period, less adept in their understanding of the law or at play crafting, perhaps both, created images of the law borrowed from their sources that they misunderstood and incorporated poorly. These they included in their works either to follow the fashion or to appeal to their legally minded patrons. In either case, there is a heretofore relatively underworked plethora of legal images and motifs significantly placed within the period drama.

Much of this imagery has been ignored, either through timidity or neglect. When it has been noticed, it has been regularly attacked as an improper subject for commentary by a number of scholars who have apparently viewed it as too perplexing, incidental, peripheral, or contrary to their critical agendas. It has been misanalyzed in abortive efforts to demonstrate, *inter alia,* that Shakespeare might have been a Templarian. It has been reconstituted into legal fictions by modern commentators seeking to create simplistic and unhistorical terminology for labyrinthine concepts. The legal imagery under consideration, however, yields significantly important opportunities to comprehend the Renaissance drama from many perspectives—aesthetic, linguistic, historic, social, and political, as well as legal and dramatic—and, as such, has been too long beset, wrongly appraised, or avoided. To echo the good Gonzalo, "Here's a maze trod indeed through forthrights and meanders," and we are best advised to follow.

Notes

INTRODUCTION

1. Paul S. Clarkson and Clyde T. Warren. *The Law of Property in Shakespeare and the Elizabethan Drama*. (New York: Gordian Press, 1968), p. xxv.

2. See, e.g., William Lowes Rushton, *Shakespeare a Lawyer* (London, 1858) and *Shakespeare's Legal Maxims* (Liverpool: Henry Young and Sons, 1907; reprinted 1973); John, Lord Campbell, *Shakespeare's Legal Acquirements Considered*. (Buffalo: William S. Hein, 1987) and *Shakespeare as a Lawyer* (Boston: Little, Brown and Co., 1883); Cushman Kellogg Davis, *The Law in Shakespeare* (St. Paul, 1884); Rocellus Sheridan Guernsey, *Ecclesiastical Law in Hamlet* (New York: AMS Press, 1971); Charles E. Phelps, *Falstaff and Equity* (Boston: Houghton Mifflin, 1901); Clarkson and Warren. *The Law of Property;* Edward J. White, *Commentaries on the Law in Shakespeare* (Buffalo: William S. Hein Co., 1987); B. J. Sokol & Mary Sokol, *Shakespeare's Legal Language: A Dictionary* (London: Athlone Press, 2000).

3. *The Law of Property,* xxv.

4. Malone stated his opinion thus: "There were at that time, in Stratford, at least six attorneys in this court, beside Mr. Henry Rogers, the steward or town-clerk, who was also an attorney. In the office of this person . . . I suppose our poet to have been placed for two or three years. . . . [H]is knowledge and application of legal terms, seems to me not merely such as might have been acquired by the casual observation of his all-comprehending mind; it has the appearance of technical skill; and he is so fond of displaying it on all occasions, that there is, I think, some ground for supposing that he was early initiated in at least the forms of law. Of this notion, which perhaps professional habits first suggested to me, I shall subjoin below, I will not say the proofs, but such circumstances as seem to me to render it extremely probable." ("Prolegomena," *The Life of William Shakespeare* [London, 1790]).

5. See, e.g. Richard Grant White, "Shakespeare, Attorney at Law and Solicitor in Chancery,"*Atlantic Monthly* 4 (1859); H. T., "Was Shakespeare a Lawyer?" *Law Journal* 6 (reissued, London: Longmans, Green & Co., 1871): 81; John T. Doyle, "Shakespeare's Law: The Case of Shylock," *The Overland Monthly* (July 1886); [Sir James Plaisted Wilde]), *The Bacon-Shakespeare Controversy* Lord Penzance, London: Sampson Low, Marston & Co., 1890): 47 (refers to "Shakespeare's perfect familiarity with . . . English law . . . so perfect and intimate that he was never incorrect, and never at fault"); James T. Foard, "On the Law Case:

Shylock v Antonio," *Manchester Quarterly* (1899): 268; William G. Devecmon, *In Re Shakespeare's Legal Acquirements* (New York: Shakespeare Society of New York, no. 12, 1899): 7 ("Shakespeare had no knowledge of the technique of law, and no just appreciation of those fundamental principles of justice which are the basis of all law"); Charles Allen, *Notes on the Bacon-Shakespeare Question* (Boston, 1900): 12 ("The Bacon argument from the legal knowledge shown in the plays is of slight weight"); Homer B. Sprague, "Shakespeare's Alleged Blunders in Legal Terminology," *Yale Law Journal* 11 (1902): 304 (A point-by-point attack on Devecmon's *In Re Shakespeare's Legal Acquirements* concludes Shakespeare had a finely developed legal sense); Granville George Greenwood, "Lawyers in Shakespeare," *The Westminster Review* 159 (1903): 161 (Shakespeare's legal knowledge was far beyond what could be attained by "the Stratford player"); J. C. Collins, "Was Shakespeare a Lawyer?" *Studies in Shakespeare* (1904); Granville George Greenwood, *In Re Shakespeare* (London, 1909), Granville George Greenwood, *Shakespeare's Law and Latin* (Chapel Hill: University of North Carolina Press, 1913), and *Shakespeare's Law* (London, 1920) (Shakespeare had no more legal knowledge than any other dramatist of his day, in fact not so much); Richard Bentley, "Shakespeare's Law," *Law Times* 155 (1923): 23 (It matters not "whether . . . we decide he had legal education—and this seems to the writer the most reasonable conclusion—or whether he had none"); H. Cunningham, "Shakespeare and a Great Legal War," *The Bookman's Journal* 14 (April 1926): 1; Dunbar Plunket Barton, *Links Between Shakespeare and the Law* (London, 1929); J. E. G. de Montmorency, "Shakespeare's Legal Problems," *Contemporary Review: Literary Supplement* (1930): 797 ("Shakespeare's law as exhibited in numberless passages, [is] obviously written by a layman who moved in legal circles"); Clara Longworth de Chambrun, "Shakespeare and the Elizabethan Statutes," *The Dublin Review* (January 1936); T. M. Wears, "Shakespeare's Legal Acquirements," *Canadian Bar Review* 16 (1938); Francis Lyman Windolph, *Reflections of Law in Literature* (Philadelphia: Pennsylvania University Press, 1956): 22 ("I would not favor the adoption in real life of the legal system prevailing in his enchanted country"); Donald F. Lybarger, "Shakespeare and the Law: Was the Bard admitted to the Bar?" *Cleveland Bar Review* 36 (March 1965); George William Keeton, "Shakespeare's Legal and Political Background," *Law Quarterly Review* 84 (1968); Richard A. Posner, *Law and Literature: A Misunderstood Relation* (Cambridge: Harvard University Press, 1988).

6. See, e.g., Penzance, *The Bacon-Shakespeare Controversy,* and the musings of Sir Edwin Durning-Lawrence, Bart., in his *Bacon* is Shakespeare (New York: The John McBride Co., 1910), and his *The Shakespeare Myth* (London: Gay & Hancock, Ltd., 1912); Edward J. Castle, *Shakespeare, Bacon, Jonson, and Greene* (Port Washington, N.Y.: Kennikut Press, 1970). The notion is nicely handled by Clarkson and Warren in the General Introduction to *The Law of Property in Shakespeare and the Elizabethan Drama,* a work in which they demonstrate that the plentitude of legalisms in Shakespeare's works was not unique, or even remarkable, in early modern drama.

7. Earnest scholarship spent arguing the straw-man authorship question includes J. M. Robertson's *The Baconian Heresy* (New York, 1913); and Samuel Langhorne Clemens [Mark Twain], *Is Shakespeare Dead?* (New York, 1909). The

argument led James Beck in the Foreword to D. P. Barton's *Links between Shakespeare and the Law* to cry, "[T]here is only one man who is more unreasonable than the Baconian, and that is the man who attempts to argue the question with him" (xvi).

8. George Malcom Young, "Shakespeare and the Termers," *Proceedings of the British Academy* 33 (1947): 12.

9. See, e.g., White, *Commentaries,* 260 ("This is one of the earliest modes of conveyance used in common law").

10. *Black's Law Dictionary* defines the character of the gift as "a gift of any corporeal hereditaments to another." The noun is "feoffment."

11. *Shakespeare's Legal Acquirements,* 66.

12. Ibid.

13. Clarkson and Warren, *The Law of Property,* 111, relies upon this example from *1 Henry IV* to illustrate the concept.

14. I.e., quick to burn; cf. "soon kindled and soon burnt," *1 Henry IV,* ed. G. L. Kittredge (Boston: Ginn, 1940) 162.

15. I use the term "New Historicism" in the pointed manner described by Robert D. Hume in his "Texts Within Contexts: Notes Toward a Historical Method," *Philological Quarterly* 71, no. 1 (winter 1992).

Chapter 1. 'A Must, Then . . .

1. See, e.g., J. H. Baker, *The Third University of England: The Inns of Court and the Common-Law Tradition* (London: Selden Society, 1990), 17; and *The Legal Profession and the Common Law* (London: Hambledon Press, 1986), 95–96, where it is suggested that this group comprised the majority of students at the Inns of Court as early as the fifteenth century.

2. *Survey of London* (Oxford: Clarendon Press, 1908) 1:76–79.

3. Of obscure origin, probably nominal form from the verb *boult,* to sift, to search and try, cf. *Henry V* 2.2.137, "Such and so finely boulted didst thou seem." Stow's usage seems to refer to the sifting of legal quiddities.

4. *O.E.D.,* definition 5, *Law:* The discussion of a hypothetical case by students at the Inns of Court for practice. The word is derived from ON *mót,* meaning a public assembly or meeting. Cf. Stow's juxtaposition of "meetings" and "boltinges" infra.

5. Boltas, Moots, and the putting of cases, as is made clear by Stow's context, are three descriptions of substantially the same activity, namely, the presentation of points for argument. It is possible that the different houses had their own names for the activity and Stow here makes an attempt to be inclusive. The *Pension Books of Gray's Inn,* however, use two of the terms—Boltings and Moots—throughout. The terms, therefore, refer to three different, though related, forms of the same activity. Dunbar Plunket Barton, on page 14 of *The Story of Our Inns of Court* (London: G. T. Foulis, 1924), distinguishes "Bolts" as those "cases propounded for argument among the 'Inner' Barristers, and . . . conducted by the 'Outer' Barristers" while a "Moot would begin, after supper in the Hall, with the putting of some doubtful case by an Outer Barrister, which would

be argued by one or two of the benchers" which in turn would lead to a "kind of mimic lawsuit."

6. *Calendar of the Inner Temple Records,* ed. F. A. Inderwick (London, 1898)), 1:468–69, and H. B. Wheatley, *London, Past and Present: A Dictionary of Its History, Associations, and Traditions* (Detroit, Mich.: Singing Tree Press, 1968), 2.:261, each suggest that the number of persons professionally associated with the Inns rose from a mere 769 in 1574—two years before the Theatre opened— to only 1,040 during the Jacobean period.

7. Every important commentator to have passed judgment upon the Inns of Court and drama has come to this same conclusion. See, Links Between e.g., Dunbar Plunket Barton, *Shakespeare and the Law* (London, 1929), 18 ("The members of the Inns of Court figured amongst the constant patrons of the drama, and amongst the regular frequenters of the theatre"); A. Wigfall Green, *The Inns of Court and Early English Drama* (New Haven: Yale University Press, 1931), 18 ("[T]he Inns were the residence of the intellectual class of the great metropolis; hence they were often called upon to establish the criteria of taste even for the court. In addition, the obligation of the lawyers to entertain the royal family and the nobility required them to display great dramatic diversity and ingenuity in providing such amusement. The Inns of Court were therefore a favorite rendezvous for poets and dramatists"); Alfred Harbage, *Shakespeare's Audience* (New York, 1961) 80 ("Two groups are mentioned again and again in contemporary allusions to the theatres—the students of the Inns of Court and the apprentices of London . . . What the [Inns'] group lacked in total numbers was counterbalanced by the large proportion of those numbers possessing the money, leisure, and inclination for playgoing. A student at the Inns of Court was a well-born, affluent, university-educated young man in his early twenties. He lived in a society devoted to intellectual pursuits and well disposed towards belles-lettres. He must have made a good spectator"); Owen Hood Phillips, *Shakespeare and the Lawyers* (London: Methuen & Co. Ltd., 1972), 33 ("Lawyers in Shakespeare's time patronized the stage and attended regularly at the theatre . . . Shakespeare's audience would include young Templars who knew something of Italian as well as classical literature . . . Here we have a public which is disputatious, which can take a point, dissect a character and treasure a phrase—a society where the terms of the law were current coin"). There was, however, a bifurcation in the Inns of Court between the genteel nobleman, who attended the Inns of Court as one attends a finishing school, and the base practitioner. The split is exemplified by John Donne, who had been a member of Lincoln's Inn, in his "Satire II." The point is well handled by Ronald J. Corthell, "'Coscus onely breeds my just offense': A Note on Donne's 'Satire II' and the Inns of Court," *John Donne Journal* 6 (1987), 1:25–32. This bifurcation might explain why many plays depict the professional attorney as either a fool or a knave. See also, E. F. J. Tucker, *Intruder into Eden: Representations of The Common Lawyer in English Literature 1350–1750* (Columbia, S.C.: Camden House, 1984), 66.

8. Andrew Gurr, *Playgoing in Shakespeare's London* (Cambridge: Cambridge University Press, 1987), 4.

9. See, e.g., the diary of Edward Heath, a student of the Middle Temple, who records his attendance at forty-nine plays paying between 1*s.* 6*d.* and 2*s.* at each

and averaging one play every ten days. He also records purchasing ten playbooks at an average of one book every seven weeks from 1628 through 1629. B.L. MS. Egerton 2983.

10. This is most particularly true of William Ingram, *The Business of Playing: The Beginnings of the Adult Professional Theater in Elizabethan London* (Ithaca: Cornell University Press, 1992); Stephen Jay Greenblatt, *Shakespearean Negotiations* (Berkeley: University of California Press, 1988); and Gordon Braden, *Renaissance Tragedy and the Senecan Tradition: Anger's Privilege* (New Haven: Yale University Press, 1985).

11. William Dugdale said they were called Inns of Court "because the Students in them, did there, not only study the Laws, but use such other exercises as might make them the more serviceable to the King's Court." *Origines Juridiciales, or Historical Memorials of the English Laws, Courts of Justice, etc.* (*The Savoy,* 1671) 141.

12. Basil Brown, *Law Sports at Gray's Inn (1594)* (New York, 1921), xxiv ("My own opinion is that Gray's Inn may in truth be called the very cradle and nursery of the English Drama"); Philip J. Finkelpearl, *John Marston of the Middle Temple: An Elizabethan Dramatist in His Social Setting* (Cambridge: Harvard University Press, 1969), 25:

> It is no exaggeration to say that through their activity the translators, playwrights, and poets of the Inns of Court kept writing alive under unpropitious circumstances. When the greater writers appeared, they did not have to create an audience or to invent new forms. They merely had to do better what had already been attempted by an interconnected group of serious men intent on making the Reformation in England humanistic and its government secure and humane. Their collective effort established the Inns as an intellectual center with a special character: critical, æsthetically innovative, and politically concerned.

13. Although the play is now accepted to be a translation from the Italian *Giocasta* by M. Lodovico Dolce, it nevertheless traces its roots through that play to Euripides' *Phoenissae.*

14. I have argued elsewhere that *The Misfortunes of Arthur* may have actually influenced *The Spanish Tragedy* and could well provide a *terminus post quem* for that play. See Brian Jay Corrigan, "Introduction," *The Misfortunes of Arthur: A Critical, Old-Spelling Edition* (New York: Garland, 1992), 43.

15. Although David Bevington, in *From Mankind to Marlowe* (Cambridge: Harvard University Press, 1962), 35–38, suggests that there was little improvement in Inns of Court plays from 1562 to 1588, see Corrigan, "Introduction," *The Misfortunes of Arthur,* which argues that the eight Grayan men involved in that production were aware of the changing tastes of the audience and sought to cater to the emerging preferences.

16. D. S. Bland, "Interludes in Fifteenth-Century Revels at Furnivall's Inn," *Review of English Studies* 3 (1952): 263–68.

17. Inner Temple Society Acts of Parliament, 1505–1589, 67. John Bruce Williamson, *The History of the Temple, London* (London: John Murray, 1925), 134.

18. Edward Hall, *Chronicle* (London, 1809).

19. The description of the action is not unlike the early extant allegorical drama represented by *Magnificence* and *Respublica.*

20. The audit register of the Record Office, quoted by Albert Feuillerat in his *Documents Relating to the Office of the Revels in the Time of Queen Elizabeth* (London: David Nutt, 1908), 378, also suggests something of the richness of the 1588 production of *The Misfortunes of Arthur:*

> Anno xxx°Reg*n*i Reigine
> The Quenes Ma*ie*stie being At Grenewich ther were shewed presented and enacted before: her highnes betwixte Christmas & Shrovetide [a play] besides feat*t*es of Activitie And other shewes by . . . the gentlemen of grayes In on whom was Inployed dyverse rem*n*ant*t*es of Clothe of goulde & other stuffe oute of the Store.

George Godwin exclaims upon this point that it "would have been strange indeed had not the Inns of Court, with their concentration of wealth and talent, managed their own revels in fine style; and this they most certainly did." *The Middle Temple: The Society and Fellowship* (London: Staples Press Ltd., 1954), 72.

21. Waterhous, quoting the Bacon Report for this period, says:

> In this Christmas time they have all Manner of pastimes as singing and dancing, and in some of the Houses ordinarily they have some interlude or tragedy played by the gentlemen of the same House, the ground and matter whereof is devised by some of the gentlemen of the House. (quoted in Williamson, *History of the Temple,* 135).

22. J. D. Walker, *Black Books of Lincoln's Inn* (London, 1897), 1 vol. no. xxxiii, 344, 348, 352, 362, 374, 418; 2:55. On Candlemas of 1565 there is an order recorded that "Mr Edwards shall have in reward Liij^s, iiij^d for his plee, and his hussher x^s more to the children that pleed." In the margin the children are glossed as "Children of the Quenes Chappell." The accounts however show that £1 was paid to the boys. The play required further payment of £1 18^{s2d} for the supper, torches, clubs, and necessaries associated with the performance.

23. John Payne Collier, *The History of the English Dramatic Poetry to the Time of Shakespeare: An Annals of the Stage,* (London, 1821), 1:191.

24. I premise my assumptions regarding the dearth of information during this period upon the remarkable fact that, although the Middle Temple's elaborate Great Hall was opened around 1574, there is no record of any inaugural celebration. This point has raised comment by the Middle Temple historian, Williamson, q.v. at pp. 229, 233. In *The Middle Temple,* Godwin suggests that, besides *Twelfth Night* in 1601 at the Middle Temple, "it can scarcely be doubted that there were other performances in the Hall during the reign of Elizabeth whose affection for the Temple is very well known" (68). Godwin, at p. 53, includes a description of a Middle Temple feast from 1577 which suggests that a play was performed that year at least:

> at the high end of the hall, which is somewhat raised, both to signify the exalted status of the Benchers and for the convenience of the play actors, are seated the members of the Privy Council and the peerage.

25. R. J. Fletcher, *The Pension Book of Gray's Inn* (1901), 78.

26. James Spedding, *The Letters and the Life of Francis Bacon* (London: Longman, Green, Longman, and Roberts, 1862), 9:370.

27. This is true unless we postulate that one of the masques is *Catiline* and the other *The Misfortunes of Arthur.* I have elsewhere argued that one of

the "masques" referred to might well be *The Misfortunes of Arthur.* "Introduction," 1.

28. *Gesta Grayorum 1688,* ed. W. W. Greg, *The Malone Society Reprints* (Oxford: Oxford University Press, 1914), 29–30. The reason given for attendance at the Theatre, as well as "the better sort of Ord'naries for Conference," was to serve the Prince,

> whereby they may not only become accomplished with Civil Conversations, and be able to govern a Table with Discourse; but also sufficient, if need be, to make Epigrams, Emblems, and other Devices appertaining to His Honour's [the *Prince of Purpoole's*] learned Revels.

The practice, of course, would also help fit the student for a career in the sovereign's court as well. The phraseology of the Grayan pronouncement is not unlike Stow's discussion of legal sports, quoted above, wherein students "frequent readings, meetings, boltinges, and other learned exercises, whereby growing ripe in the knowledge of the lawes, and approued withall to be of honest conuersation, they are . . . selected and called to the degree of *Vtter Barresters,* and so enabled to be common counsellors, and to practise the law."

29. The argument has been advanced that, in the revels of the *Gesta Grayorum,* Gray's Inn actually invented the "Jonsonian" Masque. Enid Welsford, *The Court Masque* (Cambridge: Cambridge University Press, 1927), 163–64.

30. The actors included playwright and Middletonian collaborator, William Rowley, then thirty-four years of age, as Plumporridge. Joseph Taylor played Doctor Almanac, J. Newton portrayed A Fasting Day, H. Atwell presented New Year, and W. Carpenter was Time.

31. Plays performed at the royal court and at universities were also exempted from Harrison's general censure of common players. I. J. Semper, "The Jacobean Theatre through the Eyes of Catholic Clerics," *Shakespeare Quarterly* 3 (1952): 47.

32. The evidence of the Inner Temple record from 1631, "That no play shall be continued within the House upon any Saturday night or upon Christmas even, at night, after twelve of the clock," probably refers to dicing and gaming play rather than to dramatic performances. See Green, *The Inns of Court,* 95. H. L. Bellot notes of the Inner Temple that "[f]rom 1605 to 1640 plays were performed in our Hall twice a year, at Allhallows and Candlemas, with the exception of a short interval, when 'Anticks or puppets' were substituted on account of the 'great disorder and scurrility brought into this House by lewd and lasciuious plays" (*The Inner and Middle Temple* [London: Methuen & Co., 1902]), 196, citing on page 89 the Inner Temple Society Acts of Parliament 1589–1638. The order Bellot refers to is from February 1610. On November 24 of the same year (Acts of Parliament 1589–1638: 1595) the order was repealed:

> Whereas of late yeares uppon the two festivall dayes of All Saints and Candlemasse playes have been used after dinner for recreacon which have lately been layd downe by order in parliament, it is now ordered that the same order shall henceforth stand repealed.

During the revels of 1635/36 it was decreed

> that noe person or persons whatsoever shall medd[le] in Poetry for that they have gathered with industry phrases out of Shakespeare Marston or the like.

Bodlein MS. Tanner 88, 121–122. The phraseology is reminiscent of the speeches by Purpoole's king-at-arms of 1594 and the Prince d'Amour's champion of 1599, indicating the probability of dramatic interest in the Inns of Court up to the decade preceding the Interregnum.

33. *Shakespeare's Sonnets Dated, and Other Essays* (New York: Oxford University Press, 1949), 37 et seq. Hotson's argument is predated by that of Peter Alexander, who examined the entry by Roberts in the *Stationer's Register,* the two contradictory title pages, the argument of the dedicatory Epistle to the Quarto, and internal evidence of the play in order to demonstrate its Inns of Court connection. His examination won the cautious approval of W. W. Greg. *Library* IX (1928–29), 267–86. Recently W. R. Elton has taken up the cry in his *Shakespeare's Troilus and Cressida and the Inns of Courts Revels* (Brookfield, Vt.: Ashgate Press, 2000).

34. Leslie Hotson, *Mr. W. H.* (London: R. Hart-Davis, 1964), 230 et seq.

35. Hotson, *Shakespeare's Sonnets Dated,* 56.

36. *Shakespeare and the Lawyers,* 28–29.

37. See also Philip Finkelpearl, "John Marston's *Histrio-Mastix* as an Inns of Court Play: A Hypothesis," *Huntington Library Quarterly* 29 (1966): 223–34; and M. C. Bradbrook, "The Comedy of Timon: A Reveling Play of the Inner Temple," *Renaissance Drama* 9 (1966): 83–103.

38. E. K. Chambers, *The Elizabethan Stage* (Oxford, 1923), 4:280.

39. Harl. MS. 7392, 97. Chambers, 2:98–99.

40. The order, dated 11 July, reads:

> Item, Parr Stafferton gentleman of Grayes Inne for that he that daye brought a dysordered companye of gentlemen of the Innes of Courte & others, to assalte Arthur Kynge, Thomas Goodale, and others, servauntes to the Lord Barkley, & players of Enterludes within the Cyttye, was by this Courte committed to the Compter in Wood street, and the said players lykewyse. And aswell the sayd players as the sayd Parre Stafferton, weare by this Courte commanded to set downe in wrytinge the maner how the same quarell began.

In July of the same year Henry Lord Berkeley wrote to the Lord Mayor asking that his players be released from the Counter:

> My very good Lord, ther is lately fallen owt some broile betwixt certaine of my men and some of the Innes of Courte, sought onely by them . . . Whereupon ther is some of my men comitted to warde . . . behauing them selues honestly in euery respecte, as I cannot learne to the contrary, sauing that they played on the sabothe daie contrary to your order & commaundment vnknowen to them, in respecte of that I yelde them faultie and they them selues craue pardon. So ame I now to desier your Lp. to sett them at libertie, whoe are vpon going into the Countrie to auoide querrell or other inconuenience that mought followe. (quoted in Chambers, 4:282)

41. Thomas Nashe, *Pierce Penilesse* (London: n.d.), F_3^v.

42. Robert Krueger advances the hypothesis that Davies' *Orchestra* was performed, perhaps as a play or disputation. "Sir John Davies: *Orchestra* Complete, *Epigrams,* Unpublished Poems," *Review of English Studies* 13 (1962): 2–29, 113–24.

43. *O.E.D.,* definition 4(b), *Fry:* "a [collective] 'swarm' or crowd of [young or insignificant] persons." Cf. Beaumont and Fletcher's *The Woman-Hater* 3.3. of

1607, "The whole *frie* in a Colledge, or in an Inn of Court." Davies' use of the word here may be simply a standard cant description, as the Beaumont and Fletcher quotation tends to suggest, but it might also suggest the sheer number of young Inns of Court men at the play, as the adjective "clamorous," and the description of them filling up the most expensive, private rooms implies.

44. *Epigrammes* 3, "In Rufum."

45. I.e., Alleyn at the Rose and Burbage at the Curtain.

46. *The Scourge of Villainy* (London, n.d.), G_7^v, H_4^r.

47. Thomas Dekker, *The Gull's Hornbook,* chapter 6, 2:246–47 in *Non-Dramatic Works,* ed. Alexander B. Grossart (New York: Russell & Russell, 1963).

48. Thomas Overbury, *The Overburian Characters,* ed. W. J. Paylor (Oxford: B. Blackwell, 1936), 45.

49. *Microcosmographie,* D_4^r, H_3^v.

50. F[rancis] L[enton], *The Young Gallants Whirligig,* as quoted in Gurr, *Playgoing,* 237.

51. B.L. Ms. Egerton 2983.

52. A_4^v. The lament is both humorous and telling as there were about forty weeks of vacation and only twelve of term time during the year. Hillary Term lasted three weeks, January 11–31; Easter was a movable term lasting three weeks during a period between April 15 and May 8; Trinity Term lasted the three weeks from May 22 through June 12; Michaelmas Term lasted November 2–25.

53. E. M. Symonds, "The Diary of John Greene (1635–57)," *English Historical Review* 43 (1928): 386–89.

54. Quoted by William A. Armstrong in *The Seventeenth-Century Stage,* ed. Gerald Eades Bentley (Chicago: University of Chicago Press, 1968), 219.

55. See, e.g., Henk Gras, "*Twelfth Night, Every Man Out of His Humour,* and the Middle Temple Revels of 1597–98," *Modern Language Review* 84 (July 1989): 546; and Andrew J. Gurr, "The Many-Headed Audience," *Essays in Theatre* 1 (1982): 52–62.

56. Tucker, "Satire, Legal Education, and the Inns," chapter 2, *Intruder into Eden;* Gurr, *Playgoing,* 154.

57. Raman Selden, *English Verse Satire,* 1590–1765 (London, 1978), 72.

58. See, e.g., Philip Finkelpearl, "The Use of the Middle Temple's Christmas Revels in Marston's *The Fawne,*" *Studies in Philology* 44 (1967): 199–209.

59. Brian Gibbons, *Jacobean City Comedy,* 2nd ed. (London: Methuen, 1980), 34.

60. Manningham is certainly not to be classed among the fantastic Inns of Court play fanciers, either. Tucker holds him up as an example of the religious common lawyer, having recorded some forty-two sermons in two years, (*Intruder into Eden,* 20).

61. See D. S. Bland, "Arthur Broke, Gerard Legh, and the Inner Temple," *NQ* 214 (1969): 453–55.

62. See, e.g., Robert Seufert, "'The Decorum of These Daies': Robert Wilmot and the Idea of Theatre," *Iowa State Journal of Research* 58, no. 3 (February 1984), 319–27, wherein the author demonstrates that Inns-of-Court man's attempt to influence contemporary theatre.

63. Quoted in Gregory Smith, *Elizabethan Critical Essays* (Oxford: Clarendon Press, 1904), 1:80–81.

64. See, e.g. Bertil Johansson, *Law and Lawyers in Elizabethan England as Evidenced in the Plays of Ben Jonson and Thomas Middleton,* Acta Universitatis Stockholmiensis, Stockholm Studies in English 18 (Stockholm: Almqvist & Wiksell, 1967).

65. For a link between *Twelfth Night,* Jonson's play, and the Inns of Court see Gras, "Middle Temple Revels."

66. Green, *The Inns of Court,* 6. Cecil Headlam asserts the truth of this legend in *The Inns of Court* (London: Adam & Charles Black, 1909), 112, and identifies the gatehouse of Old Square as the project on which Jonson worked.

67. Finkelpearl, *John Marston.*

68. Many Webster scholars accept his Middle Temple connection without reservation. See, e.g., Elizabeth M. Brennan, ed., *The White Devil,* New Mermaids edition (New York: W. W. Norton, 1966) vi; and D. C. Gunby, ed., *John Webster: Three Plays* (Harmondsworth, England: Penguin Books, 1972), 1. But see M. C. Bradbrook, *John Webster: Citizen and Dramatist* (London: Widenfeld and Nicolson, 1980). Bradbrook does not accept the connection without first discussing the evidence in favor of so doing (see p. 28 et seq.).

69. See Campion's *Observations in the art of English Poesy* and also Daniel's reply, *Defense of Rhyme.*

70. Brian Morris, "Introduction," *The Broken Heart,* New Mermaids edition (London: Ernest Benn Ltd., 1965), ix. Martin Butler comes to the same conclusion in his *"Love's Sacrifice:* Ford's Metatheatrical Tragedy," in *John Ford: Critical Re-Visions,* ed. Michael Neill, (Cambridge: Cambridge University Press, 1988).

71. Writes Butler:

> Very little is known about the life of John Ford, but the little that is certain establishes firmly his long and intimate connection with the Inns of Court . . . playwriting seems to have been incidental to a career in one of the legal professions . . . this [legal] environment must have had an effect on his writing . . . [and] this factor closely associates his literary work with that of the other two significant dramatists produced by the Middle Temple, Marston and Webster. (*Love's Sacrifice,* 206)

72. Shirley was rewarded by being given membership to Gray's Inn (Butler, "*Love's Sacrifice,*" 204).

73. *Histriomastix,* F3v.

74. Edward Hyde's roommate in his apartments at the Middle Temple through 1628 was the playwright William Davenant. State Papers, Domestic, Chas. I 126/42, reads,

> Mr Dauenant lodging in ye Middle Temple wth M^r. Hide; sonne to my Ld Chief Justice elder brother.

Another friend of Hyde was the dramatist Thomas May, author of *The Heir; Antigone, the Theban Princess; Julia Agrippina, Empress of Rome; Cleopatra, Queen of Egypt;* and *The Old Couple.* He took up lodgings in Gray's Inn on 6 August 1615.

75. 1:51–63. Whitelock became the lord keeper of the Great Seal. He also left behind a comment indicating his own passing interest in the public theatre:

Whenever I came to [Blackfriars] (as I did sometimes in those days), though not often, to see a play, the musicians would presently play *Whitelock's Coranto,* and it was so often called for that they would have played it twice or thrice in an afternoon. (qtd. in Charles Burney, *A General History of Music from the Earliest Ages to the Present Period* [London, 1782–89], 2:299).

76. Qtd. in Alan Wharam, *Treason: Famous English Treason Trials* (Gloucestershire, England: Alan Sutton Publishing Ltd., 1995), 12.

77. Lacey Baldwin Smith, *Treason in Tudor England: Politics and Paranoia* (Princeton: Princeton University Press, 1986), 268–69.

78. Brian Jay Corrigan, "The Legal Landscape of the Playhouse World." Paper presented at the thirtieth annual meeting of the *Shakespeare Association of America,* Minneapolis, 22 March 2002.

79. Andrew J. Gurr, "Ford and Contemporary Theatrical Fashion," *John Ford: Critical Re-Visions,* ed. Michael Neill, ed., (Cambridge: Cambridge University Press, 1988), 82.

80. A fascinating history of this venture may be found in S. P. Cerasano, "Competition for the King's Men? Alleyn's Blackfriars Venture," *Medieval and Renaissance Drama in England,* 4 (1989), 173–86.

81. See Gurr, *Playgoing,* 31. Davenant received the patent for the playhouse on 16 March 1639. It would probably have been built close to Temple Bar.

82. See, e.g., Jonson's *The Poetaster* and *Every Man Out of His Humour, Gismunde of Salerne, The Lover's Melancholy, The Roman Actor, Love's Sacrifice, The Picture, The Inner Temple Masque,* and *The Triumph of Peace.* It may also be worthy of note that Heminges and Condell's Epistle to the Reader of the First Folio seems to be appealing to readers of a legal turn of mind. It draws upon an obvious legal motif while referring to the two playhouses most favored by the law students:

> [T]hough you be a Magistrate of wit, and sit on the Stage at *Black-Friers,* or the *Cockpit,* to arraigne Playes dailie, know, these Playes haue had their triall alreadie, and stood out all Appeales; and do now come forth quitted rather by a Degree of Court, then any purchas'd Letters of commendation.

83. E.g. Quarlous from *Bartholomew Fair* refers to himself as a former member of the Inns of Court at 3.5.278; both Manly and Wittipol from *The Devil is an Ass* are living at Lincoln's Inn; Shallow, from *2 Henry IV,* is from Clement's Inn, an Inn of Chancery, and is probably a Grayan; Falstaff went to Clement's Inn; Richard Plantagenet lives at the Temple in *1 Henry VI;* the Præludium to Goffe's Salisbury Court play, *The Careless Shepherdess,* portrays "Spark, an Inns of Court gentleman" as a character/playgoer who is *au courant* with "the Laws of Comedy and Tragedy"; Throte from Barry's *Ram-Alley* refers to his days in the Inns of Court; Templars abound in Jasper Mayne's *The Citie Match,* and Inns-of-Court men are routinely ruined in Middleton's *Father Hubbard's Tales.*

84. For example, the famous rose scene from *1 Henry VI* occurs in the Middle Temple garden; Gray's Inn is referred to as the locus of the infamous fight between Shallow and Stockfish in *2 Henry IV;* and Lincoln's Inn figures prominently in the wooing scene from *The Devil is an Ass.* The pivotal scene in *The Staple of News* occurs in the Apollo Club of the Devil's Tavern, which was located within the precincts of the Middle Temple. Face, in *The Alchemist,* agrees

to meet Partinax Surely at the Round in the Temple. It is also possible that Prospero's speech in *The Tempest,*

> Our Revels now are ended. These our actors,
> As I foretold, were all spirits and
> Are melted into air, into thin air;
> And, like the baseless fabric of this vision,
> The cloud-capped towers, the gorgeous palaces,
> The solemn temples, the great globe itself,
> Yea, all which it inherit, shall dissolve,
> And, like this insubstantial pageant faded,
> Leave not a rack behind,

refers both to the revels popular among the gentry and to the areas along the Thames associated with revelry—the Tower (which often shot ordnance during the mock progresses of the Christmas Princes), Greenwich, Whitehall, Richmond palaces, the Middle and Inner Temples, and the Globe theatre. The suggestion has been made that Gray's Inn's *Russian Masque* of Twelfth Night, 1594/95, provided the inspiration for the action of Muscovites and blackamoors in 5.2 of *Love's Labour's Lost* (Richard David, *Love's Labour's Lost,* 4th ed. Arden [London: Methuen Press, 1951], xxx–xxxi). It is also possible that the visored, flambeaux-carrying law students who paraded through London during their revels inspired the two sets of masquing young gentlemen in *Romeo and Juliet* and *The Merchant of Venice.*

CHAPTER 2. TRICKS AND QUILLETS

1. Joseph Quincy Adams, *Shakespearean Playhouses* (repr., Gloucester, Mass.: Peter Smith, 1960). 65–66.
2. The Red Lion venture featured its own series of litigations involving Brayne with his carpenters, the details of which are to be found in William Ingram, *The Business of Playing: The Beginnings of the Adult Professional Theater in Elizabethan London* (Ithaca: Cornell University Press, 1992).
3. Qtd. in Adams, *Shakespearean Playhouses,* 61.
4. Ibid., 64–65.
5. C. W. Wallace, "The First London Theatre: Materials for a History," 13 *University Studies* 13, nos. 1, 2, 3 (1913, Lincoln, Nebraska).
6. Ibid. See also Herbert Berry, "A Handlist of Documents about the Theatre in Shoreditch," *The First Public Playhouse: The Theatre in Shoreditch 1576–1598,* ed. Herbert Berry (Montreal: McGill-Queen's University Press, 1979).
7. William Ingram, *A London Life in the Brazen Age: Francis Langley, 1548–1602* (Cambridge: Harvard University Press, 1978).
8. Ibid., 108.
9. E. K. Chambers, *The Elizabethan Stage* (Oxford, 1923), 4:316.
10. Adams, *Shakespearean Playhouses,* 164. Adams relies upon the survey of the Manor of Paris Garden made in 1627, which depicts the site of the playhouse.

11. This is, of course, De Witt's famous description of the most eminent (*omnium prestantissimum*) and most ample (*amplissimum*) amphitheatre in England, the Swan (*cignus [vulgo Le Theater off te cijn]*). Transcription from Joyce I. Whalley, "The Swan Theatre in the 16th Century," *Theatre Notes* 20, no. 2 (winter 1965/66), 73. Also qtd., with orthographic variants, in Chambers, *Elizabethan Stage*, 2:362.

12. Chambers, *Elizabethan Stage*, 2:131 et seq.

13. Ibid., 2:132–33. This reasonable assumption is likewise reached by W. W. Greg in his *Henslowe's Diary* (London, A. H. Bullen, 1904–1908), 2:186–87; and Ingram, Brazen Age, 187.

14. Chambers, *Elizabethan Stage*, 2:132–33.

15. All quotations from the suit are taken from C. W. Wallace, "The Swan Theatre and the Earl of Pembroke's Players," *Englische Studien* 43 (1911): 340 et seq. A cogent description of these legal proceedings is to be found in Ingram, *Brazen Age*, 187–91.

16. For a more complete discussion of the merits of the players' replies see Brian Jay Corrigan, "Of Dogges and Gulls: Sharp Dealing at the Swan (1597) . . . and Again at St. Paul's (1606)," *Theatre Notebook* 55, no. 3 (2001): 219–29.

17. Carol Chillington Rutter, ed., *Documents of the Rose Playhouse* (Manchester, England: Manchester University Press, 1999), 125–26.

18. Chambers, *Elizabethan Stage*, 2:133.

19. Qtd. in Adams, *Shakespearean Playhouses*, 175.

20. For an analysis of the playhouse, its management, and history see Herbert Berry. *The Boar's Head Playhouse* (Washington, D.C.: Folger Books, 1986); and C. J. Sisson, *The Boar's Head Theatre: An Innyard Theatre of the Elizabethan Age*, ed. Stanley Wells (London: Routledge & Kegan Paul, 1972).

21. Ingram, *Brazen Age*, 239.

22. Ibid.

23. Ibid., 241.

24. Ibid., 265.

25. Ibid., 267.

26. Public Record Office (PRO), C.2.Jas I/L.13/62, Browker's answer.

27. See, e.g., Samuel Rowlands's *The Letting of Humours Blood in the Head-Vaine*, Satire 4. 63 (*Works*, I):

> What meanes *Singer* then?
> And *Pope* the Clowne, to speak so Boorish, when
> They counterfeit the Clownes vpon the Stage?

28. *Shakespeare in the Public Records,* Pulbic Records Office Handbook No. 5, (London: Her Majesty's Stationery Office, 1964), 13–14. See also Brian Jay Corrigan, "A Legal Dodge in the Business Practices of the Original Globe and Drury Lane Theatres," *Theatre Notebook* 51, no. 2 (spring 1997): 72–74. In the latter work, I labored under the misconception that the partners were attempting to create a use in the property. While a use was certainly employed in the Drury Lane transfer, which is the point of the article, this discussion supersedes my earlier assumption that such was also the case with the Globe.

29. William Blackstone, *Commentaries on the Laws of England*, vol. 2 (repr., Chicago: University of Chicago Press, 1979), 180–82.

30. *Witter v. Heminges,* 1619–20, qtd. in C. W. Wallace, "Shakespeare's Money Interest in the Globe Theater," *The Century Magazine* 80, no. 4 (August 1910): 507.

31. Blackstone, *Commentaries,* 2:193.

32. Ibid., 2:186, citing Thomas Littleton, *Tenures* §304.

33. Wallace, "Shakespeare's Money," 510.

34. See Leslie Hotson, "John Jackson and Thomas Savage," in his *Shakespeare's Sonnets Dated, and other essays* (New York: Oxford University Press, 1949), 127.

35. Qtd. in E. A. J. Honigmann and Susan Brock, *Playhouse Wills 1558–1642* (Manchester, England: Manchester University Press, 1993), 74.

36. Edwin Nungezer has noted this as a punning allusion to the Globe transaction. See his *Dictionary of Actors* (Ithaca: Cornell University Press, 1929), 219.

37. See, e.g., Andrew J. Gurr, *The Shakespearean Stage 1574–1642,* 3rd ed. (Cambridge: Cambridge University Press, 1992), 45–49.

38. Mark Eccles, "Elizabethan Actors II: E-J," *NQ* 30 (December 1991): 458.

39. Honigmann and Brock, *Playhouse Wills,* 86, 87.

40. Adams, *Shakespearan Playhouses,* 238.

41. *Coram Rege Rolls,* Easter, 7 James I, membrane 456.

42. Irwin Smith, *Shakespeare's Blackfriars Playhouse: Its History and Design* (New York: New York University Press, 1964), Doc. 40, p. 516.

43. Cf. Harold Newcomb Hillebrand, "The Child Actors," *University of Illinois Studies in Language and Literature* 11, no. 2 (Urbana: University of Illinois Press, 1926), 205 ("[Kirkham] waited until all was quiet and to some extent forgotten and his erstwhile partner Kendall was dead, before stirring up old history with the hope of extracting some tidbits for himself.")

44. Smith, *Shakespeare's Blackfriars Playhouse,* Doc. 17, p. 467.

45. Ibid., 468.

46. Chambers, *Elizabethan Stage,* 2:41–42.

47. Ibid., 182.

48. *Star Chamber Proceedings,* Elizabeth, Bundle C 46, No. 39 (qtd. in Smith, *Shakespeare's Blackfriars Playhouse,* Doc. 24, pp. 484–86).

49. *Chancery Proceedings,* James I, Bills and Answers, K 5, No. 25. See Smith, *Shakespeare's Blackfriars Playhouse,* Doc. 43, p. 534–46.

50. *Keysar v. Burbage et al., Court of Requests Proceedings,* James I, uncalendared. Printed in Smith, *Shakespeare's Blackfriar's Playhouse,* Doc. 41, pp. 520–26.

51. W. Reavley Gair, *The Children of Paul's: The Story of a Theatre Company, 1553–1608* (Cambridge: Cambridge University Press, 1982), 155. But see William Ingram, "The Playhouse as an Investment, 1607–1614: Thomas Woodford and Whitefriars," *Medieval & Renaissance Drama in England* 2 (1985), 225, 227–28, wherein the author suggests that Woodford had very little contact with Paul's and in fact did nothing more than broker the purchase for performance of Chapman's *Old Joiner of Aldgate.*

52. *Coram Rege,* Easter, 4 James I, fol. 536:

London. Thomas Woodforde gen*erosus* queri*tur* de Edwardo Peerce in Custo*dia* Mar*rescalli* Marescal*sie* domi*ni* Regis coram ipso Rege existen*te* de eo q*uo*d ipse secundo die

Decembris Anno Regni d*omi*ni Jacobi nunc Regis Angl*ie* secundo vi & armis &c in ip*sum* Thomam Woodforde apud london ... in pace dei & d*i*cti d*omi*ni Regis adtunc & ib*i*d*e*m existen*tem* insult*um* fecit Et ip*sum* Thomam adtunc & ib*i*dem ver*b*erauit vulnerauit & maletratauit Ita q*uo*d de vita eius des*per*abat*ur* Et alia enormia ei intulit contra pacem d*i*cti d*omi*ni Regis nunc ad dampn*um* ipsius Thome Centu*m* librar*um,* etc.

53. Note Paul's remarkable stock that was liquidated in the three-month period from May to August 1607 (table is adapted from Hillebrand, "Child Actors," 213.

Play	*Author*	*Licensing Date*
Satiromastix	Dekker	11 November 1601
Blurt, Master Constable	Dekker(?)	7 June 1602
Westward Ho!	Dekker & Webster	2 March 1605
Parasitaster	Marston	12 March 1606
The Phoenix	Middleton	9 May 1607
Michaelmas Term	Middleton	15 May 1607
The Woman Hater	Beaumont & Fletcher	20 May 1607
Bussy D'Ambois	Chapman	3 June 1607
Northward Ho!	Dekker & Webster	6 August 1607
The Puritan	Middleton(?)	6 August 1607
Trick to Catch the Old One	Middleton	7 October 1607
A Mad World, My Masters	Middleton	4 October 1608

54. Brian Jay Corrigan, "Middleton, *The Revenger's Tragedy,* and Crisis Literature," *Studies in English Literature* 38, no. 2 (spring 1998), 281–95.
55. See Smith, *Shakespeare's Blackfriars Playhouse,* 192.
56. See Ibid., 190–91. The annuity was probably a combination of a Royal gift (to be paid by others) and a gratuity from the syndicate for Daniel's efforts in acquiring the patent.
57. Gair, *Children of Paul's,* 185.
58. Adams, *Shakespearean Playhouses,* 217; Nungezer, *Dictionary of Actors,* 227–28.
59. Frederick Gard Fleay, *Biographical Chronicle of the English Drama 1559–1642* (New York: Burt Franklin Press, 1891), 1:91; Chambers, *Elizabethan Stage,* 2:52; Smith, *Shakespeare's Blackfriar's Playhouse,* 192–93.
60. *Decl. Accts.,* Pipe Office Roll 543, fol. 137:

To Samuel Daniell and Henrie Evans uppon the Counsells warraunte dated at thee Courte at Whitehalle xxiiij^{to}die ffebruarij 1604 [1605] for two Enterludes or plaies presented before the kinges Ma*ies*tie by the Queenes Ma*iest*s Children of the Revells the one on Newyers daie at night 1604 [1605] and the other on the third daie of Januarie followinge xiij^{li}vj^{s}viij^{d}and by the waye of his highnes rewarde vj^{li}xiij^{s}iiij^{d}in all xx^{li}.

61. Chambers, *Elizaethan Stage,* 2:51.
62. Although Harbage and Schoenbaum in their *Annals of English Drama 975–1700* list *Bussy D'Ambois* as a Paul's play, they are relying upon this court performance to mark it so. Chapman, like Marston, was a playwright for the Blackfriars children at this time and even predated Marston as such. With the singular exception of the specially commissioned play, *The Old Joiner of Aldgate* (1603), Chapman was remarkably steady with the Blackfriars company. From 1602 to 1610 he appears to have written all of his single-authored works only

for them, even surviving the transfer from Evans to Keysar and then to Rosseter. For a complete rehearsal of the peculiar commission for *The Old Joiner of Aldgate* see Gair, *Children of Paul's,* 147–51.

63. See, inter alia, Hillebrand, "Child Actors," 196.

64. William Ingram, "Robert Keysar, Playhouse Speculator," *Shakespeare Quarterly* 37, no. 4 (winter 1986), 476–85.

65. Public Records Office, REQ. 2/155/13. See Ingram, "Robert Keysar," 480.

66. Book O, pp. 130–32; 153, 179, 222, 274, 305, 320, 325, 335, 336, 398, 414, 433, 441. See Ingram, "Robert Keysar," 481 et. seq.

67. Harold Newcomb Hillebrand, "Thomas Middleton's *The Viper and Her Brood,*" *MLN* 42, no. 1 (January 1927), 35–38.

68. Ingram, "Robert Keysar," 482.

69. Smith, *Shakespeare's Blackfriars Playhouse,* 546.

70. Hillebrand, "Child Actors," 200.

71. Qtd. in Chambers, *Elizabethan Stage,* 3:257–58.

72. Robert M. Wren, "Salisbury and the Blackfriars Theatre," *Theatre Notebook* 23, no. 3 (spring 1969), 103–9, esp. 107.

73. Qtd. in Chambers, *Elizabethan Stage,* 2:53–54.

74. See Ingram, "Playhouse as Investment."

75. The particulars of the King's Revels venture may be found in Chambers, *Elizaebethan Stage,* 2:64–68; and in Debra Brown Young, "King's Revels," Ph.D. diss. 30, Tulane University, 1986.

76. Qtd. in Ingram, "Playhouse as Investment," 211.

77. Ibid., 212.

78. Ibid.

79. C. L'Estange Ewen, *Lording Barry, Poet and Pirate* (London, 1938).

80. Burbage testified on 2 November 1612 that "about the first year of his Majesty's reign—there having been . . . great visitation of sickness . . . and by reason thereof no such profit and commodity raised and made of and by said playhouse as was hoped and expected, the said Evans, as it seemed, grew weary and out of liking with the interest and term of years which he had in the said playhouse, and thereupon some speech and treaty was had with [Burbage] about the surrendering and giving up of the said lease." Qtd. in Smith, *Shakespeare's Blackfriars Playhouse,* 539.

81. Ibid., 532.

82. Ibid., xxx.

83. Qtd. in, with interpolation by, Adams, *Shakespearean Playhouses,* 219.

84. See Wren, "Salisbury and the Blackfriars Theatre."

85. John Day, *The Ile of Gvls,* Shakespeare Association Facsimiles, No. 12, 1936, Sig. B.

86. Wren, "Salisbury and the Blackfriars Theatre," 108.

87. Court of Requests Proceedings, James I, uncalendared. The text of the suit may be found in Smith, *Shakespeare's Blackfriars Playouse,* 520–26.

88. Rejoinder of the defendants dated 19 June 1610.

89. See discussion above at note 65.

90. Qtd. in Smith, *Shakespeare's Blackfriars Playhouse,* Doc. 36, p. 509.

91. *Chancery Proceedings,* James I, Bills and Answers, Bundle E4, No. 9, §18.

92. From a purely legal standpoint, had these litigants been as hostile as many commentators assert, we should expect to find a writ of attachment, or

indeed several such writs, seeking sureties of the peace against one another. See, e.g., Public Records Office, Handbook No. 5 (London: Her Majesty's Stationery Office, 1964), 8. "Many thousands of such writs issued to the Sheriffs of the different counties in Elizabethan England." That none are found on the Controlment Roll may not be dispositive, but such absence is certainly suggestive that these litigants were not in fear of one another nor necessarily attempting to harass each other with nuisance arrests, fictitious complaints, and annoyance bonds of surety.

93. M. E. Smith, "Personnel at the Second Blackfriars: Some Biographical Notes," *NQ* 30 (October 1978): 442.

Chapter 3. Thy Love's Use Their Treasure

1. It would, however, appear that Shakespeare was far more interested in the doctrine of the use as an image than a legal document. Note his bawdy rendering of the legal concept in the final couplet of Sonnet 20:

> But since she [Nature] prick'd thee out for women's pleasure,
> Mine be thy love, and thy love's use their treasure.

Here Shakespeare suggests that the beloved male make the poet *feoffee to uses* of his love while women have the beneficial enjoyment of the young man's body.

2. 4.1.379–84 [emphasis supplied]. The use was tied up with another legal concept called a perpetuity. This passage has often been cited in that light. Sir Dunbar Plunket Barton, in his *Links Between Shakespeare and the Law* (Boston: Houghton Mifflin, 1929), p. 76, sees another contemporaneous reference to *Chudleigh's Case* (also called the *Case of Perpetuities*) in *All's Well That Ends Well* 4.3.292–95, when Parolles says that the Captain "for a carecue . . . will sell the fee-simple of his salvation, the inheritance of it, and cut th'entail from all remainders, and a perpetual succession for it perpetually."

3. Jan Lawson Hinley, "Bond Priorities in The Merchant of Venice" *Studies in English Literature* 20 (1980): 228.

4. Marc Shell, "The Wether and the Ewe: Verbal Usury in The Merchant of Venice," *Kenyon Review* 1, no. 4 (1979): 65 [interpolation in the original].

5. J. R. Brown, ed., *Arden Shakespeare Edition: The Merchant of Venice*, (Cambridge: Harvard University Press, 1955), 119.

6. This sort of conveyance is not, in fact, a use at all. If Antonio were asking Shylock to divest himself of the rents and profits of his estate in Antonio's favor while retaining the title, he would be asking for a grant with a reservation from Shylock. The controlling precept in such a case would be *reservatio non debet esse de proficuis ipsis, quia ea conceduntur, sed de reditu novo extra proficua*. Antonio, however, clearly states that he is requesting a use. Shakespeare appears to have known the difference between a use and a reservation. In *King Lear* the essential transfer of land to Goneril and Regan is such a grant with a reservation. Lear creates the reservation patently:

> I do invest you jointly with my power,
> Pre-eminence, and all the large effects

> That troop with majesty. Ourself, by monthly course,
> With *reservation* of an hundred knights,
> By you to be sustained, shall our abode
> Make with you by due turn. Only we shall *retain*
> The name, and all th' addition to a king. The sway,
> Revenue, execution of the rest,
> Beloved sons, be yours.
>
> (1.1.132–40) [emphasis supplied]

Therefore, Lear is reserving the literal title of king along with one hundred knights to himself while conveying the governance and inccme of the realm to his sons-in-law. Later, Shakespeare has Lear iterate his legally-correct expression:

> I gave you all ...
> Made you my guardians, my depositories,
> But kept a *reservation* to be followed
> With such a number.
>
> (2.4.249–52) [emphasis supplied]

The conveyance Antonio requires must not be one in which Shylock retains the title—as in a *King Lear*-type reservation—but rather one that aliens his title to a *feoffee to uses* and conveys the use to a *cestui que use,* either to someone else or to himself, in accord with the purpose of a use.

7. Although I developed this interpretation of the use conveyance in *The Merchant of Venice* independently, I have since discovered that my reading is attested in both George Williams Keeton, *Shakespeare's Legal and Political Background* (New York: Pitman, 1967), 146; and Owen Hood Phillips, *Shakespeare and the Lawyers* (London: Methuen, 1972), p. 117. The latter work relies upon the findings of the former in this instance.

8. Kenelm Edward Digby, *An Introduction to the History of the Law of Real Property,* 3rd ed. (Oxford, 1884). 284–85; Richard C. Maclaurin, *On the Nature and Evidence of Title to Realty* (London: C. J. Clay, 1901), 137. In his *History of English Law* (London: Methuen, 1936–1971), 4:425–26, W. S. Holdsworth demonstrates that consideration of natural love and affection was not accepted as sufficient consideration to raise a use until the late sixteenth century, just before the writing of *The Merchant of Venice*. The relevant case law is found in *Sharington v. Strotten* (1565), Plowden, 298; *Callard v. Callard* (1597), 2 Anderson, 64.

9. Alice N. Benston, "Portia, the Law, and the Tripartite Structure of The Merchant of Venice." *Shakespeare Quarterly* 30 (1979): 379.

10. Sir Frederick Pollock and Frederic William Maitland, *History of the English Law Before the Time of Edward I,* 2nd ed. (reissued, London: Cambridge University Press, 1968), 2:234.

11. Alfred William Brian Simpson, *An Introduction to the History of the Land Law,* 2nd ed. (Oxford: Oxford University Press, 1973), 174.

12. See the discussion infra at note 22 and accompanying text for the Renaissance dramatic rendering of this particular problem.

13. E. W. Ives, "The Genesis of the Statute of Uses," *English Historical Review* 82 (1967): 673. The statute caused dissent because it disallowed the separation of the legal title, formerly held by the *feoffee* to uses, from the equitable

estate, formerly held by the *cestui que use*. The statute was primarily aimed at raising money for the Crown by preventing the avoidance of feudal dues. The Crown's intervention caused unrest because avoidance of feudal dues was the very reason many landowners created the use in the first place. The statute had a secondary effect of preventing fraud against private persons (as when a use was created to avoid levy against property in a private suit). This secondary effect was, in itself, unobjectionable; but the statute also prevented devise of land by will, tacitly reinstating a rule of primogeniture and removing the other major reason a landowner might wish to create a use.

14. Sir Francis Bacon, *Reading on the Statute of Uses* (New York: Garland, 1979), 416. Edward Coke had earlier, in 1593, planned a reading on the Statute of Uses before the Inner Temple. See John Bruce Williamson, *The History of the Temple, London* (London: John Murray, 1925), 209–10.

15. Ibid.

16. Simpson, *History of the Land Law,* 188.

17. Bacon, *Statue of Uses,* 395.

18. Coke's 1593 Reading on the Statute of Uses at the Inner Temple was canceled due to a visitation of the plague, which sent the Temple parliaments to St. Albans in November. A.P. 2:16–17; D.232.

19. Indeed, according to Paul Clarkson and Clyde Warren, "The Statute of Uses was passed little more than fifty years before Shakespeare began writing, and of course uses and the Statute were very live and important subjects to lawyers throughout the period of the drama considered." *The Law of Property in Shakespeare and the Elizabethan Drama* (New York: Gordian Press, 1968), 139.

20. Barbara Everett, "Antony and Cleopatra," *The Complete Signet Classics: Shakespeare,* gen. ed. Sylvan Barnet (New York: Harcourt Brace Jovanovich, 1972), 1273.

21. Anthony S. Brennan, "Excellent Dissembling: Antony and Cleopatra Playing at Love," *Midwest Quarterly* 19 (1977–78): 314.

22. Although the Statute of Uses was modified by the Statute of Enrollment, which required conveyances in use to be "made by writing indented, sealed, and enrolled in one of the King's Court of Record" (27 *Henry VIII,* c. 16 [1535]), the requirement of written proof was easily circumvented by employing a device known as lease and release. See Clarkson and Warren's excellent discussion of these maneuverings in *Law of Property,* 137–39.

23. Michael Jamieson says, "This speech of Dame Purecraft's is the greatest admission of Puritan deviousness in the play." *Ben Jonson: Three Comedies* (Harmondsworth, England: Penguin Books Ltd., 1985), 487.

24. It is helpful to bear in mind that Jonson was the first playwright in English history to have designed a volume of his works for study. It has been pointed out that he intended "to be *read,* not merely heard." Douglas M. Lanier, "The Prison-House of the Canon: Allegorical Form and Posterity in Ben Jonson's *The Staple of News," Medieval & Renaissance Drama in England,* 2 (New York: AMS Press, 1985), 253. See also Richard Helgerson, "The Elizabethan Laureate: Self-Presentation and the Literary System," *ELH* 46 (1979): 206–7, and *Self-Crowned Laureates: Spenser, Jonson, Milton, and the Literary System* (Berkeley: University of California Press, 1980), 145–47.

25. Jonson apparently believed that his audience was familiar enough with the concept of use conveyances to develop an off-handed, bawdy joke around a use transfer, "A to B for the use of A." In *Epicoene (circa* 1609) *(Regents Renaissance Drama Series,* ed. L. A. Beaurline, [Lincoln: University of Nebraska Press, 1966]), Truewit says,

> This too, with whom you are to marry, may have made a conveyance of her virginity aforehand, as your wise widows do of their states, before they marry, *in trust* to some friend, sir.
>
> (2.2.132–35)

This is not unlike the jest recorded in Middleton's *The Phoenix (circa* 1604) (ed. John Bradbury Brooks [New York: Garland, 1980]) which also relies upon the audience's understanding of the legal term to appreciate the pun:

> FALSO. Here are the foils; come, come, sir; I'll try a law-bout with you.
> TANGLE. I am afraid I shall overthrow you, sir, i'faith.
> FALSO. 'Tis but for want of use then, sir.
> TANGLE. Indeed, that same odd word, *use,* makes a man a good lawyer, and a woman an arrant.
>
> (2.3)

26. *The Complete Plays of Ben Jonson,* ed. G. A. Wilkes (Oxford: Clarendon Press, 1982), 1.2., 1.5.16–18.

27. 3.3.132–34. Most editors and many commentators have scrupulously avoided the legal imagery in this play. It is interesting to note, as an example, the Yale Studies in English edition of *The Devil is an Ass,* ed. William Savage Johnson (New York: Henry Holt and Company, 1905). Although it was written during the height of the Bacon-Shakespeare controversy, when legal imagery in Renaissance drama should have been of primary interest, the Yale edition is entirely silent on this crucial point. Not one of the passages quoted in this discussion is noted in that edition.

28. 4.5.15–16. Clarkson and Warren are quick to point out that "although Jonson speaks of feoffment, deed of feoffment, feoffee, and letter of attorney for livery of seisin, there was here no livery of seisin by either Fitzdotterel or his attorney." *Law of Property,* 117. This problem need not presuppose Jonson's misunderstanding of the conveyance in use. Indeed, Jonson seems well able to use the law accurately in other plays as well as in this play. Fitzdotterel's description of the legal arrangements must be weighed with other instances of his inability to understand what is happening around him. Further, the lawyer in question is not Fitzdotterel's attorney, but Merecraft's—see 4.5.13–14. The discussion of the legal arrangement, therefore, should be looked upon as yet another occasion to demonstrate Fitzdotterel's inability to function in a world where cozeners outstrip even the Devil.

29. 4.6.42–46, 50–52. Clarkson and Warren suggest that "Meercraft is perfectly correct in saying that a feoffment to the 'Spanish lady' would not be valid. In the first place, there was no Spanish lady; and, in the second place, even apart from any fraud, the mistake would be sufficient to invalidate it." *Law of Property,* 117, citing Maclaurin, *Title to Realty,* 36; and Bracton, *On the Laws and Customs of England,* ed. George E. Woodbine, trans. Samuel E. Thorne (Cam-

bridge: Harvard University Press, 1968), f. 396b. The reference may also be to the incapacity of an alien to hold real estate, according to Clarkson and Warren, n. 80.

30. This would be true except, as will be discussed, Mrs. Fitzdotterel has no jointure and may well lose the estate entirely.

31. 3.3.64–67, 73–74. Middleton, in *A Chaste Maid in Cheapside,* seems to allude to the same injunction against dueling when a servant says to Whorehound, who has been wounded in a duel, "You're like to lose your land / If the law save your life sir, or the surgeon" (5.1.139–40). This evidence tends to support Richard Levin's argument favoring a later date, perhaps around 1614, for Middleton's play. Richard Levin, *The Multiple Plot in English Renaissance Drama* (Chicago: University of Chicago Press, 1971), 247.

32. Clarkson and Warren ask, "[W]hy should Fitzdotterel resort to a feoffment in trust at all, instead of simply making a will? The answer to this is that dramatically a will would not fit in with the frauds being practiced by Meercraft." *Law of Property,* 141. While their point about fraudulent intent in the play is well taken, they seem to have nodded in regards to the will. If Fitzdotterel is successful and kills Wittipol in the duel, the king's edict and proclamation would act to seize his estate and leave him nothing. It is also possible that his estate would be confiscated even if he lost the duel. The law on the matter is unclear, but the conveyance in use is certainly the most obvious trick to keep his land while breaking the law.

33. Ibid., 140–41.

34. Ibid.

35. An attempt that would not have worked in any case. The rules in *Beverley's Case,* 4 Co. Rep. 123b, 73 Eng. Reprint, 1118; *Thompson v. Leach,* Comb. 438, 90 Eng. Reprint, 577; and *Thompson v. Leach,* 12 Mod. 173, 88 Eng. Reprint, 1243, all hold that in cases of *non compos mentis* a feoffment could be set aside by a committee for the grantor or the grantor's heir, but not by the grantor himself after he has recovered his mental capacity. See the discussions in Digby, *Law of Real Property,* 359 n. 1; Maclaurin, *Title to Realty,* 152 n. 1; Joshua Williams, *Principles of the Law of Personal Property, Intended for the Use of Students in Conveyancing* (London: S. Sweet, 1848), 357; and Clarkson and Warren, *Law of Property,* 119. It is possible that Jonson attempts to create such a committee of Eitherside, Gilthead et al. in act five. But because Fitzdotterel is then in the throes of trying to prove his mentally deficient condition (by reason of satanic possession much like Voltore in the final act of *Volpone*) it would be impossible for them to determine whether he was *non compos mentis* at the time of the transfer.

36. 4.7.78–9. The use has made him a financial cuckold rather than the usual meaning of the word. A paramour has usurped his place with his wife in a financial dealing. As such, the play demonstrates a far different sort of morality, and Jonson succeeds at exactly the point where Knoll says he fails (Robert E. Knoll, *Ben Jonson's Plays: An Introduction* [Lincoln: University of Nebraska Press, 1964], 169). Says Knoll, "In place of cuckolding Fitzdotterel, his avowed purpose in the early acts of the play, Wittipol now suddenly rescues Mistress Fitzdotterel and awakens her husband to an awareness of his own foolishness. For constancy's sake, if for no other reason, Wittipol should have persisted in

his plans: Fitzdotterel deserved cuckolding and his wife had earned a lover." Not only does Mrs. Fitzdotterel refuse Wittipol as a lover in the relevant earlier scene but also Fitzdotterel is cuckolded in a far more sophisticated manner, leading again to Jonson's thesis in the play that the Londoners have vices and devices far beyond the ken of devils.

37. This construction of the working of the use within the plot accounts for the otherwise confusing explanation Manly offers in the final line of the play when he suggests both Mr. and Mrs. Fitzdotterel share the property:

> His land is his: and never, by my friend,
> Or by myself, meant to another use,
> But for her succours who hath equal right.
>
> (5.8.163–65)

38. Eugene M. Waith, "Things as They Are and the World of Absolutes," *The Elizabethan Theatre IV,* ed. George Hibbard (Hamden, Conn.: Archon Press, 1972), 116.

39. Ben Jonson, *The Staple of News,* ed. Anthony Parr (Manchester, England: Manchester University Press, 1988), 60 n. 113. All line references are to this, the Revels edition.

40. Dryden included it among Jonson's other late plays when he referred to the aging poet's "dotages." Madeleine Doran, in her *Endeavors of Art: A Study of Form in Elizabethan Drama* (Madison: University of Wisconsin Press, 1954), 365, pronounced it "intolerably dull." However, Swinburne considered it the "last magnificent work of his maturest genius." *The Complete Works of Algernon Charles Swinburne,* vol. 12: *A Study of Ben Jonson,* 54, ed. Edmund Gosse and Thomas James Wise (London: W. Heinemann, Ltd., 1926). The play seems to have been performed only twice during Jonson's lifetime and was withdrawn. See Parr's discussion in Jonson, *The Staples of News,* ed. Anthony Parr, 49–50.

41. 1.2.15, 18. The copyhold is an estate given by and at the will of the lord of the manor. William Blackstone, *Commentaries on the Laws of England* (Chicago: University of Chicago Press, 1979), 2:95. Therefore, this is the first of many suggestions of Pennyboy Junior's prodigality concerning the land he thinks he has inherited. It is, completely in keeping with Junior's character, a grandiose gesture that he may just as grandly retract.

42. 1.1.18–19. For a discussion of the double entendre, which does not affect this discussion, see Parr at p. 75 n. 19, Cf. *1 Henry IV,* 4.3.62, wherein Hotspur refers to Bolingbroke's former return from exile by saying he returned "to sue his livery."

43. *Law of Property,* 142.

44. 5.1.51. Parr glosses "hum" as "the 'buzz' of rumour," underscoring the specious nature of its full accuracy.

45. 5.1.99–104.

46. Note the significant double entendre.

47. 5.1.87–88. Note the possible allusion to the action preceding the restoration of the use conveyance in Philip Massinger's "A New Way to Pay Old Debts," (*the Selected Plays of Philip Massinger,* ed. Colin Gibson [New York: Cambridge University Press, 1978]), which may have been produced as early as five years

before *The Staple of News*. The relevant passage is discussed at note 73, *infra*, and in the accompanying text.

48. 5.1.108–11 [emphasis supplied]. The syntax is convoluted and the comma in line 109 troubling. The sense, however, is reasonably clear. Picklock is saying, "Have faith (trust) in the conveyance I have obtained (the trust/use). It is the trust (and the near impossibility of proving it was not a conveyance with livery of seisin) that will secure (for) you the absolute deed to the property in question." In line 110 the italicized phrase is the actual admission of the conveyance in use. The reason the document is constantly referred to as a trust rather than a use is twofold. First, Jonson uses the word *use* throughout the play (especially in the Pennyboy Senior sequences) to mean interest got of usury, and to apply the technically correct term, use, to the conveyance runs the risk of some confusion even among the lawyers in the audience. Second, Jonson generally prefers to nominate conveyances under the Statute of Uses as trusts, as discussed throughout this chapter, and that appellation is not incorrect. The term, trust, and its connotations of fair dealing and faithfulness, linguistically supports his misanthropic view of business dealings. Cf. Lanier, "Prison-House of the Canon," 266 n. 21, "*Trust* is a key word in the final act. It occurs only in the fifth act and there twenty times, plus a pun on 'truss'd.'"

49. 5.3.12, 14–15. Note the homophonic pun that Middleton also used in a similar situation in *A Trick to Catch the Old One* (ed. G. J. Watson [London: Ernest Benn Ltd., 1968]). See page 141, *infra,* and accompanying discussion.

50. For a full discussion of this theme, see Parr's discussion in his "Introduction" to *The Staple of News* at pp. 12–14, where he discusses the "resurrection of values which transform both the prodigal and the miser into liberal men" and concludes that Jonson offers "an unsentimental demonstration that prodigality is capable of being moderated into liberal virtue."

51. 4.3.13–15 [emphasis supplied]. Pecunia's relation to real property is underscored by Mirth, who identifies her in her emblematic context as "the daughter of earth." 2.int.29.

52. The ribbon bands holding the wax seal.

53. Spread open as legal documents.

54. See, e.g., Lanier, "Prison House of the Canon," 257 ff.

55. *Ben Jonson's Plays*, 173.

56. Ibid.

57. Lanier, "Prison-House of the Canon," 262, "By accenting the means of Picklock's overthrow, Jonson can stress that Pennyboy Canter's ideal of moderation *is* possible, that the moral man need not be vulnerable to men of policy if he approaches the question of moderate action pragmatically."

58. See the discussion of *The Phoenix* at note 25, supra.

59. Interestingly, the play seems to start where *Michaelmas Term* ends. In *Michaelmas Term,* Easy is cheated out of his country estate by play's end and is angry with himself at having been stupid enough to allow his own cozening. *A Trick to Catch the Old One* begins with such a disgruntled character learning the niceties of the law in order to gull his guller. The latter play, therefore, requires greater attention to the legal ramifications of cozenage. Consequently, law plays an important part in the imagery of the play, as can be detected in the quotations used in this discussion, but additionally the protagonist specif-

ically says, "Any trick, out of the law [i.e., anything legal]), now would come happily to me" (1.1.25–26). This requires the character to know the law in order both to use it and avoid running afoul of it.

60. Middleton's pun on the word, which means both "quibble" and "parcel of land."

61. Middleton, *A Trick to Catch the Old One,* 1.1.7–12. For "præmunire" see Blackstone's *Commentaries,* 4:103–17. A writ ultimately issued for any heinous offenses, but originally developed under Edward I to penalize papal usurpation of the king's authority in the domain.

62. Middleton only hints at this precise conclusion, which may be arrived at by comparing the following evidence:

> HOARD. Thou . . . canst defeat thy own nephew, Lucre, lap his lands into bonds, and take the extremity of thy kindred's forfeitures, because he's a rioter, a wastethrift, a brothel-master, and so forth. (1.2.25–28);
>
> LUCRE. For my strict hand toward his mortgage, that I deny not, I confess I had an uncle's pen'worth: let me see, half in half, true. I saw neither hope of his reclaiming, nor comfort in his being, and was it not then better bestowed upon his uncle, than upon one of his aunts? (2.1.6–11);
>
> LUCRE. (*ironically*). Why, do you think, i'faith, he was ever so simple to mortgage his lands to his uncle, or his uncle so unnatural to take the extremity of such a mortgage? (2.1.106–8).

63. When Lucre first learns of the wealthy widow and determines to reestablish a relationship with Witgood he says, "I hope he has not so much wit to apprehend that I cozened him: he deceives me then" (2.1.164–65).

64. See note 6, supra.

65. 4.2.60–63. Charles Barber's edition of the play (Berkeley: University of California Press, 1968) suggests that "[p]erhaps (since the Host is still present) the lines are spoken aloud, to force his uncle's hand" (95). If this interpolation is true, as seems likely under the circumstances, this action only demonstrates the dangers of raising the use orally and privately. The need to have the mortgage delivered freely, fully, and before witnesses is paramount if Witgood is to regain his property and live up to his name.

66. See note 22, supra, and accompanying discussion of lease and release.

67. This image of the guller gulled is a foil for the secondary plot line wherein Lucre's enemy-in-cozenage, Hoard, is allowed to trick himself into marrying the false widow, who is actually Witgood's punk.

68. *See* Marston Stevens Balch, *Middleton's A Trick to Catch the Old One and Massinger's A New Way to Pay Old Debts* (1633) (Salzburg: University of Salzburg, 1981), which demonstrates Massinger's reliance on Middleton's work in general.

69. Massinger, "A New Way to Pay Old Debts," 4.2.118–24, 26–27. One difficulty with reading a use conveyance of the land into this dialogue arises in the phrase, "urge him to produce / The deed in which you pass'd it over to him." There need not be any writing in the creation of a use conveyance. Again, as in both *A Trick to Catch the Old One* and *The Staple of News,* the question of who has the actual papers for the property becomes essential. The writing Overreach has would probably not detail the fact that the transaction was a use rather than a deed of sale. Overreach—the *feoffee to uses*—clearly intimates that he intends to

characterize the transfer as a feoffment with livery of seisin. The document in question, therefore, is most probably the original deed to the land, which was conveyed to Overreach (cf. "Wellborn was apt to sell" at 2.1.48 and "the witnesses are dead" at 4.1.200), but the relevant lines may be spoken ironically or deceitfully depending upon how one reads the context. However, because the document seems to have been drawn up specifically for the conveyance, two other possible explanations exist for this rather uncertain document (besides the distinct possibility that Massinger was not interested in the legal technicalities of his dramatic image). First, Overreach, with the aid of Marrall, has merely forged a document, which he now claims is the deed Wellborn passed over to him (the death of the "witnesses" therefore is a matter of convenience). If this is the case, Wellborn is being clever in suggesting that the forged document in Overreach's possession was given to him *in use,* which he may suspect will tie up the property in a lengthy court battle and render his uncle a Pyrrhic victory. Second, the deed could be understood to be the use conveyance as recorded under the Statute of Enrollments transferring the land that Overreach now incorrectly claims he is seized of by action of the Statute of Uses. In either case, the use is being employed to underscore the intrinsic character traits of both parties.

70. 5.1.165. Whether this deed is good or not, Overreach's modus operandi is to claim title to land he wants and then allow the rightful owner to spend all his means in court attempting to prove clear title. Although the *cestui que use* had a protected interest in the courts of Chancery after the fifteenth century, Chancery was notoriously expensive and slow to act. See, e.g., Overreach's boast earlier in the play in another context:

> I'll make my men break ope his fences,
> Ride o'er his standing corn, and in the night
> Set fire on his barns, or break his cattle's legs.
> These trespasses draw on suits, and suits expenses,
> Which I can spare, but will soon beggar him.
> When I have harried him thus two or three year,
> Though he sue *in forma pauperis,* in spite
> Of all his thrift, and care, he'll grow behind-hand.
>
> (2.1.35–42)

Dickens's description of Chancery's injustices in *Bleak House* was as relevant to the seventeenth century as to the nineteenth. Overreach may easily force Wellborn into court on a use conveyance without the necessity of setting fire to any barns and, owing to the vagaries of use conveyances in general, obtain the property by order of the court. This, of course, assumes that the conveyance really is in use, which is an area of some doubt.

71. 5.1.330–31. It might be significant to note that Massinger at this point took at least some pains to represent the rudiments of documentary conveyance accurately. When the box is opened and the "fair skin of parchment" revealed, Wellborn observes, "Indented, I confess, and labels too, / But neither wax, nor words" (5.1.185–86). The need for indention, sealing (with wax and ribbons (the latter often referred to as bands or labels)), and words is standard in such conveyances. Compare the relevant passage in the Statute of Enrollment, which requires use conveyances to be documented with "writing indented, sealed, and enrolled." See note 22, supra.

72. Michael Neill, "Massinger's Patriarchy: The Social Vision of *A New Way to Pay Old Debts*," *Renaissance Drama*, vol. 10, ed. Leonard Barkan (Evanston, Ill.: Northwestern University Press, 1979), 205.

73. The opening line of *A New Way to Pay Old Debts* is radically different from the opening of *A Trick to Catch the Old One*. In the latter instance Witgood is beaten and sorrowful, but he nevertheless demonstrates a caring affection for the young woman he has wronged. Wellborn is first seen in a tavern bellowing, "No booze? Nor no tobacco?" and engaging in a brawl requiring him to be thrust out of doors.

CHAPTER 4. I KNEW A WENCH

1. See, e.g., G. R. Hibbard, "Love, Marriage and Money in Shakespeare's Theatre and Shakespeare's England," *The Elizabethan Theatre VI*, ed. G. R. Hibbard (Waterloo, Ont.: Archon, 1975); Margaret Scott, "'Our City's Institutions': Some Further Reflections on the Marriage Contracts in *Measure for Measure*," *ELH* 49 (winter 1982): 790–804; Ann Jennalie Cook, *Making a Match: Courtship in Shakespeare and His Society* (Princeton: Princeton University Press, 1991), 185, 190–94.

2. Anne Barton, "'Wrying but a little': marriage, law and sexuality in the plays of Shakespeare," *Essays, Mainly Shakespearean* (Cambridge: Cambridge University Press, 1994), 4–5. What is of course missed in arguing that Shakespeare never calls a *de præsenti* union "marriage" is Biondello's line in *Shrew* wherein he says that he knew "a wench *married* in an afternoon as she went into the garden for parsley to stuff a rabbit" (4.4.99–101) [emphasis added]. This line in context, juxtaposed as it is to Biondello's news of a clandestine ceremony for Bianca and Lucentio to which he must "[t]ake the priest, clerk, and some sufficient honest witnesses" (4.4.94–95), clearly indicates that Shakespeare was not opposed to placing both forms of union into the category of marriage. Moreover, it must be noted, Shakespeare does not say that a *de præsenti* union *isn't* marriage. As the following arguments should reveal, he often clearly suggests the contrary.

3. For example, William Harrington, *Commendacions of matrymony* (1528), arguing on A4–A4^v that secret marriage "is forboden by the lawe," although if "one of the same [e.g., spouses created through such a union] forsake the other and take other they lyue in a dampnable aduoutry," and continues to say that a man so contracted

> maye not possesse the woman as his wyfe nor the woman the man as her husbonde nor inhabyte nor flesshely meddle togyther as man and wyfe: afore suche tyme as that matrymony be aproued and solempnysed by oure mother holy chyrche and yf they do in dede they synne deadly.

Harrington must be read as stating the Church's view rather than the State's. This is a minority view of the Church in viewing the sin as deadly—a sin of lust—rather than venial, which it was held by the time of the drama under consideration. The breach was often excused on payment of a fine or by public penance or both. The fourteenth-century *Instructions for Parish Priests* by John

Myre, Cotton MS Claudius A.II, fol. 129ᵛ, does follow an admonition to have couples wed in church and avoid irregular marriages with a separate, distinct injunction against lechery, "Of lechery telle hem ryght thys / That dedly synne for sothe hyt ys." Irregular marriages are earlier described as "cursed," to be sure, but not deadly. Erasmus called it a "little sin."

4. The most greatly misused of which is Henry Swinburne's *Treatise of Spousals or Matrimonial Contracts: Wherein All the Questions Relating to that Subject are Ingeniously Debated and Resolved,* a quarto edition of which was printed in London in 1686 but written before 1623, the date of Swinburne's death. Swinburne was an ecclesiastical lawyer, proctor of the ecclesiastical court at York, later commissary of the exchequer and judge of the consistory court. Though a treatise has a great deal of probative value, and a learned work like Swinburne's is most helpful, it must not be relied upon exclusively as a statement of the law. Like any published Observation or Commentary, Swinburne's work is not dispositive. It occupies a legal niche analogous to modern Supreme Court's *dicta* and is not in itself legally binding. It does represent an approach to a question at law, which seems to its author to have the effect of law. In drama, as in law school lectures, one should probably begin with what is called, in American jurisprudence, Black Letter law—that is, the illustrative or definitional approach to the law. If appropriate, and the facts at nand so require, one may veer from the absolute statements of the law and into the permutations and gray areas favored by students "putting of cases" at moots. The problem with Swinburne's *Treatise* has been its attractiveness to researchers in literature. Nearly every commentator on the marriages in *Measure for Measure,* for example, has used Swinburne's *Treatise* to discuss the troubling marriage contracts in that play. They have swallowed the attractive bait whole, and, like Claudio's rat, grown thirsty for the Truth, which its application to the play might reveal, drunk deeply, and died.

5. See, e.g., Cook, *Making a Match,* 191 n. 21, in which she cites Swinburne's *Treatise* §XIV to support her contention that secret marriages would not undermine subsequent public marriages. Though Swinburne does, indeed, say that this is the status of the law in certain circumstances, in the section in question Swinburne strongly opposes the philosophy underlying that law and cites the practice with extreme disapproval.

6. Margaret L. Ranald, "'As Marriage Binds, and Blood Breaks': English Marriage and Shakespeare," *Shakespeare Quarterly* 30 (winter 1979): 68–81; and also her *Shakespeare and his Social Context* (New York: AMS Press, 1987). See also Barton, "Wrying but a little," 10–11 (relying on Ranald). Ranald's discussion on this point fails to incorporate the legal need for an *exchange* of vows in 2.1, side-stepping the issue by suggesting that "Kate remains silent, and by the legal principle that 'silence means consent' she is considered to have agreed to the contract." This is clearly not a vow tantamount to matrimony, as Ranald contends, but rather a humorous railroading of Kate into a marriage set for Sunday to which she has *not* consented. Kate's final word on the matter, in fact, is, "I'll see thee hanged on Sunday first." Only Petruchio's fiction and Baptista's "give me your hands . . . 'Tis a match" create the betrothal. This engagement, however, falls far short of a present union. See, e.g., Swinburne's reference to canon law that "the single promise of either party alone doth not make spousals . . . the promises must be mutual" (§II.2).

7. Another Shakespearean Kate is also railroaded in like fashion. When King Henry V says, "Now, welcome, Kate; and bear witness all, / That here I kiss her as my sovereign queen" (5.2.357–58) he certainly seems to intend to be then and there married to her. The Queen's lines following seem to support this view of instant marriage, for she speaks of "God, the best maker of all marriages," and she says, "so be there 'twixt your kingdoms such a spousal." However, Henry then alludes to having to prepare "for our marriage, on which day . . . shall I swear to Kate." The context of the latter lines would appear to suggest that this sequence is to be understood as a betrothal cast in the form of a *de futuro* promise. The French princess, like Petruchio's Kate, offers neither assent at this time our objection. In both instances, Shakespeare does not seem overly concerned with questions of mutuality because in each instance no present marriage is required, the church service being specifically mentioned within the promises.

8. 5.2.31–43. Rosalind seems obsessed with the idea of incontinence after the contracting of marriage, and one of her most famous sequences includes a description of "who Time trots withal":

> Marry, he trots hard with a young maid between the contract
> of her marriage and the day it is solemnized: if the
> interim be but a sennight, Time's pace is so hard, that
> it seems the length of seven year.
>
> (3.2.304–7)

9. A further hint at the contract may be picked out of Oliver's earlier reference to "my sodaine wooing [and] her sodaine consenting" (5.2.7–8). Marriage *per verba de futuro* will be discussed below in detail.

10. H. C. Hart, *New Shakespeare Society Translation* (1877–79), (3:471).

11. See the discussion in the text accompanying notes 49 and 51.

12. Richard Whytforde, *A Werke for Husholders* (1530), warns that the devil "doth decyue many persones by the pretence and colour of matrimony, in pryuate and secrete contractes" (sig. E iii). Houlbrooke's comment on the quoted passage points to Whytforde's fear of the easy repudiation of such contracts "once lust was slaked" (*Church Courts,* 66).

13. See, e.g., Ralph Houlbrooke, "The Making of Marriage" in "Mid-Tudor England: Evidence from the Records of Matrimonial Contract Litigation," *Journal of Family History* (winter 1985): 339–52.

14. This admittedly strained quibble is occasioned by the juxtaposition of Schmidt's lexicographical entry 2, citing to this passage, and 3, which suggests a holder of an office on a commission. S.v. "Commission," in Alexander Schmidt, *Shakespeare Lexicon* (New York: Walter De Gruyter, 1971).

15. In an attempt to test the obscurity of this interpretation, I directed a production of *As You Like It* in the spring of 1992 with this interpretation firmly in mind. The performance for a non-legal audience did, indeed, demonstrate that a gratifying number of spectators understood that the two had married, at least in Rosalind's mind. This intuitive understanding of informal marriage is also attested by Lady Martin, in "Shakespeare's Female Characters," *Blackwood's Magazine* (October 1884): 428, when she says relevant to this passage, "I could never speak these words without a trembling in the voice, and the involuntary rushing of happy tears into the eyes, which made it necessary for me to turn my

head away from Orlando." It is perhaps not too great a leap to say that if a modern audience intuits a vague form of nuptial from these lines that an Elizabethan audience would have even more readily grasped the significance of this formally correct creation of a *de præsenti* contract.

16. Hymen refers to it as a wedding at l.147; Duke Senior at l. 173, and earlier at 5.2.15; Touchstone refers to the day as that in which he and Audrey will be married at 5.3.2; Orlando calls it the day Oliver and "Aliena" will marry at 5.2.46.

17. One might favorably compare this to the wedding masque Prospero stages for Miranda and Ferdinand in *The Tempest.* There again is Juno, this time with Ceres and Iris. Before that sequence Prospero utters his Miranda warning to Ferdinand not to break her virgin knot until the marriage can be solemnized (4.1.14–23). The end of that play also refers to the solemnization set for their marriage in Naples (5.1.307–9). No such future solemnization is mentioned in the pagan wedding feast of *As You Like It.*

18. William Blackstone, *Commentaries on the Laws of England,* vol. 1 (repr., Chicago: University of Chicago Press, 1979), 421–24.

19. Lord Hardwick's Marriage Act of 1753.

20. Pope from 1198 to 1216.

21. Blackstone, *Commentaries,* vol. 1, ch. 15, sec. 4. Cf. Swinburne's statement on the same topic:

> It is the consent alone of the parties whereby the knot is tied, and whereby this *desponsation* or *affiance* is sufficiently wrought, being the very substance (and as it were the Life and Soul) of this contract (§II.4).

22. Frederick Pollock and Frederic William Maitland, *History of the English Law, Before the Time of Edward I,* 2nd ed. reissued, (London: Cambridge University Press, 1968), 2:368–74; Richard Henry Helmholz, *Marriage Litigation in Medieval England* (Cambridge: Cambridge University Press, 1974), 38. But see Harold J. Berman, *Law and Revolution: The Formation of the Western Legal Tradition* (Cambridge: Harvard University Press, 1983), 226–30, wherein a convincing argument is made that the Canon law is, itself, a self-interested codification of convenient customary law. Hence, an initial problem arises as to the marriage law's earliest character, whether civil or ecclesiastical.

23. *Dictum* ad C. 27 q. 2 c. 34.

24. X 4.1.25; the Roman law formulation is *"Nuptias non concubitus, sed consensus facit."* Dig. 50.17.30 [Helmholz' note]. *Marriage Litigation,* 26. See also Swinburne §IV.3.

25. See, e.g., Lyndwood, *Provinciale,* 276 s.v. *clandestina: "Scias tamen quod in quolibet casuum predictorum tenet matrimonium contractum quoad deum nisi aliud perpetuum impedimentum obstet."* See also Willystine Goodsell, *A History of Marriage and the Family* (New York: Macmillan Co., 1935), 223.

26. *Die festi apostolorum Philippi et Jacobi ultimo preteriti fuit annus elapsus, fuit iste iuratus presens in domo Willelmi de Burton, alutarii Ebor, hora post nonam dicti diei quasi tertia, ubi et quando Johannes Beke sadeler Sedens super scannum, anglice "Le Sidebynke" dicte domus, vocavit ad se dictam Marioram de qua agitur et dixit sibi, "Sede mecum." Que dictis verbis acquiescens sedit; cui dictus Johannes dixit, "Marioria, vis tu esse uxor mea?" Ac illa re-*

spondit, "Volo si vos velitis." Et accipiens incontinenti dictus Johannes dexteram manum dicte Mariore dixit, "Marioria, hic accipio te in uxorem meam pro meliori et deteriori habendam et tenendam usque ad finem vite mee; te ad hoc do tibi fidem meam." Cui dicta Marioria respondit, "Hic accipio vos Johannem in virum meum habendum et tenendum usque ad finem vite mee, et ad hoc do vobis fidem meam" (Borthwick Institute of Historical Research, York Cause Papers, 121 [1372]).

27. M. M. Sheehan, "The Formation and Stability of Marriage in Fourteenth-century England: Evidence of an Ely Register," *Mediæval Studies* 33 (1971): 249–50.

28. Dean and Chapter Library, Canterbury Ecclesiastical Suit, no. 300 (1292).

29. Dean and Chapter Library, Canterbury Sede Vacante Scrapbook III, no. 35 (1293): *"in quodam campo . . . sub quadam arbore que vocatur haghelthorn."*

30. Dean and Chapter Library, Canterbury Y.1.1., Act book f. 103^r (1375): *"et fatetur se contraxisse matrimonium per verba de presenti cum Elizabeth Sontwyk de eadem et huiusmodi contractus fiebat in regia strata."*

31. York Minster Library, Dean and Chapter Court book f. 17^r (1382).

32. Dean and Chapter Library, Canterbury, Deposition book, f. 15^r (1412).

33. Ibid., f. 54^r (1414), and f. 121^v (1420).

34. *Hokerigge v. Lucas,* Dean and Chapter Library, Canterbury, Deposition book, fols. 95^r–95^v (1417), where the marriage was contracted *"ad quandam parvam silvam vocatam a grove."*

35. Borthwick Institute of Historical Research, York, Cause Papers, 172 (1427).

36. Ibid., 181 (1439).

37. Ibid., 252 (1472).

38. Ibid.

39. Guildhall Library, London, MS. 9065, Liber Examinationum, f. 51^v(1489).

40. F. J. Furnivall, *Child-Marriages, Divorces, and Ramifications etc. in the Diocese of Chester, A.D. 1561–66,* Early English Text Society, Original Series no. 108 (1897), li.

41. Houlbrooke, "The Making of Marriage," 339–52.

42. George Chapman, *The Gentleman Usher,* ed. John Hazel Smith (Lincoln: University of Nebraska Press, 1970), 4.2.122–47.

43. Henry Swinburne, *Treatise of Spousals or Matrimonial Contracts: Wherein All the Questions Relating to that Subject are Ingeniously Debated and Resolved,* (London, 1686), §IV.1.

44. This is perhaps the most consistently recurring theme in Swinburne's published opinion. See, e.g. §§XVI.6; XVI.9; XVII.6; XVII.11–20. See also Cook, *Making a Match,* 191–92.

45. A. Esmein, *Le Marriage en droit canonique* (Paris, 1891), 1:142–49. It is important to note that in a number of fifteenth- and sixteenth-century cases that do not apply a *res ipsa loquitur* treatment where coitus is admitted fail to do so because the defendants deny that a promise of marriage preceded the act. See, e.g., *Syblil Balkhurst v. Randle Ramshae,* 31 Jan. 1565/6, quoted in Furnivall, *Child-Marriages,* 210. See also Swinburne's comment at §XVII.22.

46. Precedent for this is found in a case out of Ely from 1379. Cambridge University Library, Registrum Primum, Act book, Ely, 1374–82, f. 119^v:

Dictus Philipus proposuit oretenus quod ipse et prefata Johanna matrimonium adinvicem contraxerunt per verba de presenti mutuum consensum eorum exprimencia, videlicet per ista verba, Ego volo habere te in uxorem et super hoc posuit fidem suam in manibus cuiusdam Johannis filii Thome de March, et ego volo habere te in virum.

Despite the niceties of the linguistic dispute, the court held for the validity of the marriage contract. But see Houlbrooke, "The Making of Marriage," 348, where Norwich records from the relevant period demonstrate defendants succeeding over plaintiffs at a rate of four to one because most plaintiffs "did not have enough witnesses or produced irrelevant or insufficient evidence."

47. See, e.g., the case cited *supra* at note 26, in which a witness relates the exchange of vows between John Beke and Marjory.

48. See the excellent treatment of this question by Eric Josef Carlson, "Marriage Reform and the Elizabethan High Commission," *Sixteenth Century Journal* 21 no. 7 (1990): 437–51, which concludes that

> the commissioners [who had been delegated the authority of the Supreme Governor of the Church of England] consistently upheld the authority of ordinary ecclesiastical courts to decide matrimonial litigation. As well, they reaffirmed the medieval canons as the basis upon which those cases would be decided, shutting and bolting the door against any possibility that England would follow the Protestant churches of the continent and of Scotland in reforming the law of marriage. Ultimately the commissioners took their instructions from the ever-conservative queen.

Carlson's conclusions, which are probably correct, only point to the state of confusion surrounding secret unions. Although the courts upheld evolving church authority in such cases, they applied the static medieval constructions of the ecclesiastical marriage law to do so.

49. E.g., *Ex officio c. Roebech,* Essex Act book, qtd. in Richard Henry Helmholz, *Roman Canon Law in Reformation England* (Cambridge: Cambridge University Press, 1990), 72

("[Roebech] was present at the marriage of the aforesaid Jane Chapman privately in her chamber," and thereby subject to penalties requested by the Church in its rôle of plaintiff *ex officio.*)

50. See. e.g., Helmholz, *Marriage Litigation,* 31, where his evidence quite clearly demonstrates that "The court records show the tenacity of the belief that people could regulate their own matrimonial affairs, without the assistance or the interference of the Church."

51. See, e.g. the case of Richard and Anne Stockley from 26 March 1621/2 in Walton parish, who were seen by a Thomas Woofal being married in a field by a Master Kendricke, "according to ye forme layd down in the booke of Common prayer, with the vse of a ringe." Other such marriages are quoted in Furnivall at pp. 56, 59, and 65–67, occurring in 1561, 1562/3, and 1565.

52. Ernest Schanzer, in a fairly convincing discussion in which he finds Angelo and Mariana's contract a *de futuro* contract, argues in favor of another type of *de futuro* contract. He refers to this separable type of *de futuro* contract as a *sponsalia iurata*. This is, according to Swinburne (at §XVI.1), a *de futuro* contract combined with an oath, or a sworn contract which could not be unilater-

ally canceled (Swinburne, §XVI.5). "The Marriage-Contracts in *Measure for Measure*," *Shakespeare Survey* 13 (1960): 85. Schanzer's argument will be discussed in the treatment of *Measure for Measure*, infra.

53. Swinburne devotes his §XIV to distinguishing between public and private spousals. Public spousals are those created before a witness (¶1) while private spousals are unwitnessed. Of the private spousal Swinburne has much to say. There are two competing theories regarding such contracts; the first theory holds the pact void for two causes:

(a) *Nullum pactum, nullum conventionem, nullum contractum inter eos videri volumus subsequuurum, qui lege contrabere prohibente, contrahunt.* A man may not do secretly what the law would not allow him to do publicly. [Swinburne's gloss here is to suggest that persons so contracting do so because they would be estopped from contracting publicly for some legal reason such as consanguinity of the parties or a preexisting marriage.] (b) *Idem est in lege non esse & non apparere.* To the law it is the same not to be as not to appear to be. As a private contract cannot be proved, it cannot exist in the cognizance of the court and is therefore void. (Swinburne §XIV.2)

The second theory holds the pact enforceable on the theory that

Clandestina conjugia contra leges quidem fiunt, contracta tamen dissolvi non possunt. Despite the illegality of secret marriages, they are indissoluble because the fundamental requirement of mutual consent has been met. Solemnities are but accidentals to the spousals. Swinburne §XIV.3

Swinburne's *dicta* on the cause favors the latter view so long as there are no impediments that would otherwise nullify the contract such as consanguinity of the parties (¶¶4–5). The York and Norwich courts are firm in their application of the former argument (Swinburne's §XIV.2(b)); here is a clear demonstration of the tensions between the letter and spirit of the law upon which the playwrights of the period focus.

Henry VIII tried to have the matter laid to rest by statute in 1540 (32 Henry VIII, *circa* 38) which made solemnized marriages enforceable over proved but unsolemnized, prior *de præsenti* unions. Because of the sinfulness inherent in elevating man's law over God's, however, the statute was repealed nine years later by 2 & 3 Edward VI, *circa* 23. The repeal clearly favors the argument presented by Swinburne at §XIV.2(c). Even on the state level, a binding contract of marriage—even if secretly entered into—was a binding contract.

54. On a misunderstanding of this technicality, J. Birje-Patil argues that Juliet and Claudio's contract in *Measure for Measure* was a *de futuro* contract. "Marriage Contracts in *Measure for Measure*," *Shakespeare Studies* 5 (1969): 106–11. Cf. Swinburne's *dicta* at §III.3, "Spousals *de præsenti* are *improperly* called *spousals,* being in nature and substance, rather matrimony than spousals . . . a man may contract present matrimony, and yet refer the solemnization thereof till another time, in respect of this future solemnization; the contract *de præsenti* may justly be defended and verified to be *futurarum Nuptiarum repromisso,* a promise of future marriage."

55. Ralph Houlbrooke has presented evidence from the mid-sixteenth century, "The Punishment of Incontinence," in his *Church Courts and the People During the English Reformation 1520–1570* (Oxford: Oxford University Press, 1979), 65 n. 39, wherein he arrives at the same conclusions. A court might en-

force disciplinary proceedings, such as specific performance, in such cases of incontinence after contracting, but there is no hint of the copulation being deemed fornication.

56. Bishop Thomas Watson, last Catholic bishop of Lincoln, was also of the opinion that solemnization was primarily required for proof of the marriage. See his work, *The Seven Sacraments of Christ's Church* wherein he refers to solemnization not as essential or requisite but merely "expedient for sundry causes."

57. A recorded case from Norwich is illustrative. Robert Gyles was held to marry Joan Sylvester, "according to [his] promise," when the two of them were apprehended in July 1551 "doyng and commytting the crime of incontinencye." Deposition Books 5B:221–223^r. Qtd. in Houlbrooke, "The Making of Marriage," 345.

58. Robert Fabyan, *The New Chronicles of England and France,* ed. Henry Ellis. (London: F.C. & J. Rivington, 1811).

59. The argument, because of the very nature of secret marriage, must of necessity remain one of purest conjecture. For an argument that asserts and argues the secret marriage of Shakespeare and Anne Hathaway as fact, see Joseph William Gray, *Shakespeare's Marriage* (London: Chapman & Hall, 1905), 59.

60. See John Semple Smart, *Shakespeare: Truth and Tradition* (Oxford: Clarendon Press, 1966), 61.

61. Arthur Scouten, "An historical approach to *Measure for Measure,*" *Philological Quarterly* 54 (1975): 68–84.

62. Cf. the two such cases mentioned at note 33, supra.

63. This despite the findings of Houlbrooke "The Making of Marriage," 340), that "the amount of matrimonial contract litigation declined substantially between the fourteenth and seventeenth centuries." Both Houlbrooke and Carlson's evidence can be reconciled, however. Though the overall bulk of litigation did, indeed, dwindle over the three-hundred-year-period, the final decades of the sixteenth century demonstrate a palpable reversal of the downward trend noted by Houlbrooke.

64. Carlson, "Marriage Reform," 448–50.

65. See Helmholz, *Roman Canon Law,* 169 ff.

66. Birje-Patil, "Marriage Contracts in *Measure for Measure,*" 107.

67. Ibid. 106.

68. Ibid. 107–8.

69. Scott, "'Our City's Institutions,'" 791.

70. Scott here misquotes her source, A. D. Nuttall, "'Measure for Measure': The Bed-Trick," *Shakespeare Survey* 28 (1975): 51–56, who, at page 53, is clearly not discussing the marriage law, of which there was a law quite "like" it in England, but rather the penalty attached to its transgression in Shakespeare's Vienna. Says Nuttall, "The consummation of an espousal before matrimony may have been an offence in strict law [in James's England] but there was never any question of a death penalty. This is *story-book* law."

71. Scott, "Our City's Intitutions," 792. In point of contention, S. Nagarajan, in *"Measure for Measure* and Elizabethan Betrothals," *Shakespeare Quarterly* 14 (1963), relies upon an *Encyclopædia Britannica* for his legal knowledge—as Margaret Scott condones—and arrives at the entirely wrong conclusion that "only a *de præsenti* contract allowed any sexual union" (117–18 and n. 3).

72. Scott's twisted syntax requires the elisions in the text in order to clarify this point. To avoid the charge of manipulation, however, I present the quotation in its original form here. Scott has raised the prohibition of clandestine marriage created in 1563 by the Counsel of Trent to suggest that the law in Shakespeare's Vienna would not view the clandestine marriage in the same light as would the law in Shakespeare's England. She refers to Lucio and Claudio's exchange in 1.2 of the play when she says:

> At this stage in the play it is difficult to escape the conclusion that Shakespeare has invoked Vienna's allegiance to Rome in order to remind us that English Protestant law, while inevitably shaping our responses, cuts no ice at all in Vincentio's state.

The problem with this argument, of course, is that Scott has only just finished ridiculing the idea that a Protestant English audience would be aware of its own law regarding marriage. Now she suggests that the same Protestant English audience would have no trouble acknowledging, accepting, and understanding a post-Reformation Catholic doctrine arrived at on the Continent. Moreover, it was a doctrine that was not itself promulgated on much of the Continent (for the discussion of which, see Lewis Stockton's work, *Marriage Considered from Legal and Ecclesiastical Viewpoints* [Buffalo, N.Y.: Huebner-Bleistein, 1912], 84. There Stockton quotes the enforcement section of the Tridentine Decree, demonstrating that it did not go into force *proprio vigore* and correctly concludes that "this decree was never promulgated in England. It was never promulgated in most parts of Europe. It was never accepted in France"). Additionally, according to Scott, the English audience would have little trouble applying this unpromulgated foreign doctrine to what was, six pages earlier, a fictional Vienna ruled by story-book law. Furthermore, as she admits that Protestant law is inevitably shaping our responses, it seems irrational to dismiss an in-depth examination of that law in favor of the *Encyclopædia Britannica* entry.

73. Ranald, "'As Marriage Binds, and Blood Breaks,'" 81.

74. Karl P. Wentersdorf, "The Marriage Contracts in 'Measure for Measure': A Reconsideration," *Shakespeare Survey* 32 (1979): 131.

75. I am indebted in part to Eileen Z. Cohen for this conclusion. See her "'Virtue is Bold': The Bed-trick and Characterization in *All's Well That Ends Well* and *Measure for Measure*" *Philological Quarterly* 65 (spring 1986).

76. One of the arguments current during this period, which Swinburne discusses at some length before rejecting, held that the law could not take notice of contracts made in secret because they could not be proved. See note 53, argument §XIV.2(b), *supra,* and accompanying text.

77. Schanzer, "Marriage-Contracts in *Measure for Measure,*" 83 (citing the Catholic Churchman William Harrington's *Commendacions of matrymony* (1528), A4–A4[v]). See also Edgar Innes Fripp, *Shakespeare: Man and Artist* (London: Oxford University Press, 1938), 2:613, where he makes the remarkable comment that the Puritans, long the enemy of the public theatre, exercised their influence upon the writers to raise a sense of moral condemnation within the bosom of the audience members concerning such libertine attitudes as were depicted on the stage.

78. James Orchard Halliwell-Phillips, *Outlines of the Life of Shakespeare* (London: Longmans, Green & Co., 1883), 1:62; Joseph Quincy Adams, *Outlines*

of the Life of Shakespeare (London: Constable, 1923), 69; W. W. Lawrence, "*Measure for Measure* and Lucio," *Shakespeare Quarterly* 9 (1950): 450. One need only look to Shakespeare's own marriage to learn the poet's personal attitude toward premarital sexual relations.

79. See Helmholz, and Furnivall, *Marriage Litigation; Child-marriages.*

80. Condemning the practice, a seventeenth-century puritan divine states categorically that, in reference to secret marriage, "Many make it a very marriage, and thereupon ... take libertie after a contract to know their spouse, as if they were married." William Gouge, *Of Domesticall Duties* (London, 1622), 202. Compare again Prospero's warning to Ferdinand not to break Miranda's virgin knot before solemnization of their marriage in Naples (4.1.14–23). Such admonition would not be necessary if post-contractual consummation were not common, or at least foreseeable.

81. Cf. also Isabella's reaction to the news that Claudio has impregnated Juliet. Her reaction, "Oh, let him marry her," could well indicate her ecclesiastically biased admonition to solemnize their pact, as some commentators have read it, but it is more likely that it is a desperate solution to what she believes is simple fornication devoid of any precontract. After all, the Church itself would view Claudio and Juliet's act as incontinence, not fornication, if all the facts were known, which tends to indicate that all of the facts are not known.

82. Schanzer, "Marriage-Contracts" in *Measure for Measure*"; Ranald, "'As Marriage Binds, and Blood Breaks.'"

83. Nagarajan, "*Measure for Measure* and Elizabethan Betrothals," 115–19; Birje-Pati, "Marriage Contracts in *Measure for Measure*."

84. See, e.g., E. R. C. Brinkworth, *Shakespeare and the Bawdy Court of Stratford* (London: Phillimore, 1972), 14–18, 75, 80, 87. N.B. Although Juliet confesses her "sin" in 2.3, she herself never uses that word, but says only it is her "shame." Again, the text is full of such vagaries that a fully conclusive argument cannot be made. No single approach can ever address all of the problems presented. I beg only to suggest that performance interpretation could certainly support a textual interpretation indicating that Juliet is cowed and simply accepts the duke/friar's assumption that she has sinned although she herself does not inwardly believe it. In another vein, however, Juliet could, indeed, be either ignorant enough of the status of the law or devout enough to believe her confessor's assertion that consummation before solemnization is sin in fact.

85. The dichotomy was a commonplace in the period. Cf. the warning that "they which dare play man and wife onely in view of heauen, and closet of Conscience, let them be aduised ... for on earth if the Priest see no celebrated Marriage, the Judge saith no legitimate issue, nor the Law any reasonable or constituted Dower." *The Lawes Resolutions of Womens Rights* (London, 1632), 117. See also Swinburne's opinion at §XIV.5, "[N]ot to appear, and not to be, are both one in Law, that's true *Jure fori, non jure poli,* Before Man, not before God; for the Church indeed doth not judge of secret things, whereof there is no appearance. But most true it is, that Almighty God being Καρδιογνοςης, [sic] before him bare Conscience alone is a thousand Witnesses."

86. See, e.g., Schanzer, "Marriage Contracts" in *Measure for Measure,"* 84. Schanzer makes the mistake of seeing the antecedent of "'tis" as being "the words of heaven," when the context and number of the verb clearly point to "the

demigod authority," which will not show mercy but upon those it so chooses, according to the context of the scripture to which Claudio alludes, Romans 9:15.

87. Cf. The foolish Elbow, who leans on justice (2.1.49); "vice ... should meet the blow of justice" (2.2.30); "O just but severe law" (2.2.41); the showing of pity "most of all when I show justice, For then I pity those I do not know, Which a dismiss'd offence would after gall" (2.2.100–102); "My brother justice have I found so severe, that he hath forced me to tell him he is indeed Justice" (3.2.267); "You think you have made no offence, if the duke avouch the justice of your dealing" (4.2.200); "She hath been a suitor to me for her brother Cut off by course of justice" (5.1.35); "My brother had but justice, In that he did the thing for which he died" (5.1.453). In each case, justice is not viewed as evil, but strict, blindly laying down precepts to follow without acknowledging mitigating factors.

88. Nagarajan, "*Measure for Measure* and Elizabethan Betrothals."

89. Scott, "'Our City's Institutions.'"

90. Birje-Patil, "Marriage Contracts in *Measure for Measure*."

91. *See* his §XIV.3 and the discussion, supra, at note 53 and accompanying text.

92. Swinburne §§III.4, XII.8–9, XVII.8.

93. 3.1.223–24, "the nuptial appointed, between [the] time of the contract and limit of the solemnity."

94. Swinburne §XVIII.3. Though one may infer that the date of the nuptial has passed, nothing in the play suggests that it has, or, if it has, how long ago it did. Of more importance, however, this objection is never raised in the play. Though pedantically tenable from a purely legal point of view, this fact demonstrates that Shakespeare was more interested in informing the action of *Measure for Measure* with the law in question than in developing a fully realized *exemplar* of secret marriage breach for his audience. Either Shakespeare was unaware of this objection, indicating that he informed himself of the law only to a degree that it could be useful to him, or he simply ignored a troubling point in the law in order to keep the action lean and swift. In either case, this instance demonstrates the necessity of proceeding with caution in the Shakespearean legal world.

95. There is, in fact, evidence of a similar situation in the casebooks. In the case of *Jane Walkden v. Richard Lowe,* 12 December 1561, Lowe had secretly promised Walkden marriage, which she promised him in return. They then "had carnall dole together." She afterward requested him to repeat his promise of marriage before witnesses, her friends, which he did. Her "frendes p*r*omysed hym a pece of good, and wold not p*er*forme hit, so that this *respond*ent was lothe to marrie." Lowe went on to marry one Ellen Stones, who left him when she learned of his precontract with Walkden. Walkden was delivered of a girl, the issue of her copulation with Lowe. Despite the nondelivery of the promised goods by the friends, Lowe's consummated *de futuro* contract with Walkden was upheld over his subsequent *de præsenti* contract with Stones.

96. Swinburne §XVIII.3. The comment that Angelo "swallowed his vows whole" seems pejorative in nature. *Cf. As You Like It,* 5.4.152–53, wherein Phebe, tricked into a match with Silvius, honorably responds, "I will not eat my word."

97. Swinburne §XVIII.4. Again, I bring up a point clearly defined in law—that of limitation—which is conspicuously absent from the dramatic text. One is left merely to conjecture why Shakespeare found it necessary to attach a specific, five-year period to Mariana's suffering. It is probably meant to demonstrate the callous nature of Angelo or the patience of Mariana. But it may also hint, to a legally aware audience member, at the lapsing of a stated legal limitation that now requires a special, equitable intervention from the sovereign in order to see merciful justice done.

98. This sense of Isabella's pronouncement is underscored at the end of 3.2 when the duke says he plans to set a trap for Angelo with his "old betrothed but despised" in order to "pay with falsehood false exacting, And perform an old contracting." The performance of the old contract will, according to the duke's reasoning, perfect it. Cf. Black's Law Dictionary, "Perfect: Complete; finished; executed; enforceable;" with "Perform: To perform an obligation or contract is to execute, fulfill, or accomplish it according to its terms." See note 44, supra, and accompanying text for a full discussion of the concept of perfecting a *de futuro* marriage contract.

99. For this vision of Isabella I have relied upon the excellent character analysis found in Cohen's article, "'Virtue is Bold.'"

100. Nuttall, "The Bed-Trick," p. 54.

101. E.g., *Registrum Primum,* Act book, Ely, f. 136ʳ(1380) in which the respondent argued that "*antequam ipsam carnaliter cognovit protestabatur se nolle ipsam habere in uxorem.*" His protest before carnal knowledge that he could not take the woman as his wife was ignored by the court in favor of the precontract entered into before the subsequent protestation. Swinburne is also quite clear on this issue, at §XVII.11, "Spousals *de futuro* do become matrimony by carnal knowledge"; ¶13, "albeit parties betroathed should protest before the act done, that they did not *intend* thereby, that the Spousals should become matrimony, yet this protestation is overthrown by the fact following; for by lying together, they are presumed to have swarved from their former unhonest protestation; And so the former Spousals are now presumed honest matrimony"; ¶14, "so strong is the presumption of law in favor of matrimony, as [an *ex post facto*] confession [denying the coitus created matrimony] doth not work any thing against it"; ¶19, "Spousals do become matrimony by carnal knowledge, albeit the man were constrained through *fear of death* to know the woman."

102. See supra, notes 53 and 54 and accompanying text. Ranald's suggestion ("'As Marriage Binds, and Blood Breaks,'" 79) that Angelo could raise a defense of *error personæ* may be correct technically, but the presumption of matrimony would invalidate even that defense. Nevertheless, Ranald's point that the "Duke's insistence on having the religious ceremony performed" removes that defense is well taken. If her *de futuro* marriage had been effectively dissolved—that is, if Mariana had been dishonest in fact or the dowry had been an enforceable condition—it would not become matrimony with subsequent coitus. Swinburne §XVIII.15.

103. Without understanding the workings of the marriages, Janet Adelman builds her argument around this very point when she observes that "[t]he bed tricks thus offer to save Bertram [in *All's Well*] and Angelo from their own fantasies [for they are] presented with legitimate sexuality as a *fait accompli.*"

"Marriage and the Maternal Body: On Marriage as the End of Comedy in *Measure for Measure*" *Critical Essays on Shakespeare's Measure for Measure,* ed. Richard P. Wheeler (New York: G. K. Hall & Co., 1999), 121.

104. The context indicates that the mystical experience occurs when *de futuro* spousals are translated into matrimony. I am indebted to Nuttall's preliminary findings for this interpretation of *Measure for Measure.* "The Bed-Trick," 55.

105. For an excellent discussion on how this solemnization acts as a test for Mariana's truth and mercy see Ranald, "'As Marriage Binds, and Blood Breaks,'" 79.

106. Black's Law Dictionary. The definition would refer not to restoring her to her ante-precontract condition, which would be clearly hostile to the intention of the law since Juliet is pregnant, but rather to restore her to her ante-proscription condition, which would be as Claudio's wife. Read in this way, Vincentio is ordering Claudio to be faithful to his true contract.

107. *The Miseries of Enforced Marriage,* ed. Glenn H. Blayney, (Malone Society Reprints 107) (Oxford: Oxford University Press, 1963).

108. By the time of Wilkins's play the idea of heaven witnessing, recording, and blessing the secret marriage was a commonplace. Cf. Juliet's lament in *Romeo and Juliet* 3.5.207–10:

> My husband is on earth, my faith in heaven.
> How shall that faith return again to earth
> Unless that husband send it me from heaven
> By leaving earth?

109. Cf. later, similar protestations at lines 983–86; 1402–8; 2485–86.

110. Swinburne's §XV deals with spousals contracted by signs. The text as presented to us, however, gives no indication that Scarborrow and Clare are exchanging tokens such as rings, which would indicate present consent. With only their words preserved as a guide, there is at least the argument that they could, on the technicality of their verb tenses and conditional phraseology, legally dissolve their agreement.

111. See, e.g., Uncle William's advice to Scarborrow at lines 474–80:

> You are his ward, being so, the Law intends,
> He is to haue your duty, and in his rule
> Is both your marriage, and your heritage,
> If you rebell against these Iniunctions,
> The penalty takes hold on you, which for himselfe,
> He straight thus prosecutes, he wasts your land,
> Weds you where he thinkes fit.

112. For discussions of the interesting wardship question see Glenn H. Blayney, "Wardship in English Drama (1600–1650)," *Studies in Philology* 53 (1956): 470–84; and David Atkinson, "Marriage Under Compulsion in English Renaissance Drama," *English Studies* 67 (1986): 483–504.

113. This difficulty is attested in Swinburne, who suggests it several times, and in reference to a man who marries one woman secretly and then another woman publicly that "albeit this Question may seem to appertain to the determination of Divines, yet will I adventure to signifie mine own Opinion." §XIV.8.

NOTES 233

114. *The Moral Vision of Jacobean Tragedy* (Madison: University of Wisconsin Press, 1960), 118.

115. Upon this point the law was clear. A *de futuro* contract did not produce a husband and wife, "except in certain cases" which here do not apply, and could be dissolved by mutual consent or an intervening *de præsenti* spousal. Swinburne §IV. ¶2.

116. See, e.g., the article by Theodora Jankowski, which reinvents the legal figuring of secret marriage in order to demonstrate a pet hypothesis regarding female empowerment. She argues that the *de præsenti* marriage was legal; however, "their promises are followed by a physical consummation which was not allowed partners in a *de præsenti* spousal." She continues by stating categorically that "[i]t is clear, then, that although the Duchess's marriage to Antonio *itself* is legal, the *consummation* of it is irregular and would open the couple to ecclesiastical penalties" ("Defining/Confining the Duchess: Negotiating the Female Body," *Studies in Philology* 87 [1990]: 221–37). The period law is fairly clear on quite a different point. The secret union and the consummation are both "legal," particularly so in a *de præsenti* union, but may be open to penalties *not* for copulation but rather for failure of ecclesiastical sanction of the union itself. In arguing that the Duchess "scorns accepted legal practices" via a secret marriage, Jankowski uses her language imprecisely. The *de præsenti* marriage was both socially accepted and legal in the temporal court. It simply was not *licit* in the eyes of the Church. See also Nuttall's comment in "The Bed-Trick," 52–53, that "the Duchess's remark does not suggest that she is referring to matters so familiar as hardly to need mentioning. . . . In fact the old distinction of the canonists proved too fine-grained for the courts and *a fortiori* that which magistrates and jurists had difficulty in applying clearly can hardly have been immediately perspicuous to the man in the street." Nuttall must then use an example drawn from one of the most problematic cases to prove his point. Quite the contrary, as this chapter should make clear, the sheer number of dramatic renderings of secret marriage demonstrates conclusively the degree of familiarity the theatre patron must have had with the concept. The Duchess's direct statement should be seen not as exposition of an unfamiliar concept, as Nuttall supposes, but as a specific and conscious choice to avoid public declaration of private love.

117. See, e.g., Murial C. Bradbrook, *Themes and Conventions of Elizabethan Tragedy,* 2nd ed. (Cambridge: Cambridge University Press, 1952), 186–212. Bradbrook suggested the audiences would not approve of the marriage; Robert Guy Howarth, *Literature of the Theater: Marlowe to Shirley* (Sidney: Holstead Press, 1953), 195 et seq. Howarth views the play as a revenge tragedy reacting against marriage below one's class; Clifford Leech, "An addendum to Webster's Duchess" *Philological Quarterly* 37 (April 1958): 253–56. Leech also claims that the Duchess's marriage beneath her is the prime motivation for her downfall.

118. See, e.g., Frank W. Wadsworth, "Webster's Duchess of Malfi in the Light of Some Contemporary Ideas on Marriage and Remarriage," *Philological Quarterly* 35 (1957): 394–407. Wadsworth responds in the negative to Leech's suggestions, above; Robert Guy Howarth, *Modern Language Review* 59, no. 4 (1964): 633. Howarth, reversing his earlier opinion while reviewing Leech's work, decides that Webster preferred worth to birth; Robert B. Heilman,

Tragedy and Melodrama: Versions of Experience (Seattle and London: University of Washington Press, 1968): 61–72, 197–98, wherein the Duchess is described as an innocent victim of evil men, who neither deserves nor earns her fate; Katherine H. James, "The Widow in Jacobean Drama," Ph.D. diss., University of Tennessee, Diss. Ab. 34 (1973): 1246A. James sees the marriage as both innocent and the cause of the tragedy; Philip G. Kuchnert, "Will and Fate in Four English Renaissance Tragedies," Ph.D. diss., University of Utah, Diss. Ab. 35 (1974): 1626A. Kuchnert sees in the Duchess a stoic endurance elevating the human spirit above worldly concerns; Margaret L. Mikesell, "Matrimony and Change in Webster's *The Duchess of Malfi*," *Journal of the Rocky Mountain Medieval and Renaissance Association* (1981): 97–111. Mikesell sees a conflict in the play between old and new views of marriage, the Duchess preferring a love relationship to marriage of position; Richard F. Hardin, "Chapman and Webster on Matrimony: The Poets and the Reformation of Ritual," *Renaissance and Reformation*, new series, 4 (1976): 65–73, in which the private ceremony is seen as morally superior to the brothers' brutality; Harriett Hawkins, "The Morality of Elizabethan Drama: Some Footnotes to Plato," *English Renaissance Studies Presented to Dame Helen Gardner*, ed. John Carey (Oxford: Clarendon Press, 1980), 12–32. Hawkins demonstrates the injustice of narrow, orthodox moral assumptions, especially concerning marriage, working within the play.

119. "The Duchess of Malfi: Styles of Ceremony," *Essays in Criticism* 12 (1963): 73–84.

120. "Merit and Degree in Webster's The Duchess of Malfi," *English Literary Renaissance* 11 (1981): 70–80.

121. Ibid., 73 n. 6.

122. "The Witch: Stage Flop or Political Mistake?" in *"Accompaninge the players": Essays Celebrating Thomas Middleton, 1580–1980,* ed. Kenneth Friedenreich (New York: AMS Press, 1983), 172.

123. The spousal cannot be *de futuro* because that promise to be married would have been dissolved by the intervening marriage between Isabella and Antonio. Swinburne ¶IV.2. The situation is precisely the same as that in *The Atheist's Tragedy* with this important difference: while Sebastian in this play is frantic to keep his *de facto* wife from engaging in an adulterous liaison with the man she believes is her husband, Charlemont has no such anxiety. Though Charlemont is upset by what he perceives to be Castabella's infidelity to their vows, and though Tourneur's moralism keeps her chaste through the expedient of the wasting sickness of her *de facto* husband, nowhere in *The Atheist's Tragedy* do we find the sort of soul-damning apprehension we find in the breached *de præsenti* unions of *Miseries of Enforced Marriage* or *The Witch*.

124. Lancashire, "Stage Flop or Political Mistake?" 169.

125. Barton, "Wrying but a little."

126. All references are to *A Fair Quarrel*, ed. R. V. Holdsworth (London: Earnest Benn, Ltd., 1974).

127. E. H. Sudgen, *A Topographical Dictionary to the Works of Shakespeare and His Fellow Dramatists* (Manchester, England: Manchester University Press, 1925), 387. Pancridge was known also as St. Pancras, which Holdsworth accounts a "disreputable" suburb south of Cheapside (*History of English Law,* 127 n. 358) and Fran C. Chalfont identifies as a "disreputable" place "two miles

northwest of St. Paul's" (*Ben Jonson's London* [Athens: University of Georgia Press, 1978], 136). It is, in fact, in North London. The term "Pancridge Parson" was apparently a popular expression. It can be found in Fields's *A Woman is a Weathercock* (2.1.92), Nabbes's masque, *The Spring's Glory* (*Works,* 2:232), and also in his *Tottenham Court* (5.6). Jonson, in his *A Tale of a Tub,* introduces Canon Hugh as "Vicar of Pancrace" (*dramatis personæ* and again at 4.1.81–82) and the hasty marriage action of John Clay, Audrey Turfe, and Justice Preamble heads "to Pancrace, to the Vicar" (2.6.38). St. Pancras Church was not, of course, the only place to fly for irregular marriages. In his play *A Chaste Maid In Cheapside,* Middleton uses Barn Elms on the southwest corner of St. James's Park as the intended nuptial retreat for Moll and Touchwood, Jr. Middleton's 1613 play also refers to *de præsenti* contracting at 4.1.227 et seq. The entire Moll-Touchwood, Jr. plot revolves around the two young lovers' attempts to steal away and be secretly married.

128. Standish Henning, *A Mad World, My Masters* (Lincoln: University of Nebraska Press, 1965).

Bibliography

Adams, Joseph Quincy. *Outlines of the Life of Shakespeare.* London: Constable, 1923.

———. *Shakespearean Playhouses.* Reprint, Gloucester, Mass.: Peter Smith, 1960.

Adelman, Janet. "Marriage and the Maternal Body: On Marriage as the End of Comedy in *Measure for Measure.*" *Critical Essays on Shakespeare's Measure for Measure.* Edited by Richard P. Wheeler, 120–44. New York: G. K. Hall, 1999.

Alexander, Peter. "Measure for Measure: a case for the Scottish Solomon." *Modern Language Quarterly* 28 (1967): 478–88.

Allen, Charles. *Notes on the Bacon-Shakespeare Question.* Boston, 1900.

Andrews, Mark Edwin. *Law versus Equity in the Merchant of Venice.* Boulder: University of Colorado Press, 1965.

Armstrong, Walter P., Jr. "Shakespeare and the Law," *Tennessee Bar Journal* 27 (1991): 26–31.

Armstrong, William A. *The Seventeenth-Century Stage.* Edited by Gerald Eades Bentley. Chicago: University of Chicago Press, 1968.

Atkinson, David. "Marriage Under Compulsion in English Renaissance Drama." *English Studies* 67 (1986): 483–504.

Bacon, Sir Francis. *Works.* Edited by James Spedding, Robert Leslie Ellis, and Douglas Denon Heath. London: Longman, 1872.

———. *Reading on the Statute of Uses.* New York: Garland, 1979.

———. *Essays* (1625). Edited by Michael J. Hawkins. London: J. M. Dent, 1994.

Baker, John H. "The Common Lawyers and the Chancery: 1616." *Irish Jurist* 4 (1969): 368–92.

———. "The Use upon Use in Equity," *Law Quarterly Review* 93 (1977): 33–38.

———. *An Introduction to English Legal History,* 2nd ed. London: Butterworth, 1979.

———. *The Order of Sergeants at Law.* London: Selden Society, 1984.

———. "Law and Legal Institutions." *William Shakespeare: His World, His Work, His Influence.* Edited by John F. Andrews, 41–54. New York: Scribner's, 1985.

———. *The Legal Profession and the Common Law.* London: Hambledon Press, 1986.

———. *An Introduction to English Legal History,* 3rd ed. London: Butterworth, 1990.

———. *The Third University of England: The Inns of Court and the Common-Law Tradition.* London: Selden Society, 1990.

———. "Famous English Canon Lawyers: Henry Swinburne." *Ecclesiastical Law Journal* 3 (1993): 5–9.

———, ed. *The Reports of Sir John Spellman.* Vol. 94. London: Selden Society, 1978.

Baker, J. H., and S. F. C. Milsom. *Sources of English Legal History: Private Law to 1750.* London: Butterworth, 1986.

Balch, Marston Stevens. *Middleton's A Trick to Catch the Old One and Massinger's A New Way to Pay Old Debts* (1633). Salzburg: University of Salzburg, 1981.

Barnes, Thomas G. "Star Chamber and the Sophistication of the Criminal Law." *Criminal Law Review* 24 (1977): 316–26.

Barrett, D. S. "Plautus, *Mostellaria* 630–32 and *The Merchant of Venice*." *Classical Bulletin* 59 (1983): 60–62.

Barton, Anne. "'Wrying but a little': marriage, law and sexuality in the plays of Shakespeare." *Essays, Mainly Shakespearean,* 3–30. Cambridge: Cambridge University Press 1994.

Barton, Sir Dunbar Plunket, *The Story of Our Inns of Court.* London: G. T. Foulis, 1924.

———. *Links Between Shakespeare and the Law.* Boston: Houghton Mifflin, 1929.

Barton, J. L. "The Medieval Use." *Law Quarterly Review* 81 (1965): 562–77.

———. "The Statute of Uses and Trusts of Freeholds." *Law Quarterly Review* 82 (1966): 215–25.

———. "The Rise of the Fee simple." *Law Quarterly Review* 92 (1976): 108–21.

Bawcutt, N. W. "'He who the sword of heaven will bear': The Duke versus Angelo in *Measure for Measure*." *Shakespeare Survey* 37 (1984): 89–97.

Bean, J. M. W. *The Decline of English Feudalism.* Manchester, England: Manchester University Press, 1968.

Beck, James. "Foreword." *Links Between Shakespeare and the Law,* by Dunbar Plunket Barton. London, 1929.

Bedwell, C. E. A. *A Brief History of the Middle Temple.* London: Butterworth, 1909.

Bell, H. E. *An Introduction to the History and Records of the Court of Wards and Liveries.* Cambridge: Cambridge University Press, 1953.

Bellot, H. L. *The Inner and Middle Temple.* London: Methuen & Co., 1902.

Belsheim, Edmund O. "The Old Action of Account." *Harvard Law Review* 45 (1931): 466–500.

Bennett, Robert B. "The Law Enforces Itself: Richard Hooker and the Law Against Fornication in *Measure for Measure*." *Shakespeare and Renaissance Association of West Virginia: Select Papers* 16 (1993): 43–51.

Benston, Alice N. "Portia, the Law, and the Tripartite Structure of *The Merchant of Venice.*" *Shakespeare Quarterly* 30 (1979): 367–85.

Bentley, Richard. "Shakespeare's Law." *Law Times* 155 (1923): 23–29.

Berger, Harry, Jr. "Marriage and mercifixation in *The Merchant of Venice:* The Casket Scene Revisited." *Shakespeare Quarterly* 22 (1981): 155–62.

Berman, Harold J. *Law and Revolution: The Formation of the Western Legal Tradition.* Cambridge: Harvard University Press, 1983.

———. "The Origins of Historical Jurisprudence: Coke, Selden, Hale." *Yale Law Review* 103 (1994): 1651–1738.

Bernthal, Craig A. "Staging justice: James I and the Trial Scenes of *Measure for Measure.*" *SEL: Studies in English Literature, 1500–1900* 32 (1992): 247–69.

Berry, Herbert, ed. *The First Public Playhouse: The Theatre in Shoreditch 1576–1598.* Montreal: McGill-Queen's University Press, 1979.

———. *The Boar's Head Playhouse.* Washington, DC: Folger Books, 1986.

———. "Shylock, Robert Miles, and Events at the Theatre." *Shakespeare Quarterly* 44 (1993): 183–201.

Berry, Ralph. *Shakespeare and Social Class.* Atlantic Highlands, N.J.: Humanities Press International, 1988.

Bevington, David. *From Mankind to Marlowe.* Cambridge: Harvard University Press, 1962.

Biancalana, Joseph. "Widows at Common Law: The Development of Common Law Dower." *Irish Jurist* 23 (1988): 255–329.

Birje-Patil, J. "Marriage Contracts in *Measure for Measure.*" *Shakespeare Studies* 5 (1969): 106–11.

Blackstone, William. *Commentaries on the Laws of England.* 4 vols. Reprint, Chicago: University of Chicago Press, 1979.

Bland, D. S. "Interludes in Fifteenth-Century Revels at Furnivall's Inn." 3 *Review of English Studies* (1952): 263–68.

———. "Arthur Broke, Gerard Legh, and the Inner Temple." *NQ* 214 (1969): 453–55.

———. "Shakespeare's legal language." *Verbatim* 14 (1988): 11–13.

Blatcher, Marjorie. *The Court of King's Bench 1450–1550.* London: Athlone Press, 1978.

Blayney, Glenn H. "Wardship in English Drama (1600–1650)." *Studies in Philology.* 53 (1956): 470–84.

Bolton, W. F. "Ricardian Law Reports and *Richard II.*" *Shakespeare Studies* 20 (1988): 53–65.

Bonfield, Lloyd. *Marriage Settlements, 1601–1740: The Adoptions of the Strict Settlement.* Cambridge: Cambridge University Press, 1983.

Boose, Lynda E. "The Father and the Bride in Shakespeare." *PMLA* 97 (1982): 325–47.

Bowen, Catherine D. *The Lion and the Throne: The Life and Time of Sir Edward Coke 1552–1634.* London: Hamish Hamilton, 1957.

Boyarsky, Saul. "'Let's kill all the lawyers': What did Shakespeare mean?" *Journal of Legal Medicine* 12 (1991): 571–74.

Bracton. *On the Laws and Customs of England.* Edited by George E. Woodbine. Translated by Samuel E. Thorne. Harvard University Press, 1968.

Bradbrook, Murial C. *Themes and Conventions of Elizabethan Tragedy,* 2nd ed. Cambridge: Cambridge University Press, 1952.

———. "The Comedy of Timon: A Reveling Play of the Inner Temple." *Renaissance Drama* 9 (1966): 83–103.

———. *John Webster: Citizen and Dramatist.* London: Weidenfeld and Nicolson, 1980.

Braden, Gordon. *Renaissance Tragedy and the Senecan Tradition: Anger's Privilege.* New Haven: Yale University Press, 1985.

Brand, Paul. "The origins of the English Legal Profession." *Law and History Review* 5 (1987): 31–50.

———. *The Origins of the English Legal Profession.* Oxford: Blackwell, 1992.

Braunmuller, A. R. "'To the Globe I Rowed': John Holles Sees A Game of Chess." *English Literary Renaissance* 20, no. 2 (spring 1990): 340–56.

Brennan, Anthony S. "Excellent Dissembling: Antony and Cleopatra Playing at Love." *Midwest Quarterly* 19 (1977–78): 313–29.

Brennan, Elizabeth M., ed. *The White Devil.* New Mermaids edition. New York: W. W. Norton, 1966.

Brinkworth, E. R. C. *Shakespeare and the Bawdy Court of Stratford.* London: Phillimore, 1972.

Brodsky, Vivien. "Widows in Late Elizabethan London: Remarriage, Economic Opportunity and Family Orientation." *The World We Have Gained.* Edited by Lloyd Bonfield, Richard M. Smith, and Keith Wrightson, 43–99. Oxford: Blackwell, 1986.

Brooke, Christopher N. L. "Marriage and Society in the Central Middle Ages." *Marriage and Society: Studies in the Social History of Marriage.* Edited by R. B. Outhwaite, 17–34. London: Europa, 1981.

Brooks, C. W. *Pettyfoggers and Vipers of the Commonwealth: The "Lower Branch" of the Legal Profession in Early Modern England.* Cambridge: Cambridge University Press, 1986.

Brown, Basil. *Law Sports at Gray's Inn (1594).* New York, 1921.

Brundage, James A. *Sex, Law, and Marriage in the Middle Ages.* Aldershot, England: Variorum, 1993.

Bryson, W. H. "Law Reporting in England 1603–1660." *Law Reporting in England.* Edited by Chantal Stebbings, 113–22. London: Hambledon, 1995.

Buck, Andrew. "Rhetoric and the Law of Property in Early Sixteenth-Century England." *The Happy Couple: Law and Literature.* Edited by J. Neville, Annadale, Australia 14–24. The Federation Press, 1994.

Bullough, G., ed. *Narrative and Dramatic Sources of Shakespeare.* 8 vols. London: Routledge & Kegan Paul, 1975.

Burney, Charles. *A General History of Music from the Earliest Ages to the Present Period.* London, 1782–89.

Burt, Richard A. "'Licensed by Authority': Ben Jonson and the Politics of Early Stuart Theater." *ELH* 54, no. 3 (fall 1987): 529–60.

———. *"Licensed by Authority": Ben Jonson and the Discourses of Censorship.* Ithaca: Cornell University Press, 1993.

Butler, Martin. "*Love's Sacrifice:* Ford's Metatheatrical Tragedy." In *John Ford: Critical Re-Visions.* Edited by Michael Neill. Cambridge: Cambridge University Press, 1988.

Cacicedo, Alberto. "'She is fast my wife': sex, marriage, and ducal authority in *Measure for Measure.*" *Shakespeare Studies* 23 (1995): 187–209.

Caenegem, R. C. van. *The Birth of the English Common Law.* Cambridge: Cambridge University Press, 1973.

Calderwood, James L. "The Duchess of Malfi: Styles of Ceremony." *Essays in Criticism* 12 (1963): 73–84.

Campbell, John, Lord. *Shakespeare's Legal Acquirements Considered.* London, 1859.

Campbell, Susie. "'Is that the law?': Shakespeare's political cynicism in *The Merchant of Venice.*" *The Merchant of Venice.* Edited by Linda Cookson and Bryan Loughrey, 65–73. Essex, England: Longman, 1992.

Carlson, Cindy. "Trials of Marriage in *Measure for Measure.*" *Shakespeare Yearbook* 6 (1996): 355–81.

Carlson, Eric Josef. "Marriage Reform and the Elizabethan High Commission." *Sixteenth Century Journal* 21, no. 3 (1990): 437–51.

———. *Marriage and the English Reformation.* Oxford: Blackwell, 1994.

Castle, Edward J. *Shakespeare, Bacon, Jonson, and Greene.* Port Washington, N.Y.: Kennikut Press, 1970.

Cerasano, S. P. "Competition for the King's Men? Alleyn's Blackfriars Venture." *Medieval and Renaissance Drama in England* 4 (1989): 173–86.

———. "Half a dozen dangerous words." *Gloriana's Face: Women, Public and Private, in the English Renaissance.* Edited by Marion Wynne-Davies and S. P. Cerasano, 167–83. Detroit, Mich.: Wayne State University Press, 1992.

Chalfont, Fran C. *Ben Jonson's London.* Athens: University of Georgia Press, 1978.

Chambers, E. K. *The Elizabethan Stage.* 4 vols. Oxford, 1923. Reprinted, 1945.

———. *William Shakespeare: A Study of Facts and Problems.* 2 vols. Oxford: Clarendon Press, 1930.

Chapman, George. *The Gentleman Usher.* Edited by John Hazel Smith. Lincoln: University of Nebraska Press, 1970.

Clare, Janet. "'Greater Themes for Insurrection's Arguing': Political Censorship of the Elizabethan and Jacobean Stage." *Review of English Studies* new series, 38 (1987): 169–83.

———. "The Censorship of the Deposition Scene in *Richard II.*" *Review of English Studies* 61, no. 161 (1990): 89–94.

Clarkson, Paul S., and Clyde T. Warren. *The Law of Property in Shakespeare and the Elizabethan Drama.* New York: Gordian Press, 1968.

Clemens, Samuel Langhorne ([Mark Twain]. *Is Shakespeare Dead?* New York, 1909.

Cobbett's Complete Collection of State Trails. Vol. 1. Edited by T. B. Howell. London, 1809.

Cockburn, J. S. *A History of English Assizes.* Cambridge: Cambridge University Press, 1972.

——. "Twelve silly men? The Trial at Assizes, 1560–1670." *Twelve Good Men and True: The Criminal Trial in England, 1200–1800.* Edited by J. S. Cockburn and Thomas A. Green, 158–81. Princeton: Princeton University Press, 1988.

Cohen, Eileen Z. "'Virtue is Bold': The Bed-trick and Characterization in *All's Well That Ends Well* and *Measure for Measure.*" *Philological Quarterly* 65 (spring 1986): 171–86.

Cohen, Stephen A. "'The quality of mercy': Law, Equity, and Ideology in *The Merchant of Venice.*" *Mosaic* 27 (1994): 35–54.

Cohen, Walter. "*The Merchant of Venice* and the Possibilities of Historical Criticism." *ELH* 49 (1982): 765–89.

Coke, Edward. *A Commentarie Upon Littleton (The First Part of the Institutes of the Lawes of England).* London, 1628.

——. *Second, Third, and Fourth Parts of the Institute of the Lawes of England.* 3 vols. London, 1797.

——. *The Reports.* 6 vols. London: Butterworth and Son, 1826.

Collier, John Payne. *The History of the English Dramatic Poetry to the Time of Shakespeare: An Annals of the Stage.* London, 1821.

Collins, J. C. "Was Shakespeare a Lawyer?" *Studies in Shakespeare* (1904).

Cook, Ann Jennalie. *The Privileged Playgoers of Shakespeare's London, 1576–1642.* Princeton: Princeton University Press, 1981.

——. *Making a Match: Courtship in Shakespeare and His Society.* Princeton: Princeton University Press, 1991.

Corrigan, Brian Jay. *The Misfortunes of Arthur: A Critical, Old-Spelling Edition.* New York: Garland, 1992.

——. "A Legal Dodge in the Business Practices of the Original Globe and Drury Lane Theatres." *Theatre Notebook* 51, no. 2 (summer 1997): 72–74.

——. "Of Dogges and Gulls: Sharp Dealing at the Swan (1597) . . . and Again at St. Paul's 1606)." *Theatre Notebook* 55, no. 3 (2001): 219–229.

Corthell, Ronald J. "'Coscus onely breeds my just offense': A Note on Donne's 'Satire II' and the Inns of Court." *John Donne Journal* 6, no. 1 (1987): 25–32.

Croft, Pauline. "Wardship in the Parliament of 1604." *Parliamentary History* 2 (1983): 39–48.

Cummings, Brian. "Swearing in Public: More and Shakespeare." *English Literary Renaissance* 27 (1997): 197–232.

Cunningham, H. "Shakespeare and a Great Legal War." *The Bookman's Journal* 14 (April 1926).

Cunningham, Karen. "Female Fidelities on Trial." *Renaissance Drama* 25 (1994): 1–31.

Davis, Cushman Kellogg. *The Law in Shakespeare.* St. Paul, 1884.

Dawson, John P. "Coke and Ellesmere Disinterred: The Attack on the Chancery in 1616." *Illinois Law Review* 36 (1941): 27–52.

Day, John. *The Ile of Gvls*. Shakespeare Association Facsimiles, no. 12 (1936).

de Chambrun, Clara Longworth. "Shakespeare and the Elizabethan Statutes." *The Dublin Review* (January 1936).

Dekker, Thomas, *Non-Dramatic Works*. Edited by Alexander B. Grossart. New York: Russell & Russell, 1963.

de Montmorency, J. E. G. "Shakespeare's Legal Problems." *Contemporary Review: Literary Supplement* (1930).

Denvir, John. "William Shakespeare and the Jurisprudence of Comedy." *Stanford Law Review* 39 (1987): 825–49.

Derrett, J. Duncan M. *Henry Swinburne (?1551–1624) Civil Lawyer of York*. Borthwick Papers, no. 44. York, England: University of York Borthwick Institute of Historical Research, 1973.

Devecmon, William G. *In Re Shakespeare's Legal Acquirements*. New York: Shakespeare Society of New York, no. 12, 1899.

DeVine, Stephen. "Franciscan Friars, the Feoffment to Uses, and Canonical Theories of Property Enjoyment Before 1535." *The Journal of Legal History* 10 (1989): 1–22.

Dickinson, John W. "Renaissance Equity in *Measure for Measure*." *Shakespeare Quarterly* 13 (1962): 287–97.

Digby, Kenelm Edward. *An Introduction to the History of the Law of Real Property,* 3rd ed. Oxford, 1884.

Donaghue, Charles. "The Canon Law on the Formation of Marriage and Social Practice in the Later Middle Ages" *Journal of Family History* 8 (1983): 144–58.

Doran, Madeleine. *Endeavors of Art: A Study of Form in Elizabethan Drama*. Madison: University of Wisconsin Press, 1954.

Doyle, John T. "Shakespeare's Law: The Case of Shylock." *The Overland Monthly* (July 1886).

Draper, J. W. "Usury in *The Merchant of Venice*." *Modern Philology* 33 (1935): 37–47.

———. "Robert Shallow, esq. J.P." *Neuphilologische Mitteilungen* 38 (1937): 257–69.

———. "Dogberry's Due Process of Law." *Journal of English and Germanic Philology* 42 (1943): 563–76.

Dugdale, William. *Origines Juridiciales, or Historical Memorials of the English Laws, Courts of Justice, etc., The Savoy,* 1671.

Dunkel, Wilbur. "Law and Equity in *Measure for Measure*." *Shakespeare Quarterly* 13 (1962): 275–85.

———. *William Lambard, Elizabethan Jurist*. New Brunswick, N.J.: Rutgers University Press, 1965.

Durning-Lawrence, Sir Edwin, Bart. *Bacon Is Shakespeare*. New York: The John McBride Co., 1910.

———. *The Shakespeare Myth*. London: Gay & Hancock, Ltd., 1912.

Dutton, Richard. "Censorship." *A New History of Early English Drama*. Edited by John D. Cox and David Scott Kastan. New York: Columbia University Press 1997.

Earle, John. *Microcosmographie*. London, 1628.

Eccles, Mark. "Elizabethan Actors II: E–J." *NQ* 30 (December 1991).

Elton, W. R. *Shakespeare's Troilus and Cressida and the Inns of Courts Revels*. Brookfield, Vt.: Ashgate Press, 2000.

Erickson, Amy Louise. *Women and Property in Early Modern England*. London: Routledge, 1993.

Esmein, A. *Le Marriage en droit canonique*. 2 vols. Paris, 1891.

Eure, John D. "Shakespeare and the Legal Process: Four Essays." *Virginia Law Review* 61 (1975): 390–433.

Everett, Barbara. "Antony and Cleopatra." *The Complete Signet Classics: Shakespeare*. Sylvan Barnet, General Editor. New York: Harcourt Brace Jovanovich, 1972.

Ewen, C. L'Estange. *Lording Barry, Poet and Pirate*. London, 1938.

Fabyan, Robert. *The New Chronicles of England and France*. Edited by Henry Ellis. London: F.C. & J. Rivington, 1811.

Feuillerat, Albert. *Documents Relating to the Office of the Revels in the Time of Queen Elizabeth*. London: David Nutt, 1908.

Finch, Andrew J. "Parental Authority and the Problem of Clandestine Marriage in the Latter Middle Ages." *Law and History Review* 8 (1990): 189–204.

Finkelpearl, Philip J. "John Marston's *Histrio-Mastix* as an Inns of Court Play: A Hypothesis." *Huntington Library Quarterly* 29 (1966): 223–34.

———. "The Use of the Middle Temple's Christmas Revels in Marston's *The Fawne*." *Studies in Philology* 44 (1967): 199–209.

———. *John Marston of the Middle Temple: An Elizabethan Dramatist in His Social Setting*. Cambridge: Harvard University Press, 1969.

Fleay, Frederick Gard. *Biographical Chronicle of the English Drama 1559–1642*. Vol. 1. New York: Burt Franklin Press, 1891.

Fletcher, R. J. *The Pension Book of Gray's Inn*. 1901.

Foard, James T. "On the Law Case: *Shylock v Antonio*." *Manchester Quarterly* (1899): 268.

Fortesque, John. *De Laudibus Legum Angliae*. Edited by S. B. Chrimes. Cambridge: Cambridge University Press, 1949.

Fripp, Edgar Innes. *Shakespeare: Man and Artist*. London: Oxford University Press, 1938.

Furnivall, F. J. *Child-Marriages, Divorces, and Ramifications etc. in the Diocese of Chester, A.D. 1561–6*. Early English Text Society, original series, no. 108 (1897).

Gair, W. Reavley. *The Children of Paul's: The Story of a Theatre Company, 1553–1608*. Cambridge: Cambridge University Press, 1982.

Gesta Grayorum 1688. Edited by W. W. Greg. *The Malone Society Reprints*. Oxford: Oxford University Press, 1914.

Gibbons, Brian. *Jacobean City Comedy,* 2nd ed. London: Methuen, 1980.

Gillis, John R. *For Better, For Worse: British Marriages 1600 to the Present.* Oxford: Oxford University Press, 1985.

Glanvill. *The Treatise on the Laws and Customs of the Realm of England Commonly Called Glanvill.* Edited by G. D. G. Hall. Oxford: Clarendon Press, 1993.

Gleason, J. H. *The Justices of the Peace in England 1558–1640: A Later Eirenarcha.* Oxford: Clarendon Press, 1969.

Godwin, George. *The Middle Temple: The Society and Fellowship.* London: Staples Press Ltd., 1954.

Goodsell, Willystine. *A History of Marriage and the Family.* New York: Macmillan Co., 1935.

Gouge, William. *Of Domesticall Duties.* London, 1622.

Gras, Henk. "*Twelfth Night, Every Man Out of His Humour,* and the Middle Temple Revels of 1597–98." *Modern Language Review* 84 (July 1989): 546.

Gray, Charles. "The Boundaries of Equitable Function." *American Journal of Legal History* 20 (1976): 192–226.

———. "Reason, Authority and Imagination: The Jurisprudence of Sir Edward Coke." *Culture and Politics from Puritanism to the Enlightenment.* Edited by Perez Zagorin, 25–66. Berkeley: University of California Press, 1980.

Gray, Joseph William. *Shakespeare's Marriage.* London: Chapman & Hall, 1905.

Green, A. Wigfall. *The Inns of Court and Early English Drama.* New Haven: Yale University Press, 1931.

Greenblatt, Stephen Jay. *Shakespearean Negotiations.* Berkeley: University of California Press, 1988.

Greene, David. "*Measure for Measure:* Mythological History, Reality, and the Stage." *Law and Philosophy: The Practice of Theory. Essays in Honor of George Anastaplo.* Vol. 2. Edited by John A. Murley, Robert L. Stone, and William T. Brathwaite, 871–85. Athens: Ohio University Press, 1992.

Greenwood, Granville George. "Lawyers in Shakespeare." *The Westminster Review* 159 (1903): 161.

———. *In Re Shakespeare.* London, 1909.

———. *Shakespeare's Law and Latin.* Chapel Hill: University of North Carolina Press, 1913.

———. *Shakespeare's Law.* London, 1920.

Greg, W. W. *Henslowe's Diary.* 2 vols. London: A. H. Bullen, 1904–8.

———. *Library* IX (1928–29).

Guernsey, Rocellus Sheridan. *Ecclesiastical Law in Hamlet.* New York: AMS Press, 1971.

Gulley, Ervene. "'Dressed in a little brief authority': Law as Theater in *Measure for Measure.*" *Law and Literature Perspectives.* Edited by Bruce L. Rockwood, 53–80. New York: Lang, 1996.

Gurr, Andrew J. "The Many-Headed Audience." *Essays in Theatre* 1 (1982): 52–62.

———. *Playgoing in Shakespeare's London.* New York: Cambridge University Press, 1987.

———. "Ford and Contemporary Theatrical Fashion." *John Ford: Critical Re-Visions* Edited by Michael Neill. 81–96. Cambridge: Cambridge University Press, 1988.

———. *The Shakespearean Stage 1574–1642,* 3rd ed. Cambridge: Cambridge University Press, 1992.

Guy, J. A. "The Early Tudor Star Chamber." *Legal History Studies, 1972.* Edited by Defydd Jenkins, 122–28. Cardiff: University of Wales Press, 1975.

———. "The Development of Equitable Jurisdictions, 1450–1550." *Law, Litigants and the Legal Profession.* Edited by E. W. Ives and A. H. Manchester, 80–86. London: Royal Historical Society, 1983.

H. T. "Was Shakespeare a Lawyer?" *Law Journal* 6. Re-issued, London: Longmans, Green & Co., 1871. 81.

Hake, Edward. *Epiekeia: A Dialogue on Equity in Three Parts.* Edited by D. E. C. Yale (*circa* 1603). New Haven: Yale University Press, 1953.

Hall, Edward. *Chronicle.* London, 1809.

Halliwell-Phillips, James Orchard. *Outlines of the Life of Shakespeare.* 2 vols. London: Longmans, Green & Co., 1886.

Hammond, Paul. "The Argument of *Measure for Measure.*" *English Literary Renaissance* 16 (1986): 496–519.

Harbage, Alfred. *Shakespeare's Audience.* New York: Columbia University Press, 1941.

Harbage, Alfred and Samuel Schoenbaum. *Annals of the English Drama 975–1700.* London: Methuen & Co. Ltd., 1964.

Hardin, Richard F. "Chapman and Webster on Matrimony: The Poets and the Reformation of Ritual." *Renaissance and Reformation,* new series, 4 (1976): 65–73.

Harding, A. *The Law Courts of Medieval England.* London: George Allen & Unwin Ltd., 1973.

Harding, Davis P. "Elizabethan Betrothal and *Measure for Measure.*" *Journal of English and Germanic Philology* 49 (1950): 139–58.

Harrington, William. *Commendacions of matrymony* (1528).

Hart, H. C. *New Shakespeare Society Translation* 3 vols. (1877–79).

Haskins, G. L. "Extending the Grasp of the Dead Hand: Reflections on the Origins of the Rule Against Perpetuities." *University of Pennsylvania Law Review* 126 (1977): 19–46.

Hawkins, Harriett. "The Morality of Elizabethan Drama: Some Footnotes to Plato." *English Renaissance Studies Presented to Dame Helen Gardner.* Edited by John Carey. Oxford: Clarendon Press, 1980.

Hayne, Victoria. "Performing Social Practice: The Example of *Measure for Measure.*" *Shakespeare Quarterly* 44 (1993): 1–29.

Headlam, Cecil. *The Inns of Court.* London: Adam & Charles Black, 1909.

Heard, Franklin Fiske. *Shakespeare as a Lawyer.* Boston: Little, Brown, and Company, 1883.

———. *The Legal Acquirements of William Shakespeare.* Buffalo: William S. Hein, 1987.

Heilman, Robert B. *Tragedy and Melodrama: Versions of Experience.* Seattle and London: University of Washington Press, 1968.

Helgerson, Richard. "The Elizabethan Laureate: Self-Presentation and the Literary System." *ELH* 46 (1979):, 206–7.

———. *Self-Crowned Laureates: Spenser, Jonson, Milton, and the Literary System.* Berkeley: University of California Press, 1980.

Helmholz, Richard Henry. *Marriage Litigation in Medieval England.* Cambridge: Cambridge University Press, 1974.

———. "Support Orders, Church Courts, and the Role of *filius nullius:* A Reassessment of the Common Law." *University of Virginia Law Review* 63 (1977): 431–48.

———. "The Early Enforcement of Uses." *Columbia Law Review* 79 (1979): 1503–13.

———. *Canon Law and the Law of England.* London: Hambledon, 1987.

———. *Roman Canon Law in Reformation England.* Cambridge: Cambridge University Press 1990.

———. "Married Women's Wills in Later Medieval England." *Wife and Widow in Medieval England.* Edited by Sue Sheridan Walker, 165–82. Ann Arbor: University of Michigan Press, 1993.

Henderson, Edith G. "Relief from Bonds in English Chancery." *American Journal of Legal History* 18 (1974): 298–306.

Hibbard, G. R. "Love, Marriage and Money in Shakespeare's Theatre and Shakespeare's England." *The Elizabethan Theatre VI.* Edited by G. R. Hibbard. 134–55. Waterloo, Ont.: Archon, 1975.

Hillebrand, Harold Newcomb. "The Child Actors." *University of Illinois Studies in Language and Literature,* 11:2. Urbana: University of Illinois Press, 1926.

———. "Thomas Middleton's *The Viper and Her Brood.*" *MLN* 42, no. 1 (January 1927).

Hinley, Jan Lawson. "Bond Priorities in *The Merchant of Venice.*" *Studies in English Literature* 20 (1980): 217–39.

Holdsworth, W. S. *History of English Law.* London: Methuen, 1936–1971.

Honigman, E. A. J. and Susan Brock. *Playhouse Wills 1558–1642.* Manchester, England: Manchester University Press, 1993.

Hotson, Leslie. *Shakespeare's Sonnets Dated, and Other Essays.* New York: Oxford University Press, 1949.

———. *Mr. W. H.* London: R. Hart-Davis, 1964.

Houlbrooke, Ralph. "The Punishment of Incontinence." *Church Courts and the People During the English Reformation 1520–1570.* Oxford: Oxford University Press, 1979.

———. *The English Family 1450–1700.* Harlow, England: Longman, 1984.

———. "The Making of Marriage in Mid-Tudor England: Evidence from the Records of Matrimonial Contract Litigation." *Journal of Family History* (winter 1985): 339–52.

Howard-Hill, Trevor. "Buc and the Censorship of *Sir John Van Olden Barnavelt* in 1619." *Review of English Studies,* new series, no. 39 (1988): 39–63.

Howarth, Robert Guy. *Literature of the Theater: Marlowe to Shirley.* Sidney: Holstead Press, 1953.

———. *Modern Language Review* 59, no. 4 (1964): 633.

Hudson, John. *The Formation of the English Common Law.* London: Longman, 1996.

Hume, Robert D. "Texts within Contexts: Notes Toward a Historical Method." *Philologica Quarterly* 71, no. 1 (winter 1992): 69–100.

Hurstfield, Joel. *The Queen's Wards: Wardship and Marriage under Elizabeth I.* London: Longman, Green 1958.

Ibbetson, David. "Assumpsit and Debt in the Early Sixteenth Century: The Origins of the Indebitatus Count." *Cambridge Law Journal* 41 (1982): 42–61.

———. "Law Reporting in the 1590's." *Law Reporting in England.* Edited by Chantal Stebbings, 73–88. London: Hambledon, 1995.

Inderwick, F. A., ed. *Calendar of the Inner Temple Records.* Inner Temple Society Acts of Parliament, 1505–1589. 2 vols. London, 1898.

Ingram, Martin. "Spousals Litigation in the English Ecclesiastical Courts, c. 1350–c. 1640." *Marriage and Society: Studies in the Social History of Marriage.* Edited by R. B. Outhwaite, 35–57. London: Europa, 1981.

———. "The Reform of Popular Culture? Sex and Marriage in Early Modern England." *Popular Culture in Seventeenth-Century England.* Edited by Barry Reay, 129–65. Beckenham, England: Croom Helm, 1985.

———. *Church Courts, Sex and Marriage in England, 1570–1640.* Cambridge: Cambridge University Press, 1987.

Ingram, William. *A London Life in the Brazen Age: Francis Langley, 1548–1602.* Cambridge: Harvard University Press, 1978.

———. "The Playhouse as an Investment, 1607–1614: Thomas Woodford and Whitefriars." *Medieval & Renaissance Drama in England.* Vol. 2. (1985), 209–30.

———. "Robert Keysar, Playhouse Speculator." *Shakespeare Quarterly* 37, no. 4 (winter 1986): 476–85.

———. *The Business of Playing: The Beginnings of the Adult Professional Theater in Elizabethan London.* Ithaca: Cornell University Press, 1992.

Ives, E. W. "The Law and the Lawyers." *Shakespeare Survey* 17 (1964): 73–86.

———. "The Genesis of the Statute of Uses." *English Historical Review* 82 (1967): 673–97.

———. "Shakespeare and History: Divergencies and Agreements." *Shakespeare Survey* 38 (1985): 19–35.

James, Katherine H. "The Widow in Jacobean Drama." Ph.D. diss., University of Tennessee, Diss. Ab. 34 (1973), 1246A.

Jamieson, Michael. *Ben Jonson: Three Comedies.* Harmondsworth, England: Penguin Books Ltd., 1985.

Jankowski, Theodora. "Defining/Confining the Duchess: Negotiating the Female Body in John Webster's *The Duchess of Malfi.*" *Studies in Philology* 87 (1990): 221–37.

Johansson, Bertil. *Law and Lawyers in Elizabethan England as Evidenced in the Plays of Ben Jonson and Thomas Middleton.* Acta Universitatis Stockholmiensis. Stockholm Studies in English, no. 18. Stockholm: Almqvist & Wiksell, 1967.

Jones, N. G. "Uses, Trusts and the Path to Privity." *Cambridge Law Journal* 56 (1997): 175–200.

Jones, W. J. *The Elizabethan Court of Chancery.* Oxford: Clarendon Press, 1967.

Jonson, Ben. *Epicoene.* Edited by L. A. Beaurline. Regents Renaissance Drama Series. Lincoln: University of Nebraska Press, 1966.

———. *The Staple of News.* Edited by Anthony Parr. Manchester, England: Manchester University Press, 1988.

Jordan, William C. "Approaches to the Court Scene in the Bond Story: Equity and Mercy or Reason and Nature." *Shakespeare Quarterly* 33 (1982): 49–59.

Katz, David S. *The Jews in the History of England 1485–1850.* Oxford: Clarendon Press, 1994.

Kaye, J. M. "A Note on the Statute of Enrollments." *Law Quarterly Review* 104 (1988): 617–33.

Keeton, George William. *Shakespeare and his Legal Problems.* London: A. and C. Black, 1930.

———. *Shakespeare's Legal and Political Background.* New York: Pitman, 1967.

———. "Shakespeare's Legal and Political Background." *Law Quarterly Review* 84 (1968): 33–47.

Kelley, Donald R. "History, English Law and the Renaissance." *Past & Present* 65 (1974): 24–51.

Kiralfy, A. K. *The Action on the Case.* London: Sweet and Maxwell, 1951.

Kliman, Bernice W. "Isabella in *Measure for Measure.*" *Shakespeare Studies* 15 (1982): 137–48.

Knafla, Louis A. "The Law Studies of an Elizabethan Student." *Huntington Library Quarterly* 32 (1969): 221–40.

Knight, W. Nicholas. "Equity, *The Merchant of Venice* and William Lambarde." *Shakespeare Survey* 27 (1974): 93–104.

Knoll, Robert E. *Ben Jonson's Plays: An Introduction.* Lincoln: University of Nebraska Press, 1964.

Kornstein, Daniel J. "Fie upon your law!" *Cardozo Studies in Law and Literature* 5 (1993): 35–56.

———. *Kill All the Lawyers: Shakespeare's Legal Appeal.* Princeton: Princeton University Press, 1994.

Krueger, Robert. "Sir John Davies: *Orchestra* Complete, *Epigrams,* Unpublished Poems." *Review of English Studies* 13 (1962): 2–29, 113–24.

Kuchnert, Philip G. "Will and Fate in Four English Renaissance Tragedies." Ph.D. diss., University of Utah, Diss, Ab. 35 (1974), 1626A.

Lady Martin. "Shakespeare's Female Characters." *Blackwood's Magazine* (October 1884).

Lambard, William. *Eirenarcha: Or the Offices of the Justices of the Peace.* London, 1582.

———. *Archeion.* London, 1635.

———. *The Duties of Constables, Borsholders, Tithingmen and such other low Ministers of the Peace* (1583). Amsterdam: De Capo Press, 1969.

Lancashire, Anne. "The Witch: Stage Flop or Political Mistake?" *"Accompaninge the players": Essays Celebrating Thomas Middleton, 1580–1980*. Kenneth Friedenreich. Edited by New York: AMS Press, 1983.

Lanier, Douglas M. "The Prison-House of the Canon: Allegorical Form and Posterity in Ben Jonson's *The Staple of News*." *Medieval & Renaissance Drama in England*. Vol. 2 New York: AMS Press, 1985.

Larkin, J. F., and P. L. Hughes, eds. *Stuart Royal Proclamations*. 2 vols. Oxford: Clarendon Press, 1973.

Lawes Resolutions of Womens Rights, The. London, 1632.

Lawrence, W. W. "*Measure for Measure* and Lucio." *Shakespeare Quarterly* 9 (1950): 443–53.

Lawson, Peter. "Property, Crime, and Hard Times in England, 1559–1624." *Law and History Review* 4 (1986): 95–127.

Leech, Clifford. "An addendum to Webster's Duchess." *Philological Quarterly* 37 (April 1958): 253–56.

Levack, Brian P. *The Civil Lawyers in England 1603–1641*. Oxford: Clarendon Press, 1973.

———. "The English Civilians, 1500–1750." *Lawyers in Early Modern Europe and America*. Edited by Wilfred Prest, 108–28. London: Croom Helm, 1981.

Levin, Joel. "The Measure of Law and Equity: Tolerance in Shakespeare's Vienna." *Law and Literature Perspectives*. Edited by Bruce L. Rockwood, 193–207. New York: Land, 1996.

Levin, Richard. *The Multiple Plot in English Renaissance Drama*. Chicago: University of Chicago Press, 1971.

Lieblein, Leanore. "The Context of Murder in English Domestic Plays, 1590–1610." *Studies in English Literature* 23, no. 2 (spring 1983): 181–96.

Lybarger, Donald F. "Shakespeare and the Law: Was the Bard Admitted to the Bar?" *Cleveland Bar Review* 36 (March 1965): 9–16.

MacCullock, Diarmaid. "Bondmen Under the Tudors." *Law and Government Under the Tudors*. Edited by Claire Cross, David Loades, and J. J. Scarisbrick, 91–109. Cambridge: Cambridge University Press, 1988.

MacKay, M. "*The Merchant of Venice*: A Reflection of the Early Conflict Between Courts of Law and Courts of Equity." *Shakespeare Quarterly* 15 (1964): 371–75.

Maclaurin, Richard C. *On the Nature and Evidence of Title to Realty; a Historical Sketch*. London: C. J. Clay, 1901.

Maclean, Ian. *Interpretation and Meaning in the Renaissance: The Case of Law*. Cambridge: Cambridge University Press, 1992.

Maitland, F. W. *English Law and the Renaissance*. Cambridge: Cambridge University Press, 1901.

Malone, Edmund. "Prolegomena." *The Life of William Shakespeare*. London, 1790.

Marston, John. *The Scourge of Villainy*. London, n.d.

Massinger, Philip. "A New Way to Pay Old Debts." *The Selected Plays of Philip Massinger.* Edited by Colin Gibson. 182–270. New York: Cambridge University Press, 1978.

McIlwain, Charles H., and Paul L. Ward, eds. *Lambarde's Archeion.* Cambridge: Harvard University Press, 1957.

Merchant, W. Moelwyn. "Lawyer and Actor: Process of Law in Elizabethan Drama." *English Studies Today* 3 (1964): 107–24.

Middleton, Thomas. *A Trick to Catch the Old One.* Edited by G. J. Watson. London: Ernest Benn Ltd., 1968.

———. *The Phoenix.* Edited by John Bradbury Brooks. New York: Garland, 1980.

Mikesell, Margaret L. "Matrimony and Change in Webster's *The Duchess of Malfi.*" *Journal of the Rocky Mountain Medieval and Renaissance Association* 2 (1981): 97–111.

Milsom, S. F. C. *Historical Foundations of the Common Law,* 2nd ed. London: Butterworth, 1981.

Morris, Brian. Introduction to *The Broken Heart.* New Mermaids edition. London: Ernest Benn Ltd., 1965.

Mullaney, Steven. "Lying Like the Truth: Riddle, Representation and Treason in Renaissance England." *ELH* 47 (1980): 32–47.

Nagarajan, S. "*Measure for Measure* and Elizabethan Betrothals." *Shakespeare Quarterly* 14 (1963): 115–19.

Nashe, Thomas. *Pierce Penilesse.* London, n.d.

Neill, Michael. "Massinger's Patriarchy: The Social Vision of *A New Way to Pay Old Debts.*" *Renaissance Drama.* Vol 10. Edited by Leonard Barkan. Evanston, Ill.: Northwestern University Press, 1979.

Nungezer, Edwin. A. *Dictionary of Actors.* Ithaca: Cornell University Press, 1929.

Nuttall, A. D. "'Measure for Measure': The Bed-Trick." *Shakespeare Survey* 28 (1975): 51–56.

Ornstein, Robert. *The Moral Vision of Jacobean Tragedy.* Madison: University of Wisconsin Press, 1960.

Outhwaite, R. B., ed. *Clandestine Marriage in England, 1500–1850.* London: Hambledon, 1995.

———. *Marriage and Society: Studies in the Social History of Marriage.* London: Europa, 1981.

Overbury, Thomas. *The Overburian Characters.* Edited by W. J. Paylor. Oxford: B. Blackwell, 1936.

Patterson, Annabel. *Censorship and Interpretation: The Conditions of Reading and Writing in Early Modern England.* Madison: University of Wisconsin Press, 1984.

Penzance, Lord [Sir James Plaisted Wilde]. *The Bacon-Shakespeare Controversy.* London: Sampson Low, Marston & Co., 1890.

Phelps, Charles E. *Falstaff and Equity.* Boston: Houghton Mifflin, 1901.

Phillips, Owen Hood. "The Law Relating to Shakespeare 1564–1964." *Law Quarterly Review* 80 (1967): 172–202.

———. *Shakespeare and the Lawyers.* London: Methuen, 1972.

Plucknett, T. F. T. *A Concise History of the Common Law.* 5th ed. London: Butterworth, 1956.

Pollock, Sir Frederick. "A note on Shylock v. Antonio." *Law Quarterly Review* 30 (1914): 175–77.

Pollock, Sir Frederick, and Frederic William Maitland. *History of the English Law Before the Time of Edward I,* 2nd ed. 2 vols. Reissued. London: Cambridge University Press, 1968.

Poos, L. R. "The Heavy-Handed Marriage Counselor: Regulating Marriage in Some Later-Medieval Ecclesiastical-Court Jurisdictions." *American Journal of Legal History* 39 (1995): 291–309.

Posner, Richard A. *Law and Literature: A Misunderstood Relation.* Cambridge: Harvard University Press, 1988.

Powers, Alan. "*Measure for Measure* and Law Reform in 1604." *The Upstart Crow* 15 (1996): 35–47.

Prest, Wilfred R. "Legal Education in the Gentry 1560–1640." *Past & Present* 30 (1967): 20–39.

———. *The Inns of Court under Elizabeth I and the Early Stuarts 1590–1640.* London: Longman, 1972.

———. *The Rise of the Barristers: A Social History of the English Bar 1590–1640.* Oxford: Clarendon Press, 1986.

Purkiss, Diane, ed. *Renaissance Women.* London: William Pickering, 1994.

Ranald, Margaret Loftus. "The Betrothals of *All's Well that Ends Well*." *Huntington Library Quarterly* 26 (1963): 179–92.

———. "'As Marriage Binds, and Blood Breaks': English Marriage and Shakespeare." *Shakespeare Quarterly* 30 (winter 1979): 68–81.

———. *Shakespeare and his Social Context.* New York: AMS Press, 1987.

Read, Conyers. *William Lambarde and Local Government.* Ithaca: Cornell University Press, 1962.

Reinheimer, David A. "*The Roman Actor,* Censorship, and Dramatic Autonomy." *Studies in English Literature* 38 (spring 1998): 317–32.

Robertson, J. M. *The Baconian Heresy.* New York, 1913.

Roscelli, William. "Isabella, Sin and Civil Law." *University of Kansas City Review* 28 (1962): 215–27.

Rose, Mary Beth. *The Expense of Spirit: Love and Sexuality in English Drama.* Ithaca: Cornell University Press, 1988.

———. ed. *Renaissance Drama: Disorder and the Drama,* new series 21. Evanston, Ill.: Northwestern University Press, 1990.

Rushton, William Lowes. *Shakespeare a Lawyer.* London, 1858.

———. *Shakespeare's Testamentary Language.* London: Longman, Green and Co., 1869.

———. *Shakespeare's Legal Maxims.* Liverpool: Henry Young & Sons, 1907. Reprinted in 1973.

Rutter, Carol Chillington, ed. *Documents of the Rose Playhouse.* Manchester, England: Manchester University Press, 1999.

Saunders, Henry. "Staple Courts in *The Merchant of Venice.*" *NQ* 31 (1984): 190–91.

Schanzer, Ernest. "The Marriage Contracts in *Measure for Measure.*" *Shakespeare Survey* 13 (1960): 81–89.

Schmidt, Alexander. *Shakespeare Lexicon.* New York: Walter De Gruyter, 1971.

Schoenbaum, Samuel. *William Shakespeare: A Compact Documentary Life.* Oxford: Oxford University Press, 1977.

Schotz, Amiel. "The Law That Never Was: A Note on *The Merchant of Venice.*" *Theatre Research International* 16 (1991): 249–52.

Scott, Margaret. "'Our City's Institutions': Some Further Reflections on the Marriage Contracts in *Measure for Measure.*" *ELH* 49 (winter 1982): 790–804.

Scouten, Arthur. "An Historical Approach to *Measure for Measure.*" *Philological Quarterly* 54 (1975): 68–84.

Selden, Raman. *English Verse Satire, 1590–1765.* London, 1978.

Selzer, John L. "Merit and Degree in Webster's The Duchess of Malfi." *English Literary Renaissance* 11 (1981): 70–80.

Semper, I. J. "The Jacobean Theatre through the Eyes of Catholic Clerics." *Shakespeare Quarterly* 3 (1952): 45–51.

Seufert, Robert. "'The Decorum of These Daies': Robert Wilmot and the Idea of Theatre." *Iowa State Journal of Research.* 58, no. 3 (February 1984): 319–27.

Shakespeare in the Public Records. Public Record Office Handbooks, no. 5. London: Her Majesty's Stationery Office, 1964.

Sharpe, Kevin, and Christopher Brooks. "History, English Law and the Renaissance." *Past & Present* 72 (1976): 133–42.

Sheehan, M. M. "The Formation and Stability of Marriage in Fourteenth-Century England: Evidence of an Ely Register." *Mediæval Studies* 33 (1971): 249–50.

———. *Marriage, Family, and Law in Medieval Europe: Collected Studies.* Toronto: University of Toronto Press, 1996.

Shell, Marc. "The Wether and the Ewe: Verbal Usury in The Merchant of Venice." *Kenyon Review,* 1, no. 4 (1979): 65–92.

Simon, Sir Jocelyn. "Shakespeare's Legal and Political Background." *Law Quarterly Review* 84 (1968): 33–47.

Simpson, Alfred William Brian. "The Early Constitution of the Inns of Court." *Cambridge Law Journal* 28 (1970): 241–56.

———. *An Introduction to the History of the Land Law,* 2nd ed. Oxford: Oxford University Press, 1973.

———. *A History of the Common Law of Contract.* Oxford: Clarendon Press, 1975.

———. *A History of the Land Law,* 2nd ed. Oxford: Clarendon Press, 1986.

———. "Entails and Perpetuities." *Legal Theory and Legal History,* 143–62. London: Hambledon, 1987.

Sisson, C. J. *Shakespeare's Tragic Justice.* London: Methuen & Co., 1963.

———. *The Boar's Head Theatre: An Innyard Theatre of the Elizabethan Age.* Edited by Stanley Wells. London: Routledge & Kegan Paul, 1972.

Smart, John Semple. *Shakespeare: Truth and Tradition.* Oxford: Clarendon Press, 1966.

Smith, Gregory. *Elizabethan Critical Essays.* 2 vols. Oxford: Clarendon Press, 1904.

Smith, Irwin. *Shakespeare's Blackfriars Playhouse: Its History and Design.* New York: New York University Press, 1964.

Smith, Lacey Baldwin. *Treason in Tudor England: Politics and Paranoia.* Princeton: Princeton University Press, 1986.

Smith, M. E. "Personnel at the Second Blackfriars: Some Biographical Notes." *NQ* 30 (October 1978): 441–44.

Smith, Richard M. "Marriage processes in the English Past: Some Continuities." *The World We Have Gained.* Edited by Lloyd Bonfield, Richard M. Smith, and Keith Wrightson, 43–99. Oxford: Blackwell, 1986.

Sokol, B. J., "*The Merchant of Venice* and the Law Merchant." 6 *Renaissance Studies* (1992) 60–7.

———. "Prejudice and Law in *The Merchant of Venice.*" 51 *Shakespeare Survey* (1998) 159–73.

Sokol, B.J. and Mary Sokol. "Legal Terms Implying Extended Meanings in *As You Like It* 3.2.331–32 and *Troilus and Cressida* 3.2.89–91." *NQ* 46 (1999): 236–38.

———. "Shakespeare and the English Equity Jurisdiction: *The Merchant of Venice* and the Two Texts of *King Lear.*" 50 *Review of English Studies* (1999): 427–49.

———. *Shakespeare's Legal Language: A Dictionary.* London: Athlone Press, 2000.

Spedding, James. *The Letters and the Life of Francis Bacon.* 14 vols. London: Longman, Green, Longman, and Roberts, 1862.

Spinoza, Charles D. "Shylock and Debt and Contract in 'The Merchant of Venice.'" *Cardozo Studies in Law and Literature* 5 (1993): 65–85.

———. "The Transformation of Intentionality: Debt and Contract in *The Merchant of Venice.*" *English Literary Renaissance* 24 (1994): 370–409.

———. "'The name and all th' addition': *King Lear's* Opening Scene and the Common-Law Use." *Shakespeare Studies* 23 (1995): 146–86.

Spinrad, Phoebe S. "Dogberry Hero: Shakespeare's Comic Constables in Their Communal Context." *Studies in Philology* 89 (1992): 161–78.

Sprague, Homer B. "Shakespeare's Alleged Blunders in Legal Terminology." *Yale Law Journal* 11 (1902): 304–10.

Spring, Eileen. *Law, Land and Family: Aristocratic Inheritance in England 1300–1800.* Chapel Hill: University of North Carolina Press, 1993.

Stockton, Lewis. *Marriage Considered from Legal and Ecclesiastical Viewpoints.* Buffalo, N.Y.: Huebner-Bleistein, 1912.

Stone, Lawrence. *The Family, Sex and Marriage in England 1500–1800.* London: Weidenfeld and Nicolson, 1979.

Stow, John. *Survey of London.* 2 vols. Oxford: Clarendon Press, 1908.

Sugden, E. H. *A Topographical Dictionary to the Works of Shakespeare and His Fellow Dramatists.* Manchester, England: Manchester University Press, 1925.

Swinburne, Charles Algernon. *The Complete Works of Algernon Charles Swinburne.* Edited by Edmund Gosse and Thomas James Wise. 20 vols. London: W. Heinemann, Ltd., 1926.

Swinburne, Henry. *A Briefe Treatise of Testaments and Last Willes.* London, 1590.

———. *Treatise of Spousals or Matrimonial Contracts: Wherein All the Questions Relating to that Subject are Ingeniously Debated and Resolved.* London, 1686.

Symonds, E. M. "The Diary of John Greene (1635–57)." *English Historical Review* 43 (1928): 386–89.

Tawney, R. H., ed. *Thomas Wilson, A Discourse Upon Usury (1572).* London: G. Bell, 1925.

Thompson, Ann. "Shakespeare and Sexuality." *Shakespeare Survey* 46 (1994): 1–8.

Thorne, S.E., ed. "The Early History of the Inns of Court with Special Reference to Gray's Inn." *Essays in English Legal History.* Edited by S. E. Thorne. 137–54. London: Hambledon Press, 1985.

———. *A Discourse upon the Exposicio & Understanding of Statutes With Sir Thomas Egerton's Additions.* San Marino, Calif.: Huntington Library, 1942.

Tucker, E. F. J. "The Letter of the Law in *The Merchant of Venice.*" *Shakespeare Studies* 29 (1976): 93–101.

———. *Intruder into Eden: Representations of The Common Lawyer in English Literature, 1350–1750.* Columbia, S.C.: Camden House, 1984.

Wadsworth, Frank W. "Webster's Duchess of Malfi in the Light of Some Contemporary Ideas on Marriage and Remarriage." *Philological Quarterly* 35 (1957): 394–407.

Waith, Eugene M. "Things as They Are and the World of Absolutes." *The Elizabethan Theatre IV.* Edited by George Hibbard. Hamden, Conn.: Archon Press, 1972.

Walker, J. D. *The Records of the Honorable Society of Lincoln's Inn (Black Books).* London, 1897.

Wallace, C. W. "Shakespeare's Money Interest in the Globe Theater." *The Century Magazine* 80, no. 4 (August 1910): 500–512.

———. "The Swan Theatre and the Earl of Pembroke's Players." *Englische Studien* 43 (1911): 340 et seq.

———. "The First London Theatre: Materials for a History." *University Studies* 13, nos. 1, 2, 3 (January, April, July, 1913). Lincoln, Nebraska.

Ward, Ian. *Law and Literature: Possibilities and Perspectives.* Cambridge: Cambridge University Press, 1995.

Watkin, Thomas G. "Feudal Theory, Social Needs and the Rise of the Heritable Fee." *Cambrian Law Review* 10 (1979): 39–62.

Wears, T. M. "Shakespeare's Legal Acquirements." *Canadian Bar Review* 16 (1938): 28–37.

Welsford, Enid. *The Court Masque.* Cambridge: Cambridge University Press, 1927.

Wentersdorf, Karl P. "The Marriage Contracts in *Measure for Measure:* A Reconsideration." *Shakespeare Survey* 32 (1979): 129–44.

Whalley, Joyce I. "The Swan Theatre in the 16th Century." *Theatre Notebook* 20, no. 2 (winter 1965/66): 73.

Wharam, Alan. *Treason: Famous English Treason Trials.* Gloucestershire, England: Alan Sutton Publishing Ltd., 1995.

Wheatley, Henry Benjamin. *London, Past and Present: A Dictionary of Its History, Associations, and Traditions.* 3 vols. Detroit, Mich.: Singing Tree Press, 1968.

White, Edward J. *Commentaries on the Law in Shakespeare.* Buffalo, N.Y.: William S. Hein, 1987.

White, Richard Grant. "Shakespeare, Attorney at Law and Solicitor in Chancery." *Atlantic Monthly* 4 (1859): 84–105.

Whytforde, Richard. *A Werke for Husholders.* London, 1530.

Wickham, Glynne. *Early English Stages, 1300–1660.* Vols. 1, 2, 3 (in 4). London: Routledge and Kegan Paul, 1959–81.

Wilkes, G. A., ed. *The Complete Plays of Ben Jonson.* Oxford: Clrandon Press, 1982.

Wilkins, George. *The Miseries of Enforced Marriage.* Edited by Glenn H. Blayney. Oxford: Malone Society Reprints [107], 1963.

———. *Shakespeare's Legal Maxims.* London, 1907. Reprinted in 1973.

Williams, Joshua. *Principles of the Law of Personal Property, Intended for the Use of Students in Conveyancing.* London: S. Sweet, 1848.

Williamson, John Bruce. *The History of the Temple, London.* London: John Murray, 1925.

Windolph, Francis Lyman. *Reflections of Law in Literature.* Philadelphia: University of Pennsylvania Press, 1956.

Woodbridge, Linda, and Edward Berry, eds. *True Rites and Maimed Rites: Ritual in Shakespeare and His Age.* Urbana: University of Illinois Press, 1992.

Wren, Robert M. "Salisbury and the Blackfriars Theatre." *Theatre Notebook* 23, no. 3 (spring 1969): 103–9.

Yachnin, Paul. "A Game at Chess: Thomas Middleton's 'Praise of Folly.'" *Modern Language Quarterly* 48, no. 2 (June 1987): 107–23.

Yale, D. E. C. "Equitable Estates in the Seventeenth Century: An Explanation by Lord Nottingham." *Cambridge Law Journal* 15 (1957): 72–86.

———, ed. *Lord Nottingham's "Manual of Chancery Practice" and "Prolegomena of Chancery and Equity."* Cambridge: Cambridge University Press, 1965.

Young, Debra Brown. "King's Revels." Ph.D. diss. 30 Tulane University (1986).

Young, George Malcolm. "Shakespeare and the Termers." *Proceedings of the British Academy* 33 (1947).

Index

Admiral's Men, 58
Admiral's Men: *aka* Nottingham's Men, 58, 62, 69, 70
Alice Pierce, 57
All Hallows, 34
Allen, Charles, 196 n
Allen, Giles, 52, 53, 55
Allen, Sara, 53
Androwes, George, 84, 89, 90, 93

Bacon, Sir Francis, 19, 32, 41, 47, 108, 109, 153, 195 n, 196 n, 200 n, 213 n, 214 n
Bankside, 53, 54, 55
Barry, Lording, 88, 89, 90, 205 n, 210 n; *Ram-Alley,* 205 n
Barton, Dunbar Plunket, 196 n
Beaumont and Fletcher: *A King and No King,* 183; *The Woman-Hater,* 44, 202 n, 209 n
Beaumont, Francis, 34, 44, 47, 83, 202 n, 203 n, 209 n
Beeston, Christopher, 70
Benchers, 27, 45, 198 n
Bentley, Richard, 196 n
Berkeley's Men, 36
Betrothal, 135, 136, 149, 221 n, 222 n
Beverley's Case, 215 n
Bird (Borne), William, 56, 61
Bishop, Richard, 60
Black Joan, 57
Blackstone's Commentaries, 67, 142, 207 n, 208 n, 216 n, 218 n
Blount, Charles, 151
Boltas, 26, 197 n
Bourbon, 57
Bracery, 60
Branbolt, 57

Brayne, John, 52, 54, 55, 206 n
Brend, Nicholas, 64, 66, 67
Bridewell, 80
Bromwell, Peter, 58
Browker, Hugh, 58, 63, 207 n
Browne, Robert, 34, 45, 47, 59, 60, 61, 62, 63, 64
Burbages, the, 48, 51, 53, 55, 64, 66, 67, 69, 94, 95; Cuthbert, 52, 53, 54, 55, 64, 94, 95; James, 47, 51, 52, 53, 54, 72; Richard, 52, 54, 64, 77, 91, 93, 100
Burghley, Lord, 32, 56

Callard v. Callard, 212 n
Campbell, John Lord, 21, 195 n
Campion, Thomas, 44, 47, 204 n
Candlemas, 34, 200 n, 201 n
Case Law: *Callard v. Callard,* 212 n; *Case of Perpetuities,* 211 n; *Chudleigh's Case,* 109, 211 n; *Evans v. Kirkham,* 96, 98; *Hokerigge v. Lucas,* 224 n; *Jane Walkden v. Richard Lowe,* 230 n; *Keysar v. Burbage,* 208 n; *Kirkham and Kendall v. Daniell,* 98; *Kirkham v. Pauton,* 76, 77, 98; *Syblil Balkhurst v. Randle Ramshae,* 224 n; *Thompson v. Leach,* 215 n; *Underwood v. Manwood,* 33
Cecil, Robert, Earl of Salisbury, 92
Cestui que use, 63, 102, 105, 107, 108, 110, 112, 113, 114, 117, 118, 119, 126, 127, 129, 132, 212 n, 213 n, 219 n
Chamberlain's Men, 38, 58, 64, 69, 70
Champerty, 60

257

258 INDEX

Chancery, 26, 54, 60, 61, 89, 96, 97, 98, 99, 108, 195 n, 205 n, 208 n, 210 n, 219 n
Chapman, George, 34, 42, 47, 81, 82, 84, 86, 87, 92, 145, 146, 147, 208 n, 209 n, 224 n, 225 n, 227 n, 234 n; *Bussy D'Ambois,* 82, 209 n; The Byron plays, 86, 87, 89, 92; *The Gentleman Usher,* 144, 145, 189, 224 n
Children of Blackfriars, 80, 85
Children of the Chapel, 73, 80, 146
Children of the Queen's Chapel, 73
Children of the Queen's Revels, 80, 81, 85, 93
Christmas, 29, 31, 32, 34, 35, 40, 45, 61, 83, 93, 200 n, 201 n, 203 n, 206 n
Chudleigh's Case, 109, 211 n
Citie Match, The, 205 n
Clarkson and Warren, 18, 118, 122, 195 n, 196 n, 197 n, 213 n, 214 n, 215 n; *Law of Property,* 18, 195 n, 196 n, 197 n, 213 n, 215 n, 216 n
Clifton, Thomas, 75, 76, 79, 99
Clyomon and Clamydes, 183
Coke, Attorney General, 46, 109, 213 n
Collins, J. C., 196 n
Consideration, good, 106, 124
Consideration, valuable, 93, 106, 124
Copyhold, 216 n
Courts of Law: Chancery, 26, 54, 60, 61, 89, 96, 97, 98, 99, 108, 195 n, 205 n, 208 n, 210 n, 219 n; King's Bench, 55, 96, 98; Marshalsea Court, 60; Queen's Bench, 60; Requests, 55, 57, 208 n, 210 n; Star Chamber, 61, 75, 76, 77, 78, 79, 83, 99, 100, 208 n
Cunningham, H., 196 n
Cupid's Whirligig, 43

Damon and Pithias, 32
Daniel, Samuel, 44, 80, 81, 84, 98, 204 n, 209 n; *Philotas,* 81, 82, 84
Davenant, William, 35, 49, 204 n, 205 n
Davies, Sir John, 36, 47, 202 n, 203 n
Davis, C. K., 195 n

de la Boderie, M., 86, 87, 92
de Montmorency, J. E. G., 196 n
De Witt, Johannes, 207 n
Dead rent, 94
Deed of gift, 105
Dekker, Thomas, 37, 39, 83, 203 n, 209 n; *Blurt, Master Constable,* 209 n; *Northward Ho!,* 209 n; *Satiromastix,* 39, 209 n; *The Shoemaker's Holiday,* 183; *Westward Ho!,* 209 n
Devecmon, William, 196 n
Dickens, Charles: *Bleak House,* 219 n
Dido and Aeneas, 57
Digges, Anne, 151
Domesday book, 107
Donne, John, 151
Downton, Thomas, 56, 57
Doyle, John T., 195 n
Drayton, Michael, 85, 88, 89

Eastward Ho!, 81, 82, 84, 87
Ecclesiastical Commission, 137, 139, 152
Edward IV, 150
Elizabeth I, 30, 32, 39, 40, 47, 75, 144, 150, 151, 152, 200 n, 204 n, 208 n, 224 n
Enfeoff, 21
Epitia, 154, 155
Equity, 55, 61, 96, 100, 121, 163
Essex, Earl of, 46, 81, 151, 225 n
Evans v. Kirkham, 96, 98
Evans, Henry, 48, 51, 71, 72, 73, 74, 75, 76, 77, 78, 79, 81, 83, 84, 85, 87, 90, 91, 92, 93, 94, 95, 96, 97, 98, 99, 100, 101, 102, 103, 209 n, 210 n

Farrant, Richard, 73, 74
Feoffee to uses, 102, 104, 107, 108, 112, 113, 114, 116, 117, 118, 119, 120, 121, 122, 124, 126, 127, 129, 131, 132, 211 n, 212 n, 214 n, 218 n
Feoffment, 21, 116, 117, 122, 197 n, 214 n, 215 n, 219 n
Feudal dues, 120, 213 n
Fidei commissa, 110
Fleire, The, 34, 43
Fletcher, John, 83, 200 n, 202 n, 203 n, 209 n

INDEX

Foard, James T., 195 n
Ford, John, 44, 45, 46, 47, 204 n, 205 n;
  'Tis Pity She's a Whore, 44; *Broken Heart*, 45, 204 n; *Lady's Trial*, 44; *Lover's Melancholy*, 45, 205 n
Friar Spendleton, 57

Gascoigne, George, 40; *Jocasta*, 29, 31, 40, 46; *The Supposes*, 29, 31, 40
Gerrard, John, 98
Gesta Grayorum, 201 n
Giles, Nathaniel, master of the Chapel Children, Windsor, 74
Grant, Richard, 195 n
Gratian, 143, 148, 190
Greene, Robert, 38, 41, 196 n, 203 n
Greenwich Palace, 30
Greenwood, Granville George, 196 n
Grey, Lady Catherine, 151
Guernsey, Rocellus Sheridan, 195 n
Gurr, Andrew, 38, 198 n, 203 n, 205 n, 208 n

Hardicanute, 57
Hathaway, Anne, 151
Hawkins, Alexander, 71, 72, 74, 75, 76, 77, 78, 79, 80, 91, 95, 96, 97, 99, 100, 234 n
Heard, Franklin Fiske, 195 n
Hein, William, 195 n
Heminges, John, 64, 65, 66, 67, 68, 69, 70, 71, 91, 100, 205 n, 208 n
Henry VIII, 30, 108, 120, 213 n, 226 n
Henslowe, Philip, 44, 51, 56, 57, 58, 61, 69, 70
Heywood, Thomas, 70
Hide, John, 52
Histriomastix, 45, 204 n
Hokerigge v. *Lucas*, 224 n
Hughes, Thomas: *The Misfortunes of Arthur*, 29, 30, 32, 40, 41, 46, 199 n, 200 n, 201 n
Hunnis, William, master of the Chapel Royal, 73

Impuberes, 171
In facie ecclesiæ, 137, 142, 182, 184
Ingram, William, 55, 56, 59, 60, 62, 85, 90, 199 n, 206 n, 207 n, 208 n, 210 n

Inheritance, 65, 114, 121, 151, 211 n
Inner Temple Masque, 44
Inns of Court, 25, 27, 28, 29, 30, 31, 32, 33, 34, 35, 36, 37, 38, 39, 40, 42, 43, 44, 45, 46, 47, 48, 49, 50, 102, 107, 108, 115, 117, 127, 133, 171, 191, 192, 197 n, 198 n, 199 n, 200 n, 202 n, 203 n, 204 n, 205 n; Gray's Inn, 28, 29, 30, 31, 32, 33, 34, 35, 40, 41, 42, 44, 45, 46, 108, 109, 197 n, 199 n, 200 n, 201 n, 204 n, 205 n, 206 n; Grayans, 33, 41, 48; Inner Temple, 26, 28, 29, 30, 31, 34, 40, 42, 44, 45, 46, 198 n, 199 n, 201 n, 202 n, 203 n, 205 n, 213 n; Lincoln's Inn, 13, 31, 32, 34, 38, 41, 42, 43, 46, 48, 198 n, 200 n, 205 n; Middle Temple, 26, 29, 33, 34, 35, 37, 38, 42, 43, 44, 46, 49, 198 n, 199 n, 200 n, 203n 204 n, 205 n; Templarians, 33, 48; Furnivall's Inn, 199 n
Invasion of the Body Snatchers, 192
Isle of Dogges, 57
Isle of Gulls, 80, 81, 84, 92, 93
Ius commune, 152

James I, 80, 147, 149
Jane Walkden v. Richard Lowe, 230 n
Jointly and severally, 67, 68
Joint-tenancy, 65, 66, 67, 71
Jointure, 65, 67, 118 n, 119 n, 215 n
Jones, Richard, 56
Jonson, Benjamin, 20, 38, 39, 42, 43, 47, 81, 84, 102, 103, 113, 114, 115, 116, 118, 119, 120, 123, 126, 127, 131, 133, 196 n, 204 n, 205 n, 213 n, 214 n, 215 n, 216 n, 217 n, 235 n; *The Alchemist*, 205 n; *Bartholomew Fair*, 39, 43, 113, 114, 116, 205 n; *The Devil is an Ass*, 43, 114, 115, 133, 205 n, 214 n; *Epicoene*, 133, 214 n; *Every Man Out of His Humour*, 39, 42, 203 n, 204 n, 205 n; *Staple of News*, 43, 119, 120, 121, 123, 126, 127, 131, 133, 205 n, 213 n, 216 n, 217 n, 218 n; *Volpone*, 215 n
Jurata sponsalia, 162, 163

Kempe, William, 61, 64, 65, 66, 67, 69, 70, 71
Kendall, Thomas, haberdasher, 75, 76, 77, 80, 91, 95, 96, 98, 99, 100, 208 n
Kenilworth, Princely Pleasures of, 40
Keysar v. Burbage, 208 n
Keysar, John, goldsmith, 84
Keysar, Robert, 84, 85, 86, 87, 88, 91, 92, 93, 94, 95, 98, 208 n, 210 n
King's Bench, Court of, 55, 96, 98
King's Men, 84, 91, 93, 94, 95, 98, 205 n
King's Revels, The, 85, 88, 89, 210 n
Kinwelmarsh, Francis, 40
Kirkham and Kendall v. Daniell, 98
Kirkham v. Pauton, 76, 77, 98
Kirkham, Edward, 71, 72, 74, 75, 76, 77, 79, 80, 81, 82, 83, 84, 85, 86, 88, 91, 92, 95, 96, 97, 98, 99, 100, 208 n
Kyd, Thomas, 28; *The Spanish Tragedy,* 28, 29, 199 n

Lady Elizabeth's Men, 83
Langley, Francis, 55, 56, 57, 58, 59, 60, 61, 62, 63, 64, 206 n, 207 n
Langley, Richard, 56, 59
Lay law, 192, 193
Lease and release, 213 n, 218 n
Leveson, William, 64, 65, 66, 67, 68, 69, 70, 71
Life and Raigne of Henry IIII, The, 47
Lodge, Thomas, 41, 44, 47
Lombard, Peter, 143, 147, 190
Lowin, John, 70
Lyly, John, 73

Magister jocorum, 29
Magnificence, 30, 199 n
Malone, Edmond, 19, 195 n, 232 n
Manningham, John, 35, 39, 40, 203 n
Mark Twain, 196 n
Marriage of the Thames and the Rhine, The, 34
Marriage *per verba de futuro,* 16, 134, 135, 136, 137, 138, 141, 143, 147, 148, 149, 150, 153, 158, 162, 163, 165, 175, 176, 177, 183, 187, 222 n, 225 n, 226 n, 230 n, 231 n, 232 n, 233 n, 234 n

Marriage *per verba de præsenti,* 16, 134, 135, 136, 138, 139, 141, 142, 143, 144, 145, 147, 148, 149, 150, 151, 153, 158, 162, 166, 167, 168, 170, 171, 177, 178, 180, 181, 182, 183, 184, 185, 187, 188, 220 n, 223 n, 226 n, 227 n, 230 n, 233 n, 234 n, 235 n
Marshalsea Court, 60
Marston, John, 20, 34, 37, 42, 43, 47, 79, 81, 82, 83, 84, 85, 86, 87, 92, 93, 94, 95, 195 n, 199 n, 201 n, 202 n, 203 n, 204 n, 209 n; *The Dutch Curtesan,* 84; *The Insatiate Countess,* 87; *The Malcontent,* 45; *Parasitaster, or The Fawn,* 82, 209 n; *the silver mine play(?),* 86, 87, 89, 92
Mason, John, 89
Masque of Amity, 33
Masque of Flowers, 34
Masque of Heroes, The, 34, 42
Masque of Mountebanks, 34
Masque of Proteus, 33
Massinger, Philip, 20, 102, 130, 131, 132, 133, 216 n, 218 n, 219 n, 220 n; *A New Way to Pay Old Debts,* 130, 132, 133, 216 n, 218 n, 220 n; *The Roman Actor,* 205 n
Master of the Revels, 32, 58, 80
Menæchmi, The, 41
Mercy, 106, 159, 180
Meres, Francis, 37, 41
Middleton, Thomas, 20, 34, 42, 47, 49, 80, 82, 83, 84, 85, 95, 102, 127, 128, 129, 130, 132, 133, 174, 175, 181, 182, 183, 185, 186, 187, 189, 204 n, 205 n, 209 n, 210 n, 214 n, 215 n, 217 n, 218 n, 234 n, 235 n; *A Fair Quarrel,* 183, 184, 186, 189, 234 n; *A Trick to Catch the Old One,* 82, 85, 127, 130, 133, 209 n, 217 n, 218 n, 220 n; *A Chaste Maid in Cheapside,* 183, 215 n, 235 n; *A Mad World, My Masters,* 49, 183, 186, 187, 189, 209 n; *Michaelmas Term,* 74, 203 n, 209 n, 217 n; *The Phoenix,* 133, 209 n, 214 n; *The Puritan,* 209 n; *The Revenger's Tragedy,* 174, 209 n; *The Witch,*

175, 181, 186, 189, 234 n; *The Viper and Her Brood,* 84, 85, 210 n; *Your Five Gallants,* 85
Miseries of Enforced Marriage, The, 167, 175, 182, 183, 189, 232 n, 234 n
Moots, 197 n

Nabbes, Thomas, 38, 235 n
Nash, Thomas, 36
New Historicism, 17, 28, 197 n
Newman, John, 73
Non compos mentis, 119 n, 215 n
Norton, Thomas, 40, 204 n

Outer Barrister, 197
Overbury, Thomas, 37, 203 n
Oxford Tragedy, The, 34
Oxford's Men, 36

Palladis Tamia, Wits Treasury, 37
Pancridge Parson, 235 n
Paris Garden, 56, 58, 63, 206 n
Pauton, Edward, 99, 100
Pavey, Salathiel, 74, 79
Payne, Robert, 80
Pearce, Edward, master of St. Paul's, 74, 79, 80, 83, 94
Peckham, Edmund, 52
Pembroke's Men, 56, 57, 58, 61, 64, 207 n
Penzance, Lord, 19, 195 n, 196 n
Per my et per tout, 66
Phillips, Anne, 68
Phillips, Augustine, 64, 66, 67, 68, 70, 71
Plague, 89, 90, 174, 213 n
Playhouses: Blackfriars (first and second), 32, 38, 39, 44, 47, 48, 49, 53, 69, 71, 72, 73, 74, 75, 76, 77, 79, 80, 81, 82, 83, 84, 85, 86, 87, 88, 89, 90, 91, 92, 93, 94, 95, 96, 97, 98, 100, 101, 103, 146, 205 n, 208 n, 209 n, 210 n, 211 n; Blackfriars (Rosseter's), 49; Boar's Head, 55, 59, 60, 62, 63, 70, 207 n; Curtain, 32, 37, 47, 53, 56, 68, 203 n; Fortune, 34, 48, 49, 54, 62, 69; Globe, 38, 39, 48, 49, 55, 65, 66, 68, 69, 70, 71, 101, 206 n, 207 n, 208 n; Hope, 49; Phoenix/Cockpit, 38, 44, 48, 49; Red Bull, 48, 49; Red Lion, 47, 52, 206 n; Rose, 47, 48, 49, 56, 57, 58, 61, 69, 70, 203 n, 207 n; Rosseter's Blackfriars, 49; Salisbury Court, 48, 49, 205 n; St. Paul's, 39, 48, 49, 72, 74, 79, 80, 81, 82, 83, 84, 85, 88, 94, 207 n, 208 n, 209 n, 210 n, 235 n; Swan, 47, 48, 49, 55, 56, 57, 58, 59, 61, 63, 101, 207 n; Theatre, 28, 32, 33, 52, 53, 54, 56, 69, 198 n, 201 n, 206 n; *move to Bankside,* 54; Whitefriars, 48, 49, 84, 85, 88, 89, 90, 93, 208 n
Pope, Thomas, 58, 64, 66, 67, 68, 70, 71
Popham, Lord Chief Justice, 46
Præmunire, 128, 191
Primogeniture, 213 n
Prince d'Amour, 33, 35, 202 n
Prince of Purpoole, 32, 201 n
Privy Council, 36, 53, 58, 72, 81, 151, 200 n
Promos and Cassandra, 154, 155
Puritanism, 83
Putting of cases, 26, 197, 221 n

Queen's Bench, Court of, 60

Ralegh, Sir Walter, 151
Rastell, William, 71, 72, 75, 76, 77, 95, 96, 99, 100
Requests, Court of, 55, 57, 208 n, 210 n
Respublica, 30, 199 n
Rowley, William, 183, 186, 201 n
Rushton, William Lowes, 195 n
Russell, Thomas, 151
Russian Masque, 33, 206 n

Sackville, Thomas, 40, 46; *Gorboduc,* 29, 31, 40, 46
Samwell, Richard, 59, 60, 61, 62, 64
Satire, 36, 38, 39, 41, 49
Savage, Thomas, 64, 65, 66, 67, 68, 69, 70, 71, 208 n
Seisin, 21, 108, 116, 125, 214 n, 217 n, 219 n
Seneca, 41
Shaa, Robert, 56, 57

262 INDEX

Shakespeare, William, i, 13, 17, 18, 19, 20, 21, 22, 23, 28, 29, 32, 33, 34, 35, 36, 39, 40, 41, 45, 46, 51, 64, 65, 66, 67, 68, 69, 70, 71, 102, 103, 104, 107, 109, 110, 111, 113, 114, 127, 133, 134, 135, 136, 137, 139, 140, 141, 142, 145, 146, 149, 151, 153, 154, 155, 159, 162, 168, 187, 188, 193, 195 n, 196 n, 197 n, 198 n, 200 n, 201 n, 202 n, 207 n, 208 n, 209 n, 210 n, 211 n, 212 n, 213 n, 214 n, 220 n, 221 n, 222 n, 226 n, 227 n, 228 n, 229 n, 230 n, 231 n, 232 n, 234 n; *All's Well That Ends Well,* 211 n, 228 n; *Antony and Cleopatra,* 102, 109, 110, 111, 112, 113, 133, 213 n; *As You Like It,* 41, 134, 136, 141, 146, 152, 178, 189, 222 n, 223 n, 230 n; *Cardenio,* 183; *Comedy of Errors,* 32, 35, 39, 41; *1 Henry IV,* 20, 197 n, 216 n; *2 Henry IV,* 205 n; Falstaff, 21, 195 n, 205 n; Prince Hal, 21; *Henry V,* 197 n, 222 n; *1 Henry VI,* 205 n; *King Lear,* 45, 187, 188, 189, 211 n, 212 n; *Love's Labour's Lost,* 35, 183, 206 n; *Macbeth,* 134, 181; *Measure for Measure,* 35, 152, 153, 154, 155, 159, 163, 164, 166, 167, 172, 177, 182, 185, 189, 220 n, 221 n, 226 n, 227 n, 228 n, 229 n, 230 n, 232 n; *Merchant of Venice,* 20, 102, 103, 104, 106, 109, 110, 111, 113, 132, 133, 206 n, 211 n, 212 n; Shylock, 19, 103, 104, 105, 106, 107, 109, 110, 133, 191, 195 n, 196 n, 211 n, 212 n; *A Midsummer Night's Dream,* 40, 183; *Othello,* 44; *Richard II,* 20, 21, 46; *Romeo and Juliet,* 44, 135, 137, 149, 174, 189, 206 n, 232 n; *Sonnet 20,* 133, 211 n; *The Tempest,* 206 n, 223 n; *The Merry Wives of Windsor,* 183; *The Taming of the Shrew,* 29, 136, 151, 183, 220 n; *The Winter's Tale,* 183; *Timon of Athens,* 35; *Troilus and Cressida,* 35, 202 n; *Twelfth Night,* 33, 34, 35, 200 n, 203 n, 204 n, 206 n
Sharers Papers, 68
Sharington v. Strotten, 212 n

Sharpham, Edward, 34, 43, 44, 47, 89
Shirley, James, 35, 45, 47, 204 n, 233 n; *Triumph of Peace,* 35, 45, 205 n
Shoreditch, 28, 47, 206 n
Shrovetide, 31, 32, 33, 62, 200 n
Skialetheia, 53
Slater, Martin, 89
Southampton, Earl of, 46
Southwark, 28, 48
Spencer, Gabriel, 56
Sponsalia, 139, 146, 151, 155, 189, 225 n
Spousals, 135, 151, 153, 165, 221 n, 226 n, 232 n
Star Chamber, 55, 61, 75, 76, 77, 78, 79, 83, 99, 100, 208 n
Statute of Enrollments, 78, 213, 219 n
Statute of Uses, 108, 109, 113, 120, 126, 127, 129, 212 n, 213 n, 217 n, 219 n
Stow, John, 25, 197 n, 201 n
Stratford-upon-Avon, 36, 69
Stuart, Arbella, 151
Sturg-flattery, 57
Swinburne, Henry, 135, 147, 153, 162, 165, 171, 172, 173, 216 n, 221 n, 223 n, 224 n, 225 n, 226 n, 228 n, 229 n, 230 n, 231 n, 232 n, 233 n, 234 n
Syblil Balkhurst v. Randle Ramshae, 224 n

Tenancy in common, 65, 66
The Way to Life (A Discourse of the World), 31
Thompson v. Leach, 215 n
Tourneur, Cyril: *The Atheist's Tragedy,* 174, 175, 234 n
Treason, 46, 115, 117
Trespass, 60, 62, 63, 117

Ulysses and Circe, 34, 45
Underwood v. Manwood, 33
Unlawful maintenance, 60
Usury, 104, 217 n
Usus, 110
Utter barristers. *See* Outer Barristers

Vow Breaker, The, 183

Warwick's Men, 36
Webster, John, 20, 44, 47, 70, 83, 177, 180, 204 n, 209 n, 233 n, 234 n; *Appius and Virginia,* 44; *The Duchess of Malfi,* 134, 177, 178, 179, 180, 181, 182, 189, 233 n, 234 n; *Sir Thomas Wyatt,* 44; *White Devil,* 44, 70
What Mischief Worketh in the Mind of Man, 36
White, Edward J., 195 n, 197 n, 204 n; *Commentaries on the Law in Shakespeare,* 195 n
Wilde, Sir James Plaisted. *See* Penzance, Lord
Wilmot, Robert, 40, 47, 203 n; *Gismonde of Salerne,* 29, 31, 40; *Tancred and Gismund,* 29, 40, 183

Wilson, Robert, 58
Witch of Edmonton, The, 183
Witter, John, 68, 208 n
Wollaston, Thomas, 60
Wolsey, Cardinal, 29, 41
Woodford, Thomas, 79, 80, 85, 88, 89, 90, 208 n
Woodliffe, Oliver, 59, 61, 62, 63, 64
Worcester's Men, 61, 62, 69, 70
Writ of *subpoena,* 97, 99

Yelverton, Sir Christopher, 40, 46
Yeoman of the Revels. *See* Kirkham, Edward
Yorkshire Tragedy, The, 34